HARD TIME

HARD TIME: THE LIFE OF AN INCORRIGIBLE ON ALCATRAZ
By Charles Hopkins
As Told to Don DeNevi

Published by Creative Texts Publishers, LLC
PO Box 50
Barto, PA 19504
www.creativetexts.com

ISBN: 978-0-578-55244-6

HARD TIME

THE LIFE OF AN INCORRIGIBLE ON ALCATRAZ

BY
CHARLES HOPKINS

AS TOLD TO
DON DeNEVI

CREATIVE TEXTS PUBLISHERS

Barto, Pennsylvania

"My friend and fellow alumni Charlie Hopkins and I both graduated from America's Top Crime School- Charlie was a better student than I- He's still free!"

James "Whitey" Bulger
#1428 AZ

"Early in prison, I was classified as 'psycho' and incorrigible. It didn't matter, because I had already wasted the best part of my life racing toward hell. In the fifteen impressionable years of federal prison life that followed, I was housed daily with some of the most dangerous and notorious criminals in the annals of history. In some ways, I don't regret it, because many of them were the best friends I ever had."

Charlie Hopkins, 1999
#1186 AZ

FROM THE PUBLISHER

Although Alcatraz officially ceased prison operations in 1963, it remains the single most notorious, and possibly the most infamous, prison in the world. Even now more than 55 years after its closing as a functioning prison, the view of "The Rock" sitting alone in a tempestuous San Francisco Bay conjures up questions of what, exactly, would one have to do to be sent to such a place.

In its time, from 1934 until 1963, Alcatraz was the pinnacle of what it meant to be an escape-proof maximum-security penitentiary. Not only was Alcatraz home to thieves, bank robbers, kidnappers, and murderers, but it was home to what was considered to be the absolute worst of each type. Certainly, any federal prison is a tough environment, but to be sent to Alcatraz meant that the inmate being sent there required a level of security reserved for only 1% of all inmates, and also usually that they were either too violent or too much of an escape risk for any other maximum-security federal penitentiary.

Alcatraz, for example, was the place where men like Al Capone and "Creepy" Al Karpis were kept, both of whom were designated "Public Enemy #1" by law enforcement prior to their capture. It was also the place where Robert Stroud, "The Birdman of Alcatraz", was sent after killing a prison guard at another prison. Another notorious inmate of Alcatraz was "The Atomic Spy" Morton Sobell, who was widely publicized in the press for being a part of the network of Russian spies that were stealing American nuclear secrets after World War Two. The other two conspirators in the spy ring, a young couple by the name of Rosenberg, were sent to the electric chair, but Sobell went to Alcatraz.

Yet another notable Alcatraz inmate was Jack Twinning, who after being released from Alcatraz would go on in 1970 to participate in the murder no less than four California Highway Patrol officers in what would be dubbed the "Newhall Massacre", the single bloodiest day in the history of California law enforcement and an incident that would change the way police departments train and conduct traffic stops forever.

But lest one think that Alcatraz is ancient history because the names listed are not familiar or their crimes occurred long ago, it should be recalled that it was only fairly recently, in 2011, that the notorious Boston gangster James "Whitey" Bulger, who was himself once an Alcatraz inmate, was captured and then subsequently murdered in prison in 2018.

No, Alcatraz may not be as familiar to the public today as it was when it was an active prison, but it is not ancient history. It *is* fair to say, however, that the men that served hard time there are a dying breed. As of 2019, it is estimated that no more than six of these men are still alive and when fate does call them to their eternal destiny, all of their memories and experiences will be lost to history forever unless captured for future generations. All told only about 1500 men served hard time in Alcatraz and only a very few have told their story.

In 2018, Creative Texts Publishers signed author Don DeNevi, who, in addition to being an Ed.D., served as Supervisor of Recreation for San Quentin State Prison for more than 15 years. Don has written several books on Alcatraz, including the one that became the basis for the television movie *Alcatraz: The Whole Shocking Story* starring Telly Savales and Art Carney. What Creative Texts did not realize at the time, however, was that Don also had an unpublished manuscript, one from former Alcatraz inmate Charlie Hopkins, that he had written in 1999.

Even more remarkable than the fact that the manuscript was unpublished was the fact that Mr. Hopkins is still alive and had made the news over the past several months for being the pen pal of James "Whitey" Bulger. Several years ago, Charlie reached out to Whitey in prison to thank him for what he did for Joe Carnes. Carnes was a notable Alcatraz inmate who participated in the bloody escape attempt in 1946 that left many guards dead and sent several prisoners to the electric chair. Carnes survived to be ultimately released but upon his death was buried in an unmarked grave. Bulger found out about it and paid thousands not only to have him reburied properly but also to have him moved to the Choctaw Reservation.

In Alcatraz, Joe was one of Charlie's best friends. Years later, when Bulger went to Alcatraz, Joe was one of his best friends as well. Once acquainted through letters, Bulger and Charlie became extremely close, and one may accurately say best friends. Charlie is in possession of dozens of letters from Bulger and he is currently working on putting together a new manuscript based on those, but that is another story.

Charles Edward "Hoppy" Hopkins was Alcatraz inmate #1187 and he was far from an ordinary inmate. Charlie was born in 1932 when Franklin Delano Roosevelt was president and grew up during the Great Depression. Charlie was in and out of reform school as a boy and it was there that he met the Anglin brothers who years later would be the only inmates ever to escape from Alcatraz in 1962.

During one weekend in October 1952 Charlie and an accomplice decided it would be a good idea to do some joyriding and that joyriding trip evolved into a 3-day kidnapping spree that would encompass the capture of more than 20 people in at least 3 different states. One such person the men had kidnapped was a disabled war veteran and Charlie had a falling out with his partner over the disrespect his partner showed toward the man.

The next morning, Charlie awoke to find that his partner, aptly nicknamed "the three-gun maniac", had a gun in his ribs and told him in no uncertain terms that he was leaving him and that he was lucky he was leaving him alive. He then split, leaving Charlie to face law enforcement alone.

A huge manhunt was already on searching for the men and ironically the three-gun maniac was the first to be captured. After several days on the run, Charlie was also captured and sent to prison. Charlie was no stranger to incarceration and was a violent and angry inmate. Unable to get along with the other prisoners, he was put on chain gangs and locked in solitary confinement repeatedly. Finally, Charlie was deemed a danger to other inmates and "incorrigible" and was sent to Alcatraz.

It was at Alcatraz that Charlie became personal friends with many of the legendary inmates already listed above. His cell was next door to Al Karpis and he also became close friends with other Alcatraz legends like Joe Carnes, Robert Stroud and "Bumpy" Johnson. In Alcatraz, Charlie says that there were many guys that came in under the radar, kept their heads down, and were barely noticed by the other inmates but there was also an inner circle of men that, from a prisoner's point of view, ran the prison.

These were the "movers and shakers" of Alcatraz, the men who you didn't cross. You see, even in a maximum-security setting, Alcatraz was not without violence, and many inmates were brutally beaten and even murdered. In one instance, Charlie provided the knife that resulted in the death of one such inmate.

Needless to say, Charlie was not an inmate that flew below the radar. He was on the inside, so to speak, and was respected and liked by all of the inner circle. When asked recently about why some of the toughest, most dangerous men in the world, mostly all of which were murderers or thieves, would like him so much, Charlie responded simply "I was one of them. I belonged."

The average person cannot possibly relate to the types of men that were sent to Alcatraz, which possibly explains why so relatively few biographies have been written in collaboration with the inmate themselves. After all, would a "normal" person really want to sit down across from an unpredictable violent inmate and capture their story? Typically, this is not the case, but author Don DeNevi is no average researcher. As Supervisor of Recreation at San Quentin Don once signed a pledge that allowed the State to consider him expendable as a hostage in the event of a riot so that he could interact with the numerous lifers and even death row inmates, which included men like Scott Peterson, who is currently on Death Row for the murder of his wife, Laci Peterson. It is fair to say that Mr. DeNevi is fearless, and he has done what very few men would be willing to do, piece together the original unedited and raw story that Charlie Hopkins shared with him decades ago.

There are times in life when things are just meant to be and it is our considered judgement that the time is now is for Charlie's story to be told. Now more than 87 years old, Mr. Hopkins likes to say that his time in Springfield Penitentiary, where he was sent once he left Alcatraz, "helped calm him down a lot" and since leaving prison there is no question he has been able to live a fruitful life as a productive citizen and "stay out of trouble" from the mid-1960s until today. In speaking with Charlie now, one will find an extremely intelligent man that listens to every word that you say.

You may be surprised to know that Charlie breaks the stereotype of what one may consider a career criminal to be. He has a strong sense of right and wrong and also possesses a very strong moral code. As a young man in the Great Depression, he would watch people close to him literally starve to death, and this while grocery stores and restaurants would douse their leftover food with kerosene before throwing it out to prevent anyone from eating it. Charlie shared one story of watching his grandmother wash a kerosene-soaked cabbage with soap and water before peeling off the outside and cooking what remained for them to eat. It still tasted a bit like kerosene, but they lived.

Another story is of his first and best little friend when he was just a small boy. The boy's father could not find work and the family was starving to death. Rather than see his kids suffer, the father shot them all and then killed himself. When little more than a toddler, Charlie got the news that his little friend's father had killed him and he would never be able to see or play with him again.

It is hard to imagine the pain that these situations and many dozens more like them inflicted on young Charlie Hopkins during his formative years. Even at his worst, when angry and violent and deemed "incorrigible" by the guards, the prison psychiatrists would say "don't hurt him, there is good in this man." Perhaps it is fair to say that without anyone to care for him, he simply ended up caring for himself and tried to be loyal to some that were not worthy of that loyalty, but he himself will admit that he made many mistakes.

But now we must let Charlie tell his own story. From the Publisher's perspective, they felt they needed to warn the reader that this book is raw in its content and expresses the first hand story of Charlie Hopkins as told by Charlie Hopkins. The views and representations in it are his and his alone. One thing they can assure the reader of, however, is that Charlie is obsessed with accuracy. He painstakingly reviewed the manuscript and made sure corrections were made where needed. He also provided more than 300 pages of supporting documentation for this book, including newspaper articles, prison records, and photos.

The other thing important to highlight is that this book will read as though it was written in the 1990s because it was. Yes, Charlie is alive and it could be modernized and updated, but the Publisher felt that it would be more interesting to the reader as an unpublished time capsule, a glimpse into Charlie's mind twenty years ago when he was even closer to being the man he was when he was in Alcatraz.

Today, Charlie's memory and sense of loyalty is as strong as ever but he wants young people to know that crime does not pay and that they should stay out of trouble, stay in school and get good grades. He himself has children and as previously mentioned he has stayed out of trouble for more than five decades and has become a fruitful citizen. The final chapter of Charlie's story has yet to be written but one thing is for certain, no matter what one thinks they may know about career criminals or Alcatraz, they have never read a story like this.

Daniel A. Edwards
on behalf of
Creative Texts Publishers, LLC
August 2019

TABLE OF CONTENTS

INTRODUCTION

"In the last analysis, the essential thing is the life of the individual…"
—Carl Jung

Unlike some little boys who enjoy stepping on worms and insects or shooting small birds and animals for the sake of killing, Charlie Hopkins's conscience always intervened. Unless provoked, he would have nothing to do with death. It was as if his developing moral sense already knew the difference between sadism and reverence for life.

Decades later, Clarence "Joe" Carnes, #714AZ, one of the most respected of all Alcatraz inmates as well as Charlie's closest friend on the Rock, would say to Hopkins, "While you were among us, you were a tough little guy on the outside of yourself, but really someone else on the inside. We all laughed because you thought none of us knew it."

Although soft-hearted and vulnerable, an eradicable and unconscious wildness often consumed the cool, self-sufficient loner. Charlie knew nothing of the sweetness, safety, security, warmth, joy, and affection that most children take for granted from nurturing and nourishing parents. Hence, as a rejected boy, he lied, cheated, and stole everything in sight. As a rebellious teenager, he grew tough and violent, turning from petty thievery to armed robbery and kidnapping. Although Charlie's inner climate was essentially sunny, he might have been transformed into a power-mad, homegrown Capone capable of killing indiscriminately had he not been stopped and sent to state prison at the age of eighteen.

Because he was filled with anger and resentful of all authority, especially that found in the state and federal prison systems, where all he wanted to do "was let time carry me," he was declared "incorrigible" and ultimately dispatched to the US Federal Penitentiary at Alcatraz. "Harness him," one psychiatrist advised before Charlie left, "but do not hurt him. There is good inside this man. He is salvageable."

In June 1955, having already served several years in various juvenile reformatories, state prison road gangs, and dark, lonely isolation cells, Charlie was about to enter one of the most uncompromising tiered punishment units America ever created. Criminality, savagery, murder, homosexuality, and plots to escape were on a contorted plane hitherto unknown, even to him. Alcatraz was indeed the edge of every jailbird's void. A veteran convict from Atlanta, one of the other nineteen handcuffed and shackled inmates transferred to the notorious prison in the middle of San Francisco Bay along with Charlie, warned, "You better choose the style of time you're gonna do out there. Then, no matter what happens, live the consequences of that choice. Besides, the salt air will do you good."

The words echoed in Charlie's mind as he was raced across the continent aboard the heavily guarded, special train with steel-barred windows. On the Alcatraz dock, he and the others were loaded into the back of the prison van and driven up the steep 200 yards of rough roadway to the cellhouse's basement entrance. There, the new arrivals were escorted through the heavy doors and into the reception room of the secure penitentiary. Their shackles were removed and, for the eighth time since leaving Leavenworth, the prisoners were thoroughly searched. A cursing guard was the first to welcome Charlie to his new home.

As a sharp mid-morning sun etched every architectural detail of the heaped cellhouse masonry, the gloom within extinguished what remained of Charlie's dwindling spirit. It would take all the courage he had to resist the legendary prison's slow annihilation of what positive character a man brought with him. Inmate friends at Atlanta and Leavenworth had warned him that his life, lived thus far in grim irony, would soon become distortion. The rumors and tales about Alcatraz would somehow metamorphose into seductive reality. Inextricably ensnared in it, it, he would soon have to resign himself to spend the next five to ten years in a cell-house of tool-resistant bars, barbed wire, and steel mesh, to say nothing of the endlessly turning locks. In essence, he would have to play his role on a small stage where dramas of vicious treachery, with minor infractions of prison regulations, were reenacted daily in an eternal pageant.

Late that morning, Charlie was brought before Warden Madigan whose admonition was short and simple: "The purpose of Alcatraz is to isolate dangerous men like you from your fellow Americans. You're here because you were a one-man crime wave in Florida. At Atlanta, you were a notorious troublemaker among the inmates. You are violent. You are a kidnapper and a brute. You have come here for punishment. But I guarantee that no matter how long you are here, you will never commit the reign of terror you did at other institutions. You will be fed well—in fact, better than many Americans. You will be made reasonably comfortable, again, more so than many Americans. Alcatraz is not a vengeful place, but a preventive institution. You will never be allowed to forget for a moment that you are in a maximum-security prison. Even the tear-gas cylinders placed overhead in the dining room will remind you. I hope that you'll not bring in here your bitterness and hatred. I hope you will not be as dangerous as you were at Atlanta. Mr. Hopkins, no man can beat his own record or time."

In the recreation yard that afternoon, where most of the inmate population gathered in small groups to loaf, brag about their pasts, or get a little exercise, an old friend from Raiford ambled up to Charlie as he stretched to glimpse San Francisco and the Golden Gate Bridge. He laughed, "Not much of a view out here, kid, because fog gets in the way. And you better not stand too long where you're standing, because that area on the top tier of the steps is reserved for some special cons. Once you get to know a few things and get used to the foghorns, you'll be okay. It's the same as being in your grave, only you miss the fun of being dead. Even the rats run around with tears in their eyes."

When Charlie reclined on his bunk that night, he couldn't rid himself of the word "autopsy," which hammered over and over again in his head. For some strange reason, he picked it up years before and never let go of it. Now, he decided to look up its meaning. Later, in the Alcatraz library, he read that "autopsy" was derived from the Greek verb meaning "to see with one's own eyes." Charlie decided then and there he would do just that: record visually all the appalling intimacies of his new existence.

Within the next five years of his narrow, empty confinement, he went about the business of eating, sleeping, working, reading, growing wiser, and watching other men die. Believed by many officers to be "irreclaimable," he became the source of a growing myth. During his first year on Alcatraz, Charlie became a figure to be reckoned with, even by the toughest of the tough inmates. One guard sneered, "But don't worry; you, too, will wind up going out the hard way."

Because Hopkins was a basically psychologically healthy individual with an efficient perception of reality, he "carried" his own time, hard time, often serving months in lock-up and isolation without permanent damage to his psyche. Although he seemed elusive, strangely invincible, and someone who wished to be left alone, he made friends with a number of inmates. Some were the most dangerous in Alcatraz. Most were typical of the population: shrewd mob leaders, cruel murderers, life-serving kidnappers, escape artists, immature bank-robbers, simple burglars, clever forgers, World War II spies, and rapists. Although Charlie mingled easily, he remained aloof from them all. Charlie was his own man, observing as others grouped themselves into predatory packs. He was totally immersed in inmate routine, convinced that all the soap and water would never wash off "convict." Sure, he was branded for life, but he would survive.

By the end of 1992, more than one million visitors a year were boarding boats at San Francisco's Fisherman's Wharf to tour the "inescapable scare show" and hear accounts of Alvin "Creepy" Karpis, "Doc" Barker, George "Machine Gun" Kelly, Al "Scarface" Capone, Roy "California's Nicest Badman" Gardner, Robert "Birdman" Stroud, Martin "The Atomic Spy" Sobell, Clarence "Choctaw Kid" Carnes, Frank Morris, and the Anglin brothers. Unfortunately, when the 5,000 daily visitors depart the decaying brick cellhouse, they carry away more mystery and lore, conjecture, distortion, and exaggeration about former Alcatraz inmates than they originally brought with them. Their eerie trip down Memory Lane, although greatly aided by the hard work of federal park rangers, only partially produces insight into what life and punishment on the island were really all about.

In his memoirs, Charlie is very clear about the incomprehensibility of the Alcatraz world in the late 1950s. Most inmates incarcerated there awoke to find themselves in the same positions as the helpless insects that sometimes found their way into the cellhouse. Charlie was different from the mainstream of men who served time there. Although cooped up like the others, he was determined to live out his sentence by his own rules. He would not waste away in a cage, not because he was being emotionally starved, but because he had never found the kind of food his soul yearned for in order to survive peacefully. Thus, he had to weave an intricate existence. Almost like a cameraman relying on a visual vocabulary, he deliberately recorded, in a near-documentary approach, the rigorous truth he saw all around: a truth that some corner of his imagination insisted be told someday. Hence. we see, too, and because of that, we begin to understand and feel we are involved in his expressive range and his subsequent transformation over fifteen years.

The following account is unlike any prison portrait you will ever read. With the exception of minor editing, this intelligent and affecting autobiography was not rewritten or "touched up". The words and sentences are a former incorrigible's effort at honest workmanship. Without bothering about style, Charlie pours forth a raw, unembellished, well-meaning eyewitness narrative, remembering events as they happened more than sixty years ago.

There are no superstars in Charlie's story, no odor of brimstone or gospel. He does not have to be dramatic, because the brutal and sometimes humorous events speak for themselves. The spontaneous recollections are hardboiled, entirely frank, and completely genuine. His simple sentences say what he remembers, all of which can be corroborated by a variety of court records, documents, and other official sources. From a historical perspective, his account is of great importance. His unimpassioned memory contains sensational revelations and startling new details about men and events never before published. At Raiford, Atlanta, Leavenworth, and Alcatraz, Charlie was a member of each prison's "underworld" and witnessed more than most inmates. His chiseled words sincerely project an unblurred picture of incarceration, and you and I are stirred to move closer to a man whose fate was so different than ours.

Today, Charlie is a hardworking and respected citizen living a quiet life in Jacksonville, Florida. In Raiford State Prison and the federal penitentiary at Alcatraz, Charlie was known by fellow inmates as "good people," the highest compliment a convict can receive from his peers. Cops, judges, former prison guards, and inmates still refer to him in that way.

Charlie's practical reason for this? "You sometimes have to get mean and angry to survive. Plus being a man to yourself."

Don DeNevi
Pebble Beach, CA

CHAPTER ONE

GROWING UP STEALING

I've been caught stealing ... I enjoy stealing ...
When I want something, I don't want to pay for it ...
I walk right through the door ... Walk right through the door.
Hey, all right! If I get by, it's mine! Mine, all mine!

—from "Been Caught Stealing," written and sung by Perry Farrell

One early morning in June of 1955, nineteen of us climbed aboard a train at Leavenworth bound for San Francisco and Alcatraz Island. We were shackled in pairs, in leg irons, and our hands were chained at our waists. The railway car we sat in was specially designed and built to haul convicts. Besides the normal rows of seats at each end, it had a gun cage where a guard sat cradling a rifle. The only toilet stood exposed at one end of the coach, next to the gun cage. We tried to avoid using it because of the lack of privacy.

Our special prison coach was only one unit in the regular Southern Pacific passenger train headed west, placed as the first car behind the engine so that no one could pass through it. We stopped in Omaha that afternoon, and some guy tried to get inside our car by knocking on the door and shouting to the lieutenant in charge that he was an FBI agent. The lieutenant shouted back, "The only way I can open this door is with a direct order from the Attorney General."

As we rode along, passing from one state into another, I didn't care what lay ahead. "To hell with it," I thought. My life had always been a shambles and the one time I could have broken out of my misery by following an honest boxing career and marrying a good girl, I fucked up. I hated all authority, not because of what authority really was supposed to be, but because of how it had been used on me in my life—how it had been used on me in prison. Somehow, I wanted to attack it for my father's abandonment of our family, for my mother's neglect, and for my unhappy childhood. I wanted to blame authority for everything. And, now, I was on my way to Alcatraz, the biggest goddam authority ever invented in this country.

Throughout that journey there had been companionable chatter: all the guys talking nonsense, nobody saying anything that meant much. But once the passenger train reached Donner Summit in the California Sierras and started its descent into the San Joaquin Valley near Sacramento, nobody spoke much. A queer silence soon engulfed the coach. Some of the men hugged their knees while others half drowsed.

As the mountain terrain and small lakes passed by, my mind drifted idly. Lazy thoughts turned to the details of my doings and why I no longer felt any hope. People and incidents I had long buried, that I thought I would never bother about again, came back to hurt. I had no idea why I was stirred to recall all the garbage except that maybe it was still a living part of me and the time had finally come to face why I had wound up so deep in the federal prison system.

For the first time in a long, long time, I felt a little moisture in my eyes. Maybe, as one old walking boss in a road gang in Florida had said, "You don't live in time, son. You live in doings and deeds."

-

The earliest I can remember is when I was about five years old. The year was 1937 and I can still see my mother, Dessie, and my foster father John riding in the front seat of an old jalopy along the roads between Florida and Tennessee. Back and forth we would go: Mom, Dad, me, my three stepbrothers, and my stepsister, looking for any kind of work to make a little money.

At night, our family would camp on the side of some dirt road near a little stream, if we could find one, and cook over a campfire. We kids would fight as all kids do, or play the best way we could. My stepbrothers were Carl. Mule, and Elmo. I was closest to my stepsister, Margaret. Just like so many other Depression-era families, we had no good clothes or shoes to speak of, and we surely never had enough to eat. Even though we were always hungry, my stepfather was too proud to ask farmers nearby for food. My mother, who had conceived me when she was fourteen by some guy passing through and had married John at fifteen, told me years later that my stepfather was too religious and kind to make it in a system like ours.

John Hopkins was 32 when he took me and my mother on. Carl, Mule, Elmo, and Margaret were born soon after. John always wanted to do the right thing and depended on God to take care of the rest. John was so gentle in spirit that he allowed another man to take my mother away from him. And because that poor excuse of a wife-grabber didn't want us kids, she just left without us. She then had four more children, all by the newcomer. But six years later my mother gave all those kids away, too, when another man came along and asked her to go away with him.

But John at least had the courage to try and make it in society with the four of us and no wife. One of the haunting memories I carry occurred shortly after my mother deserted us. My friend Bobby, my first boyhood friend, was abandoned along with his brothers and sisters by his mother too. His father was so poor he had to beg from door to door in west Jacksonville, Florida, to feed his five children. One night he returned home empty handed. Because his kids were starving and crying, he shot them all and then shot himself. I think about Bobby all the time and the life he never had because his father could get no job or food. John at least wouldn't quit. Bobby's father did. From that time on, I decided that I would never, never, never give up, no matter what.

To this day, I don't hate my mother for what she did. She was a child when she brought me into the world and probably did the best she could with what little she had. At least she wasn't like some unfortunate girls in those days who in order to feed their children left them in the front seat of their broken-down car while they prostituted themselves in the back seat. I know pathetic women like that are too weak to last long in our society and it gives the federal and state governments good reason to cut them the way a farmer cuts a hog so that taxpayers don't have to support them and their unwanted children.

My family didn't suffer any more or less than thousands of other road families during the 1930s. Wives and mothers were poor, hungry, and dirty, and there was little hope that things would get better. So, if some guy came along promising a bit more, a woman was likely to take off, abandoning her husband and kids.

I learned from my grandmother that my real father was named Ridgeway. He was from the same small town as my mother, deep in the piney woods country of southern Alabama. Granny said he had a bad reputation. He apparently was tough and had once killed a black man for some trivial reason. In fact, I understand all the Ridgeways were rough people and had bad names throughout the back hills. According to Granny, all the Ridgeway hill men liked to drink, whore, and fight. Maybe this is who I inherited my fighting skills from, although I never was one for drinking and whoring.

As a young boy, I lived in the same west Jacksonville neighborhood where I was born. The area was more or less a slum where black and white families lived in relative harmony. I used to fight with black kids as much as I did white kids. Color made no difference to me. I never hated blacks as some people did. I was never taught to look down on anybody by any of my people. My feelings simply depended upon how I was treated and respected. If anyone liked me, I liked him back, regardless of his color or religion.

My stepfather never expressed any feelings about blacks and my mother was good hearted and liked everybody. I remember how in the late 1940s a black store owner would give her credit until her check from the state came in. I used to hang out in his store with Bradley, the store owner's son, the same way a lot of other boys hung out in drug stores in those days. Later, when I went to prison, I was ashamed to watch the way black inmates were treated by white inmates and white guards for no reason other than their color. In the early 1950s at Raiford State Prison and the federal penitentiary at Atlanta, the black inmates were required to take their caps off and say, "Good morning, boss man," as they passed a guard on his way to duty. Whites had to take their caps off, but they didn't have to say anything. A black farm family named Butler lived near us in the late 1940s and the father made his three boys walk the line. I remember once my mother asked one of them a question, and when he answered, "Yes," his father said, "Say 'Yes, Ma'am,' boy. Don't you ever answer a lady that way." Mr. Butler plowed fields with a mule and set a good example of hard work for his sons.

In December 1950, when I was a convict at Florida's Raiford State Prison, I was assigned to a road camp, known in those days as a chain gang. We usually dug ditches and cleared forests, but once we helped can apples in the kitchen of the state mental hospital in Chattahoochee. One hot, humid morning while I was carrying boxes of apples to the outdoor sorting tables for the mental patients to peel or reject, an elderly black woman who was a hospital supervisor asked me if I would bring her a pitcher of iced water from the kitchen refrigerator. Because the kitchen was out of bounds for the convicts, I asked the prison crew supervisor, a white man, for permission to get her some water. I began, "The lady would like..." and he shot back, "What goddamn lady? You mean that goddamn nigger? She waits until noontime." I walked back to her, trying to think of some excuse. But she heard what he said and to this day I can still see the hurt frozen on her face.

I realized early on that I couldn't have been a Hopkins, since Carl, Mule, Elmo, and Margaret never tried to steal anything. Margaret was born in December 1939. She was a pretty, blue-eyed blonde and as sweet and gentle as anyone can be. She had hard luck with men, died at age 31, and never knew much happiness. Carl was just the opposite of me and never got into any trouble at all as a kid but later he got caught moonshining, which nobody considered a crime. The sheriff said if Carl would give him a name and go to court against the moonshiner, he would drop the charges against him but my brother wouldn't do it and spent a year in jail for selling untaxed whiskey. When Carl was released, the business man he covered for put him through an electrical trade course and my brother became an electrician. Today he owns five acres of land near Jacksonville that would sell for $10,000 an acre. Each acre has a home right in the middle with road frontage. Carl's only vice, and I've told him this, is he drinks too much whiskey.

Like most delinquents, I started stealing very early. I was in the first grade at Central Riverside Elementary School in Jacksonville and I can still hear our teacher, Miss York, announce to the class, "We have a thief in this room, and I mean to find out who it is and punish him." I was scared silly, because I was the thief. I took lunch money off the kids' desks when everyone was at recess. Also, during our air raid drills twice a week (this was during World War II), I would grab money off several desks while the other kids were scrambling to get out of the room and into a shelter. I was a compulsive thief and felt no remorse about it whatsoever. I needed money desperately, and some of the kids had it.

Soon, I was stealing bicycles and shoplifting four or five comic books a day. I loved comic books and my favorites were Captain Marvel, Superman, Batman, Dick Tracy, Boy Commandos, Blackhawk, and my most favorite of all, Crime Does Not Pay. Through Crime Does Not Pay comics I became acquainted with Alvin "Creepy" Karpis. Years later when I met him at Alcatraz, I told him it seemed I had known him all my life.

A prison psychiatrist told me that all I was stealing in my childhood years was love: that I was trying to fill myself up with the love and caring my mother wasn't giving me. Maybe he was right

About this time in 1942 I became best friends with Jimmy, a boy who was older than me, and together we started demanding pennies and nickels from the other boys. One day after school we bumped into a girl going to the grocery store with a dollar bill clutched in her hand. I simply took it away from her. Within thirty minutes, the police stopped me and Jimmy. They took us to the city jail and we spent three days in the juvenile wing, frightened and wondering what was going to happen to us. Jimmy was sent home and I was released to my grandmother. Jimmy wasn't allowed to hang around me after that, so I started stealing things by myself.

My grandmother lived in the northern Florida woods and plowed fields with a mule while my grandfather was at work as a plasterer. I can honestly say I loved my grandmother more than my mother. She was the most important person in my life. She raised all her own food and kept a cow or two for our meat. She raised several of her grandchildren and made us behave by using a peach tree limb on us.

My grandmother was tough and had lots of nerve. I remember she once had a dog go mad from rabies in her house and she held him off with a chair until she could back up to where her pistol was, on a shelf. Then she calmly shot the dog. A lot of men couldn't do that. When I was seventeen, I went to her house to borrow her gun to shoot two drunks who were in my mother's house. Granny said, "Son, your mother is no good, so don't go messing your life up."

During World War II, tools and bullets were hard to come by for the ordinary person. So, I began stealing them from my second stepfather and selling them to a blacksmith. My second stepfather was a mean son of a bitch and to this day I still hate him as I did when I was a boy. He never abused the kids, but the drunken bastard never provided for them, either. I don't know what became of him. I tell Lisa, my own daughter, that people who go searching for a parent who either deserted them or gave them away as babies so they could party and whore around have the same blood running through their veins as their parent had.

I got to skipping school and stealing more and more bicycles. And soon enough I was going back and forth to the youth wing of the Jacksonville city jail. The court decided that since my mother and grandmother couldn't control me, I would be put in a foster home run for the state by Mrs. Whitney, a 70-year-old woman who provided food and lodging for five boys and four girls. The house was adequate and the old lady was decent enough. As often as I could, I would sneak into town by myself to see a movie.

One afternoon, I walked past a pool hall and saw the mother of Tom, one of the boys at the foster home, having a big time. She was surrounded by a bunch of men and all of them were boozing it up. I felt a lot of anger at that moment. I suppose the woman reminded me of my mom. Then the anger turned to disgust. I never told Tom what I saw. It would have broken his heart, because he believed his mother was up north picking fruit. Thinking of Tom and my own situation, I decided then and there that I would always go it alone and not depend on anyone. I'm still that way today. I can have just as much fun doing things alone as with someone. Being a loner would help me when I wound up in the pen, especially on the Rock.

I had a lot of respect for Mrs. Whitney. She was tough as nails, like my grandmother Maude, and she liked to talk about Buffalo Bill, whom she had once met. She had a daughter named Juanita whose father was a Mexican, and when Juanita wanted to go to the movies or anywhere else, I had to go with her. Her mother believed she couldn't meet her boyfriend this way, but she did anyway, because I never said a word about it. I came to love her like a sister, and that's probably why I have always liked Mexicans, especially Mexican women.

If I had stayed on at Mrs. Whitney's house, I probably would have ended up differently. Under her guidance I never skipped school and stayed out of trouble except for getting into fights and shoplifting whatever I wanted. Twice I got caught, and each time I told the store managers I was only trying to return something for exchange. Of course, they knew better, but they let me go anyway.

Three months before my thirteenth birthday in 1945, I was transferred to the Jacksonville Boy's Home. Leaving Mrs. Whitney's warmth and informality for the cold and rigid institution affected me deeply. I said to myself, "Fuck it," and went back to my old ways. Soon I was stealing bicycles again and sneaking out at night to break into parked cars.

The war was still on, and Jacksonville's restaurants, hotels, buses, and everything had standing room only. The downtown area was crawling with people; theaters were on every corner and booming. Traffic cops were on foot everywhere, blowing their whistles. Two blocks from the state-run boy's home, which was located at 6th and Main Streets, was the Capital Theater, which showed B- and C-rated movies. The owner let the kids from the Boy's Home in free. I've never forgotten his generosity. His kindness taught me that there are some good people on this earth who do things for other people without expecting something for themselves. He seemed to say that life isn't worth living if you can't help others, especially children. I enjoyed many Roy Rogers and Gene Autry shows there.

One day a counselor from the judge's office came to the boy's home and told me that a well-to-do family wanted to take me in. I wasn't too excited, because I knew that most of the time these "adoptions" didn't work out. The kid was frequently returned to the agency he was sent from, more hurt and frustrated than before leaving. But I said, "Sure, I'll go. Why not?"

Two weeks later the counselor came for me and together we drove to a large truck stop out on Philips Highway (US 1 South), which the couple owned. It turned out that the husband and wife were Polish immigrants named Targonski. The couple had two boys, Donald and Tony, whose ages were fourteen and twelve. Mr. Targonski was also a judge in Bayard, a nearby town. For the first time in my life I felt I was part of something solid and permanent. I had "real" brothers and got along with them. It was such a different experience for me. I was eating regularly, had good shoes and clothes, money in my pocket, and I even enjoyed going to Mass with them at the nearby Catholic Church.

The Targonskis spent all their time running their small restaurant and truck stop, so we rarely had dinner at home. We always ate at the truck stop cafe. The family always ate fish on Fridays. Donald got sick once and believed it was because he ate a hamburger on Good Friday. I remember one day he came across a pornographic comic book of Popeye having sex with Olive Oil and showed it to his girlfriend. I was present and we all laughed at Popeye, but afterwards, I felt disgusted. Ever since, I have never gotten anything out of pornography.

One day when we were alone, Mr. Targonski told me that he would leave me an equal share of the family estate. This comment meant a lot to me, because it meant I was accepted as the couple's son. But I had too many emotional problems to make it with the family, even though I loved them and enjoyed working around the truck stop. I was still depressed, anxious, and insecure. At times, I got easily upset and raised hell, not that it was the Targonski's fault. Donald, the oldest boy, tried very hard to be my brother, but I was already a confirmed loner. It was as if I said, "Don't get too close to me, because I might love you." Also, I didn't want to embarrass the family and get them involved in my troubles. A day doesn't go by that I don't reflect on those good people who tried to give me every opportunity to be a part of their family. I had been so emotionally starved and deserted by my own family that I couldn't trust or accept affection from anyone. I remember my last day with them, Donald and I got into an argument and I said I was leaving. His mom, Martha, tried to hug me, but I shook her off and left. Twice a year I visit the graves of Mr. and Mrs. Targonski and lay a wreath.

That year, I had a young school teacher by the name of Miss Duck who tried to be like a big sister, and I had genuine feeling for her. But when the end of the school year came around, Miss Duck left to teach in another city, and the little bit of love I could muster wasted away. No teacher cared for me like she did that year, and I wish I could see her again. But my emotional problems stayed with me and are not completely gone even today; they never will be. I still won't trust others much, and I keep my problems to myself.

Sadly, I returned to the boy's home in July 1945, and it wasn't long before I started roaming and prowling the Jacksonville streets and alleys at night, breaking into cars, while the other kids at the boy's home slept. One day one of my friends, Oscar, asked me if I would run away with him. I answered, 'Why not?" So, we stole two bicycles and then headed for the train yards. There, we jimmied open a box car and started to put the bikes in. But once we had one of the bikes in, a yard walker came around the freight train and yelled for us to clear out. Then, to our astonishment, the train pulled away from the siding. We cursed our luck for losing a good bike. With just one bicycle we set off anyway. With Oscar on the handlebars, I peddled more than fifty miles over two days to Stark, Florida, where we sold the bike for a dollar to one of Oscar's cousins. For a few weeks, we lived on the streets, then walked over to Oscar's relatives, who wound up taking us back to the boy's home. Again, I returned to breaking into parked cars in the dead of night, something I was good at and where I knew I could make some easy money.

Not long afterwards, in August 1945, a Yankee boy, Norman, suggested that I try running away again, this time with him. Again, I agreed, and we took off that night. No sooner had we reached the outskirts of town when a county patrol officer picked us up. That night we were placed in the juvenile section of the county jail. Little did we know that it would become our home for a month.

About the second week, a bigger and older boy named Boyette who bullied all the kids in the section came up to us, grabbed Norman by the shirt, and made some remark about Yankees. He shouted for all to hear, "Anybody in here like Yankees?" Without hesitating, I said, "Yeah, I think this here Yankee is a good old boy. What are you going to do about it?" Boyette glared at me and let my friend go. He was very angry but walked away without fighting. He went over to where a sixteen-year-old boy was sitting. The boy was bigger than Boyette, but it didn't make any difference. Boyette took off his belt and beat the kid so badly that by the time an attendant arrived, the boy was so bloodied you could hardly recognize him. The officials turned the bully over to the county jail, and it wasn't long before a judge sent Boyette to the state prison, despite his age.

I remember that another of my friends, Billy, from the boy's home, had to appear in criminal court at the age of sixteen, and in a heated exchange with the judge called him a "lying motherfucker." The judge sentenced him to a year for the original offense, plus another five years for cursing him. Billy left that courtroom with a six-year sentence for some stupid little offense. Later, Billy and I met at Raiford State Prison, where he vowed when he got out, he would find the judge and shove a shotgun up his ass.

It wasn't long before that when the same judge sent me to the reform school at Marianna, Florida, as an incorrigible delinquent. I was thirteen years old. The Marianna Industrial School for Boys had four red brick, two-story buildings called "cottages," each with a population of about thirty or forty. A cottage master and his wife had an apartment on the first floor of each cottage, and he was assisted by two inmates, who helped him run the cottage. You got up each morning and went to bed each night to the sound of a bugle. Three time a day you would line up on the sidewalk in front and to the left of the cottage for inspection. You stood with the tips of your shoes in perfect line with the edge of the sidewalk and counted off as an inmate walked the line, pointing at each boy in turn. The cottage master watched as you stood at ramrod-stiff attention until the bugle sounded again. We always said the bugle sounded like it was calling, "Soupy, soupy, soupy, come and get your slop."

No sooner did I arrive at Marianna than I got into a fist fight with another boy. One of the keepers grabbed me by the neck and led me to a low building behind the mess hall that had a row of small cells. He threw me in the first cell and made me lean over the back of a chair. He then started hitting me on the butt with a board that looked like a sawed-off boat oar. After twenty-eight licks, the guard called for help. Another man came in and held me on the cell bed while the first guy started hitting me again. I got thirty-two more licks, all within the space of ten minutes. My ass was completely black the next morning. I often think that if tough kids today had a taste of that kind of control and discipline, they wouldn't be doing the things they're doing. Today, they just think they're tough, but they've never really been tested.

It was at the Marianna Industrial School for Boys that I met Clarence Anglin who, along with his brother J. W. Anglin and Frank Morris, escaped from Alcatraz in 1962. This was 1945, and Clarence was thirteen. I liked him right away and we became friends. But he was more of a loner than I was and didn't seem to make friends with others the way most of us did. You could tell he was smart. But he was also a kind kid, never fighting or causing any type of trouble. He certainly wouldn't let anyone bullshit or take advantage of him. But he just went his own way, learning and doing as he went along. I always saw him as mature for his age.

The war was still on and the food at Marianna was awful. I guess the prison system was doing its part in the war effort by giving us poor food. When the war ended the food slowly improved, but we still didn't have heat in my cottage. The winter of 1945 was ice-cold. I was assigned to the yard crew about two months after I arrived. The old superintendent of the school died, and a twenty-one-year-old ex-marine was put in charge. The reform school today is named for him: the Arthur G. Dozier School for Boys. He made me the foreman of the yard crew because I was the best worker the reform school had. We had to cut the grass with a push mower, and I pushed that damn thing many a mile.

We alternated each day between school and work. Fortunately, we also had a good athletic program and a committed boxing coach by the name of Mr. Davis who had just gotten out of the marines. I was always in raw fist fights anyway, so I was interested to see what I could do in the ring. Boxing was fun for me, because Davis gave us professional boxing gloves. I enjoyed fighting legitimately.

Years later at Alcatraz, when my best friend Clarence "Joe" Carnes asked me why I liked boxing so much, I answered the same way Sugar Ray Robinson answered when he was asked why he kept boxing even though he was over the hill: "Because it's in my blood." For me, fighting also meant winning. And if you've been losing all your life, winning isn't half bad. By boxing and winning, I was doing something all my very own. It gave me a personal identity. I was somebody, and that recognition felt good. Plus, the bullies in the reform schools, state prisons, and penitentiaries knew enough to keep clear.

A YOUNG CHARLES HOPKINS PURSUES A PROMISING BOXING CAREER

In the spring of 1946, five boys represented the school in a Golden Gloves tournament: Donnel Rice, a bantam-weight; T. W. Holloway, a heavyweight; Maurice Hope, a middle-weight; Joe Rodriguez, a light weight; and me, a feather-weight. We all won, and Hope and Holloway received a lot of prestige. Holloway went on to the state championship and later to the national tournament in Madison Square Garden in New York. He was an inspiration to me, since I was still in the novice division.

In October 1946, I was returned to the Jacksonville Boy's Home. Before I left the reform school, the director took me aside and said that the worst possible of all mothers was better than the best possible of all institutions, and that I needed to go home. He was therefore returning me to the boy's home for a few days until he could locate my mother. They found my mother and she reluctantly agreed to take me back. But I knew it wouldn't work out, and sure enough, it didn't, for a lot of reasons.

Before long, my cousin Vernon, who was seventeen, and I took off hitchhiking. We didn't know where we were going and we didn't care. Shortly before we left, we both attended my grandfather's funeral. Vernon had been raised by my grandparents, and after the graveside service, a cemetery laborer started stomping down the grave's dirt with his feet Vernon shoved and cursed the man, shouting, "You motherfucker! That's no goddamn horse buried there! It's my grandfather!" My grandmother apologized to the gravedigger.

After walking for a few days, we got picked up by a truck driver in southern Georgia, and we rode with him to a small-town truck stop, where he bought us a meal. We headed down some railroad tracks that ended up in a huge railroad yard in Rocky Mount, North Carolina. Since it was nearing midnight and beginning to rain, we climbed into an empty gondola car. Soon we were fast asleep.

But we didn't sleep long. We were both awakened by a bright flashlight in our eyes. Neither one of us moved. The railyard worker certainly saw us, but he was probably so used to hoboes that he left without ordering us out. Vernon whispered, "I'm glad you didn't make a move. Let's get out of here." So, we found another gondola on a different track and climbed in. It was loaded with heavy steel rails, but we didn't care. We were so tired we felt we could sleep on top of anything. As we lay on the rails dozing off, an engine banged into our car and started pushing it along with several other gondola cars until all the cars were slammed into a long line of freight cars. The mild collision caused our car's load of rails to slide to the back. We were sent sprawling. I suddenly found myself pinned underneath one of the rails. The weight was so great on my chest that it took my breath away. I found myself looking straight up into the sky, unable to move or breath. Because I knew I was slowly suffocating to death, I asked God to help me out and, within seconds, whether due to God or plain old good luck, another car slammed into ours, shoving all the steel rails to the other end of the gondola. The impact freed me. For a moment I thanked God, not realizing how damaged I was. I called to Vernon in the pitch black but received no answer. As I tried to stand up, I realized my right arm was broken above the elbow. Even though I hurt all over, I managed to climb out of the gondola and collapsed on the ground. The overall pain was getting bad. I could no longer determine where it was corning from.

After a few minutes the railroad worker who had originally spotted us in the first gondola came running up. He asked, "Where is your partner?" I vaguely nodded to the car right next to us. He helped me up and almost carried me over to a switchman's office. Then he hurried back to the car where Vernon was. As he did this, several other railroad men started hovering around me, asking questions. They saw something on my leg that they tried to keep me from seeing, but I looked anyway. There was a big red hole in my leg, just below the left knee. I thought I was going to faint. But the guy who had carried me in yelled something from outside. One of the men stepped out, closed the door, then returned. He said to the other railroad worker, "Oh my God, he thinks the other boy is dead." The two then turned to me and one of them asked, "Is he any kin of yours?" I whispered that Vernon was my cousin. Then the man said, "Well, he's as dead as he'll ever be."

I was driven in a pickup truck to a hospital owned by the Southern Coastline Railroad.

Fortunately, it was less than half an hour away. A couple of days later some big official with the company came to see me and stayed about an hour. He helped all he could, and I'll never forget his genuine interest in me. He brought me the local newspaper that reported how two heavy steel rails had crushed Vernon's chest. He had died instantly.

Meanwhile, a surgeon at the hospital operated on my leg. One of the nurses told me I talked a lot of crazy talk while coming out from under ether. A day or so later I had a dream that I was standing before God, who was seated in a huge concrete chair. We were underwater and I had a strange taste in my mouth. I can't remember how the conversation went.

Years later in Alcatraz, when I told Alvin Karpis about the dream, the old convict tried to interpret it for me. He said I was dying at the time and was trying to make peace with my Maker because I felt guilty for all the trouble I had caused. But because something in my unconscious couldn't accept the peace or the role I played in the peace; the scene was enacted in slow motion— "underwater."

At that small hospital just outside Rocky Mount in North Carolina, I met some of the best people I have met anywhere. Several railroaders came to see me regularly, some even bringing me new clothes. The son of one man made friends with me and brought his friends, too. One girl kept coming back almost every day. For the first time in my life, I got close to a person. Her name was Joyce Perry. She had black hair and brown eyes and was very pretty. I came to love her because she visited me every day, but I only wrote her once after going home. She never answered and I often wonder whatever happened to her.

Soon I was able to walk around and visit other patients throughout the hospital. They were either railroad workers or the family members of railroad workers. When I was released two weeks later, two railroad policemen escorted me back to Jacksonville on one of their Southern Coastline trains and turned me over to the juvenile authorities. Judge Crisswell, who founded the Jacksonville Boy's Home, felt I would do best at my grandmother's house.

In 1948 and 1949 I lived with my grandmother, and I loved it. She was very saddened by Vernon's death. Granny cooked good country meals for me and never yelled or got mad like my mother. I was now sixteen, which meant I could fight in the open divisions of several amateur boxing tournaments in Jacksonville and east Tennessee, where some of the Ridgeway clan lived. I went over there and was winning fights right and left. The best I did was winning a lightweight title and a runner-up title. But even Granny's love for me couldn't keep me from itching for more money than pocket change. In March 1949, I was staying with some of my dad's people who lived outside Knoxville, although most of the Ridgeways lived in Chattanooga and Memphis.

I was hitchhiking with a buddy from Knoxville to Chattanooga when we committed a burglary outside a little town called Louden. Almost immediately the police picked up our trail. They chased us all day through the woods with their bloodhounds and at one point got within a hundred yards without catching a glimpse of us. About 5:00 the next morning, we came out on a dirt yard and saw a few farm houses scattered about. That didn't bother us much as we tried to find the main road. But someone must have seen us and notified the police, and sure enough, they came flying. I told the police that we were tramping and looking for farm work. The smartest of the two cops said, "Let me see your hands." After glancing at them, he snarled, "Bullshit! You don't have any calluses at all," and took out his handcuffs. But I wouldn't change my story.

The two policemen shoved us into their patrol car and drove us to the town jail. When we got there, I kept on doing all the talking. So, they put me in one room while they ordered my buddy, who was bigger and older than I was, to follow them into another room. After talking to them for a few minutes, my friend signed a confession. I was only seventeen, but I told the cops I was twenty-one to keep the juvenile authorities out of it. But they weren't stupid. One cop immediately picked up the phone to notify the FBI that I had no draft card. I tried to tell him that nobody told me you had to register. He laughed at that. So, I kept pressing the point. Finally, he put the phone down and said he would personally notify my draft board in Jacksonville. "In the meantime," he advised, "you better go down and talk to them yourself as soon as you get out of here."

My buddy and I were held in jail four months until we went to court. My court-appointed lawyer told me in the courtroom, the first and only time I saw him, that the grand jury forgot to sign my indictment. This meant I could plead guilty and get a six-month sentence, or I could wait in jail for the next term of the grand jury after January 1, 1950, six months away, at which they would re-indict me and God only knew what sentence would be handed down.

I did the six months, getting no credit whatsoever for the four months I had been waiting in jail for the trial. Swinging a sledgehammer at a rock quarry in Tennessee was no fun. In fact, I never hated anything so much, not even Alcatraz. The food was almost zero. For breakfast we got gravy in a metal pan similar to the type used for meatloaf. With the gravy came three slices of bread. At noon and evening we received a small amount of two different vegetables in the same pan. We were never given any meat Every morning, day in and day out, we were ordered onto a rickety old bus and driven to a huge rock quarry to break rocks with a sledgehammer. Eight hours a day we broke and loaded rock onto a dump truck. One day another fellow and I decided to escape. A black employee of the quarry who had been in jail half his lifetime said he would give us a signal when the shotgun guard was looking the other way. He told us if we ran on around a rock hill to our right, we would be free and clear to go on our way.

We followed the man's advice and soon found ourselves trapped on a ledge with nowhere to go. That incident taught me a lesson I never forgot. The guy tricked us and had a good laugh at our expense, but his joke wasn't funny to me. He made an enemy who doesn't forget. Here it is, more than sixty years later, and if I found him in a crack, I would show him that I don't forget.

On Friday nights, a guard in that camp and several of his buddies who were sheriff's deputies in a nearby town went out and arrested people for being drunk who weren't really drunk. In addition, they would issue traffic citations for trivial driving offenses like poking the nose of your car over the pedestrian crosswalk lines by a few inches. Then, the next morning, the town's municipal judge (they called him "The Squire") would hold court in the front room of the jail, fining the victims $12.50 for each "offense." The deputies involved got $2.50 for each arrest, while the judge, so the rumor went, got the other $10. This occurred each and every Friday and Saturday night without fail.

I saw some huge guys come into our camp. When I say they were huge, I mean they were big mountain men, as strong as apes. Most said they had not been born to break rock and were mean and ready to fight prisoners and guards alike. I watched some awesome fights between these mountain gorillas. My bunkhouse was used as a dumping ground for the more violent of them. When fights broke out at night. some of the other prisoners would call for the guards. They had to break up the fights with clubs and threaten the men with shotguns. The mountain men didn't give a damn if they lived or not. In fact, it looked to me like the harder each guy was beaten and the more blood he shed—the nearer to death he was-- the more manly he felt he had become. The rest of us just shook our heads at the mayhem.

I was released in February 1950, just after the infamous Brink's Robbery, and hitchhiked back to Jacksonville. I tried staying with my mother for three or four months, but again, it didn't work out. My mother had taken up with yet another bum, a stupid son of a bitch named Davis. He insisted she give her second set of kids away, telling her and me that the children were better off. I found more satisfaction in being on the wrong side of the law than at being at home with my mother and Davis.

It wasn't long before I met two fellows my age, Benny and Larry, who told me they had a robbery all cased out. Larry was a seventeen-year-old black kid whom I had met in Marianna. Larry and Benny said the man they were planning to rob owned a building with his living quarters on the top floor and a liquor store and lounge below.

One night the three of us entered the roof of an adjoining building and climbed down through a window into his apartment. We then waited for him to close his business at 2:00 a.m. We knew he carried a gun with him, but that didn't frighten us. There were three of us and one of him. We planned to jump him and take his pistol. In his darkened living room, we waited on each side of his apartment door and listened for him to climb the stairs. As he opened and closed the door behind him and before he could turn on the lights, we jumped him. For a moment all four of us were in a big ball, fighting and rolling all over the living room, making a lot of noise. But the guy was big and broke loose. Since we knew he still had the gun, all three of us headed for the window we entered through, jumped down to the roof of an adjoining shed, and hit the ground. It was as if we were acting simultaneously, leaping, crashing, bouncing, and running, as our intended victim was already blasting away at us from his window. Good thing it was dark and he couldn't see much. The three of us got away.

We ran, walked, and stumbled several miles while congratulating ourselves on being alive. We made it to the Lake Forest Inn, where Larry, the black kid, worked. While Benny and I waited, he went in and got all his clothes. While he was in there, he decided to take his boss's clothes too, since the man wasn't in his office or room. Through the window of his boss's room, Larry handed me a large bottle of Scotch whiskey to hold for him until he came out. But I immediately left with it and walked home. That night in my room I drank about half of it, throwing it all back up the next morning. I never was much for hard liquor, and that bout with the bottle taught me all I ever need to know about Scotch whiskey.

Later I learned that Larry and Benny planned to head home to Pennsylvania where they lived. But when Larry's boss found Larry and his stuff missing, he notified the police, who tracked Larry to a black club called the Two Spot, a place where Ray Charles used to sing when he lived in Jacksonville before he became famous. The cops caught Larry and threatened him into a confession. Then two plainclothes detectives put him in an unmarked police car and drove around my neighborhood for two days, trying to spot me. On the third morning, as I was leaving my mother's place, the two detectives caught me by surprise by easing up from behind and grabbing me. They shoved me in their car and had Larry identify me right then and there. Of course, I denied any participation in the break-in and attempted theft. I even denied taking the whiskey. I insisted I had never seen the black kid before and started telling Larry what I was going to do to him for framing me. The two detectives, meanwhile, were telling me what they were going to do to me.

So, once again I was in the Jacksonville city jail. That old jail had several sections, each containing twenty-four men, and a bullpen for those nearing trial. This bullpen consisted of four cells that held six men each and was used only during the daytime. When a new man such as myself was thrown into it, he was read a list of rules and regulations and fined three dollars. This money was supposed to be used to buy tobacco and razor blades for the use of everybody in the jail. If you didn't have any money then you worked it out by helping to keep the bullpen clean.

At night one of the prisoners in our cell would amuse the rest of us by holding a metal coffee cup near his mouth to make his voice sound as if it was coming from the speaker on the wall. He would call out the name of a man who was just brought in and say in an official tone that someone was there to post the person's bail bond. A guy down the line would then walk over and shake the fellow's cell door. The naive butt of the joke would be told to pull on his door, since it must be stuck. The unsuspecting guy would start yanking and pulling on it with little result. So, the man who had come over would say in a loud voice, "Goddammit, yank hard on the door," and the guy would yank as hard as he could. When it still wouldn't open, someone would shout, "Goddammit, throw some water on it!" The guy desperately trying to get out would take his drinking cup, get some water, and throw it on the door. This continued until the poor guy wised up or the other inmates got tired of laughing at him. Most of us laughed about it and usually the victim ended up laughing, too. But I watched one man who was in my cell get so mad that he started crying and threatened to whip everybody's ass. Then the trick wasn't so funny.

While incarcerated there, I had no money. Luckily for me, Solomon Weinhof, a fight manager from Daytona Beach, was arrested and thrown into my cell. Because I was a boxer and knew who was who in the world of boxing, we became friends and he loaned me some money for a poker game, where I won some money of my own. Later, Solomon and I would continue our friendship when I started boxing seriously.

Again, I spent months awaiting trial with no credit for time served. My mother came to court and told the judge that I had always obeyed and respected her. The judge responded, "Well, he doesn't obey and respect the laws of the state of Florida, so I'm going to put him where he will!" Then he turned and asked Larry, who was on trial too, why he gave me his bossman's whiskey. I then jumped in, saying, "To drink it, stupid! Why do you think he gave it to me?" Shocked, the judge angrily shouted back, "Well, you won't be drinking anymore. Both of you are still wet behind the ears. You both graduated from the reform school, so now you're going to college." He then sentenced me to two years and Larry to three in the Florida state prison system at Raiford.

When Larry and I arrived at Raiford we had to spend two entire weeks in a courtyard that joined the administration building. During that period, we were called in and out for processing purposes, something I felt could have been handled in two hours. But during this time, I told a black guy standing near Larry how Larry had ratted on me and that he would regret it. This guy told Larry what I had said. It was the only time in all my prison years that I ever let myself reveal anything that personal, and I regret it to this day. You never, never, never share an intention for revenge with someone you don't know.

I had always heard the food was bad at Raiford. Compared to the food in reform school or the camp in Tennessee, it was much better. The blacks were separated from the whites in every way. In fact, during our rules and regulations orientation by the captain, he ordered us whites to stay away from the "coons." The deputy warden was also a mean bastard who caused one fellow to lose an eye from a beating he administered while we were still in quarantine. Soon thereafter the son of a bitch ended up getting shot by beating up on the wrong man. But there weren't any problems between black and white prisoners, as you might expect, since the whites were told to not even talk to the blacks, although some of us did.

One morning I was working out with Billy Lima, a tough, young Cuban boxer who had fought Willie Pep. Pep was the world champion and Lima had gone the distance with him with him twice, even though he lost both fights. As Billy and I took a break from our sparring, a clean-cut looking kid about my age and body build started chatting with me, adding that his name was Bobby. I had noticed him around the gym before and saw him playing cards with Billy Kilgore a couple of times. Billy had been a top middleweight who fought regularly on television. I hadn't paid any particular attention to this Bobby but now he said he liked the way I carried myself and that he heard from Billy that I had just come off a chain gang and carried a large switchblade, a lot of hate, and more trouble than any one man could stand. In other words, I was someone to be treated with caution.

After talking further, he told me his real name was George Heroux, and it didn't take me long to see that here was a tough little kid who knew no fear. His story, as far as I'm concerned, knows no parallel in the annals of American crime.

George "Bobby" Heroux was twenty-two years old and had already been on the FBI's Ten Most Wanted list for three bank robberies and killing a state trooper in Connecticut. On the day he was arrested in Miami, the chief of police, accompanied by two officers, went to a duplex where he lived under an alias and told him they had a complaint from neighbors about his loud parties and talk that he had guns in his apartment. The chief asked him to go to the station with them on some pretext, and George said, "Sure, why not? Let me grab my jacket." George pulled a pistol from the jacket and said, "I'm George Heroux, one of the Ten Most Wanted." He then handcuffed the chief and forced him to lie on the back floor of his squad car. With one cop driving, one sitting in the back seat, and the chief on the floor, Bobby told all three to make up their minds to die if they were cornered. Then, during a running battle with other police officers who followed in their patrol cars, the chief managed to kick George on the side of his head. Angrily, Heroux turned and fired almost point-blank at the chief. This gave the cop who was driving the chance to turn the car over.

Although the chief of police survived the shooting and crash of the auto, Heroux was given the maximum prison sentence under the law and sentenced to Raiford.

For the next few months, George "Bobby" Heroux and I hung around the gym, talked, and became fast friends. He showed me pictures of his wife, Ruth, who was a real knockout of a beauty. And he told me stories about the crimes he committed with his partner, a guy called Puff. But most of all, we talked about jail life. At the time, I thought to myself, "Here is a standup guy who has an innate hatred of cops and prison workers like I do. But he's tougher than I am. He's calm under pressure, and that's what makes guys like him so dangerous. He is a remake of Babyface Nelson."

But there was another side to him that only people close to him, like his wife, Ruth, knew. For example, one morning he told me that when he was born his mother died and his aunt raised him, showering him with love. The love that he had for his aunt carried over to respect for all older women, a respect that may have saved the life of Mrs. Bennett, his landlady in Miami.

He said of Mrs. Bennett, "A few days before I was caught, Mrs. Bennett came over to our duplex claiming that we had damaged her end-tables and carpet with cigarette burns. I told her I would pay for any damage, not knowing she had already called the cops. But the cops didn't come until two days later. Meanwhile I gave her some money for the damage. When the chief and his two deputies knocked on my door, she was right there, too, running her mouth. That's when I got my jacket with the snub-nosed .38. When I pointed the gun at the cops, telling them who I was, she took off running."

I said, "Hell, Bobby, I would have probably shot that old bitch first, after all the grief she brought you."

He answered with a smile, "No, you don't harm old people. That's just the way they get."

I admired that part of his character. But, soon enough, her snitching on him cost him his life at the age of 29. Sometime during the months that followed, Ruth, Heroux's wife, somehow managed to slip a gun inside the prison by hiding it in a Kotex. In the Raiford women's restroom at the visiting park area, she managed to hide it somewhere so that an orderly could smuggle it to her husband.

The next morning, Heroux flashed the pistol at two guards who opened his cell in his semi-isolation ward when they were going to escort him to a shower. He locked one of the men in his cell and told the other that he had nothing against him and was not planning to hurt him. But if he didn't follow orders, Heroux told him he would kill him on the spot, sure as anything.

He then forced the other guard to escort him through Raiford's west gate and around a building to the hall gate leading to the deputy warden's office. The hall gate was operated by an old inmate named Oley Gritzmeyer. But as they passed through that gate and the captain's office, they were spotted. A bunch of guards immediately came running out into the corridor. As they started to make a circle around him, Heroux opened fire and hit three guards. He held them at bay with the gun while he kicked the deputy warden's door open. J. G. Godwin, the deputy warden, got up from his desk and started to run toward the rear, but Heroux fired and hit him in the back. Godwin staggered through the door of the accounting office, managing to lock it behind him. Heroux then coldly shot two other guards at almost pointblank range, broke the accounting door open, and, as other guards ran, located Godwin hiding under a desk and shot him several times in the stomach and back.

Heroux then grabbed another guard and, holding him as a shield, started to retreat down the corridor. There was no possibility of escape now. He was surrounded but he wouldn't quit. He opened fire on the surrounding guards and hit two more, including a captain. But then either George's gun jammed or he ran out of ammunition, and a large group of guards started down the corridor toward him and the officer he still held in front of him as a shield. As George rushed the guards with his bare fists, one old guard we used to call Sneaky Pete hit him over the head with his walking stick. George went down.

Meanwhile, Godwin was losing a tremendous amount blood from his various wounds and died in the prison hospital within two hours of being admitted. No doctor on duty was capable of handling the necessary surgery.

Later, the prosecutor from Miami was quoted as saying he had recommended all along that Heroux be confined at Alcatraz. George had several bank robberies against him and the killing of that state trooper in Connecticut. He told me that he wanted to be shot like Joe Cretzer, who died while trying to crash out of Alcatraz in 1946. But before he went, he wanted to kill as many guards as he could. His father was all over the newspaper front pages, crying over what Heroux did to the guards and the deputy.

George came from a good family like so many other guys at Raiford, but the difference was he had a short circuit in his brain. At the time of the Raiford shootout, I was twenty-three years old and in the US Penitentiary at Atlanta. My cell buddies woke me up at 5:00 a.m. and showed me George's picture and all the accompanying headlines on the front pages of the newspapers that had just been dropped off. I was as surprised as everyone else about the shootout and how George had specifically targeted Godwin. He sure must have hated the deputy warden. But then again, we all had hated him.

I suppose that since that early April morning before breakfast in 1955 when George Darby and another Atlanta inmate awakened me with the headlines of the Atlanta Constitution telling about what George had done, I haven't stopped thinking about him. Although my friend still had five years to live when I left him at Raiford, his life would be pure hell.

A few months after Heroux's attempted escape and his killing of Godwin, a circuit court jury convicted George of first-degree murder. But it also recommended that mercy be shown and a life sentence be given rather than the death penalty. Some jurors who admitted qualms about the death penalty felt the shooting had occurred only because George was trying to escape and that he had shown no proven premeditation. The judge in the case was Ben C. Willard, who was known throughout Florida as "the world's most lenient judge." He used to give out five-year sentences for armed robbery while others judges gave life terms for the exact same offense.

Today, as I look back upon George "Bobby" Heroux, I have mixed feelings. He was my buddy, and, right or wrong, he will always be my buddy. I wish he hadn't tried to escape and, above all, I wished he hadn't gunned down Godwin. But I know that George wouldn't have shot the deputy warden in the stomach deliberately unless Godwin had done something awful bad to him. Shooting a guy in the stomach and nowhere else means you want the guy to suffer as much pain as possible. I'll never believe George was the animal prison authorities and the newspapers made him out to be. He was better in a lot of ways than those who kept him locked up.

Heroux died on February 13, 1960, of pneumonia—at least, that's what the official records say. But if you ask me, his "pneumonia" was helped along by the way the Raiford guards treated him and the way they probably water-hosed him. See, in those days, to Raiford officials a life sentence meant solitary confinement in the "flattop" isolation building, which was actually Raiford's "death row." There, George was forced to live out his life naked in a small, concrete cell with windows you couldn't see out of because they were so heavily glazed over. A small hole in a corner of the cell was his toilet. I heard from a Raiford orderly that clean-up men or janitors chosen from the various "rat packs" in the prison helped guards hang George by his thumbs from the cell front bars so that the guards could beat him with rubber hoses and then wash him down with high-pressure hoses. If you use rubber hoses in a certain way, no bruises will show. An inmate plumber also confirmed what the orderly had confided in him. Both knew how close I was to Bobby.

In the early fall of 1992, I spoke with a former Raiford official, now in his 80s, who said he talked to George on a Thursday afternoon, asking how he was getting along. George replied, "Pretty good under the circumstances." He showed no signs of being ill. Yet, two days later, on a Saturday morning, the guards found him dead on his mattress in a corner of his cell. The warden told the press that he died of simple pneumonia.

What does common sense tell you? Why did George have several bouts with pneumonia in those last five years at Raiford unless it was because he was continually being hosed down? Someday, I hope to track George's wife, Ruth, down, and with her write the full story about George Heroux. I spent two years, 1991 and 1992, trying to locate his grave in various cemeteries throughout Florida.

Finally, when I found it in Stark, near Raiford State Prison, there was no marker, no identification, no headstone, nothing except for thick grass all over it. Ironically, Godwin's grave was less than a few hundred yards away. His grave is a lot nicer and kept up regularly. It cost me $268.00, but at least George now has a headstone. I knew him as a better person than what most saw him as and I will never forget him. Some people, good and bad, touch your life in a way that lasts a lifetime. George did that for me. I'm just sorry that both he and Godwin are dead.

In those days, the deputy warden ran everything at Raiford. If you had money you could buy yourself a soft job. If not, you got the prison's chain gang, like I did. At daylight every morning we were loaded up in trucks at Raiford's back gate and driven in different directions. We worked for ten hours a day in the hot, boiling sun. At noon we were given forty-five minutes to rest and eat cornbread and beans. This lunch never, never varied. Some of the Yankee boys would pass out from the sun. The walking bosses would pour water on their faces, saying, "Okay old buddy, let's get up and try it again." We did get a ten-minute break twice a day to smoke a cigarette. The rest of the time we were working and sweating our asses off. It was bad, because the work assigned was more than a human could do. I began bucking the guards hard, so they put leg irons on me, the kind you see in the old Paul Muni chain gang movies.

The leg irons had a metal peg permanently bradded down by using a hammer on an anvil at the blacksmith shop. This meant there was no way you could get them off. You had to learn to change your pants with them on. You pulled one pants leg down and then up the other and pulled the pants down that leg and through the inside ring of the leg irons. Once you got used to those hated leg irons you could do a lot of things.

In the early 1950s, the Florida Bureau of Prisons maintained more than sixty road camps. I was soon transferred from Raiford to a road gang in Chattahoochee, in northern Florida. No sooner had several of us climbed down out of the bus when the walking boss, an illiterate and angry son of a bitch named Casey, walked up and said, "I didn't send for a damn one of you. As far as I'm concerned, you all are trash to be thrown out." The rest of the day he walked and strutted back and forth in the camp with his walking stick, giving us dirty looks. In between, he ranted and cursed us as if we had raped his mother. Boss Casey was a real cracker and hated everybody. The first day I was there I heard from a prisoner that Casey took up with the wife of one of the inmates and paid the inmate off by making him a "trustee." While Casey was fucking his wife, the prisoner was acting like he owned the camp, ordering us around, giving us hell. If he had acted like that back at Raiford, he wouldn't have lived past the first ten minutes.

The Florida road camps were all built alike. The bunk house was shaped like a "T" with the entrance in the left corner of the "T." The guards' offices were also at the entrance, surrounded by wicker wire so that they could see in all three directions without moving. In the building was also a small mess hall, supply room, and a sweat box for punishment.

The bunkhouse was surrounded with a fifteen or twenty-foot fence, with one guard tower at the back that had a view of the whole place. The captain's office was outside the fence, near the entrance. Each morning as we walked out the gate to climb aboard a truck, the captain and his walking boss stood at the gate, counting the prisoners. We had to take our caps off as we passed them. At the black camps the blacks had to say, "Good morning, boss man," and take their hats off. In fact, they had to take their hats off every time they passed a guard.

There were between forty and sixty prisoners in our camp. We got up about five in the morning and either cleared brush off of the right of way for one of Florida's roads or dug ditches and leveled road shoulders until five in the evening. We did this five and a half days a week. You were too tired to do anything but rest when you were idle. I would love to see some of these tough gang kids today who are involved with drugs go through thirty days of that and remain tough. Most of these kids would straighten up quick.

The walking boss spent the whole day walking back and forth, cursing and intimidating you as you worked. He would be swinging his walking stick and resting his hand on his .38 revolver, hung in a gunfighter holster at his waist. If one of the prisoners passed out from the heat, he would pour water in his face, revive the poor guy, and say, "All right, ole buddy, let's get up and try it again." It was the same line used in all road camps and rock quarries, as if the State of Florida had made the fuckers memorize it.

The guards all carried state-issued twelve-gauge shotguns loaded with buck shot, and a .38 revolver. They never said anything to you unless you got too close and then they would point their shotgun at you, ready to fire. Then they would say, "Back up."

If you had to piss, you would say, "Pouring it out, boss," and he would say, "Pour it out," and you would piss right there. In those days traffic was thin, and if you had to defecate you said, "Digging a hole, boss" and he would say, "Dig a hole." You would walk over to the edge of some bushes. He would tell you to keep moving the bush as you defecated so he knew you were not moving away. On a busy road near town, the prisoners were ordered to dig a hole for a toilet and rig a canvas stall over it for privacy. But it was so hot inside, you couldn't stand it. That summer we cleared a lot of road rights-of-way. It was hot, humid, hard work, and Boss Casey tried to see just how hard he could push us. Some guys would deliberately cut their heel tendons to get out of that road camp and back into Raiford. But I never even considered such a thing. I would rather go hungry a few days than cripple myself for life.

The road camp's sweat box was about six feet from the dining room. At first, I couldn't figure this out. Then it dawned on me: the sons of bitches wanted you to smell the food cooking as you sweated out some punishment. If you were in the box, all you got were three slices of bread a day: not three slices of bread three times a day, but three slices of bread, once a day! Men had died in those sweat boxes; I was told by some of the older prisoners. Because of those deaths, the warden was ordered by the state to replace the first two boards under the roof with wicker wire so that you at least had circulating air. The unfortunate man forced into that death hole only had room to lie down or stand up. A basketball player wouldn't have survived. It was like lying in a bathtub made out of wood.

Later, in late 1967, when I happened to drop into a Jacksonville theater to see a movie, I couldn't believe what I saw in the classic feature film Cool Hand Luke, starring Paul Newman, George Kennedy, and Strother Martin. It was like I was suddenly transported back to 1950 and the Raiford chain gangs. The sweatbox that Paul Newman had to endure was exactly like the ones I had to survive. Strother Martin, playing the captain who taunted Luke with the famous line, "What we've got here is a failure to communicate," was exactly like the turkeys who ruled over us. J.D. Cannon, I believe, played the cold, murderous walking boss and was the spitting image of all the walking bosses I ever knew. In the fifties, they all wore sunglasses like Cannon did and they all stared at you the same way Cannon did. The only thing that was left out of Cool Hand Luke was the way the captains, walking bosses, and guards cursed you. Donn Pearce, who co-wrote the script, was at Raiford when I was there. As an inmate, he spent two years on a chain gang.

Naturally, I wound up in the camp's sweat box four or five times for refusing to work or arguing with a guard. Once I was in for breaking the padlock off the canteen door and stealing $15 or $20 in change from a drawer. A Yankee boy helped me in that theft. But another prisoner trying to get in good with the captain and who owed the canteen some money ratted us out. The first time I was in the sweat box, a prisoner came up and stood next to it so we could talk. I began saying what a sorry motherfucker Boss Casey was for fucking an inmate's wife and having her keep the house for him. No sooner had I said that when another prisoner came up to the sweat box and whispered that Boss Casey was listening behind the sweat box. At that I laughed and shouted as loud as I could, "Fuck Boss Casey! When I get out of prison someday, I'm gonna come back and cut his pecker off and shove it up the warden's ass. He better sleep with the lights on from now on."

Each day you spent in the box you had a half a day off. So, if you spent six days in the box, you got three days off work to build your strength back up. Every night Boss Casey would open the box's door and give the man inside a cup of milk of magnesia to drink. He laughed at me during the third time I was in the box and said, "See? If you had saved your bread, you could have had milk and bread." I shouted, "Fuck you, you miserable ball of shit." He said, "We'll see how tough you are." He kept me in there seven whole days. When I got out, I could barely walk.

One of the walking bosses' pet prisoners ratted on a buddy of mine named Ted Long for some minor thing. That night when the bunkhouse inmate-guard, or floorwalker, as the officials called them, said Ted's name, Ted asked, "Am I going to the box?" When the inmate-guard said, "Yes," Ted slugged the rat on the jaw. The inmate-guard, who was slightly crippled and walked with a cane, managed to pull a knife as he struggled to get up. I grabbed the inmate-guard's walking stick and hit him across the back. Ted grabbed the knife and threw it across the bunk house. He then started beating up on the guy until other guards rushed in and pulled Ted away.

We were both thrown in the box. The next day Ted and the rat were both transferred back to Raiford.

A couple of months later, I led my bunk house out on a work strike. Boss Casey picked out six or eight of us, with me as ring leader, and sent us all back to Raiford and there I remained until my release. My last recollection of Ted Long is that one Sunday morning during the church service, Ted put a nickel in the collection tray and took out a dollar someone had put in but the inmate usher saw him and made him put it back before anyone saw him. Ted was as hungry as any of us for a little pocket money, but the prison system only laughed.

In the mid-1920s, the nation had been shocked by revelations of barbarity in what was called Florida's "convict-lease system." Here was Florida, the state of "flowers, sunshine, and laughing waters," participating in the exploitation, neglect, and sometimes murder of small-time, unfortunate convicts with no more regard than if they were from another planet. Well, things changed over the years but when I was at Raiford and in the road camp, prisoners, as far as most of the guards were concerned, were at the very bottom of the human heap and black prisoners were regarded as subhuman. The tramp, the hobo, the vagabond, the faker, the beggar, the thief, the unskilled and unemployed workers were all several notches ahead of us. They at least were treated as human beings. They were shown pity, dignity, and a little compassion. At Raiford and in the road gang, we were stripped of any distinctive marks, of personality, of self-assertion. Not only were we just numbered flesh left to the mercy of the guards but we were also left helpless among ourselves. Nobody gave a damn if we killed each other, and whippings were so commonplace that no one, even among the prisoners, bothered to feel sorry for the man being whipped. Inmates were still hung by their thumbs in the early 1950s, with just the tips of their feet touching the floor. Prisoners were beaten with a two-foot length of garden hose. They say it bruises you on the inside instead of the outside.

The typical prison guard, as far as I was concerned, was just as neurotic or psychotic as we were. The unfortunate son of a bitch breathed daily in a strained atmosphere. He leaned on a gun all day long and was on duty from sunup to sundown. If he was lucky, he made $90 a month. This meant the job didn't attract the caring and intelligent type who could adequately guard and protect his crew of prisoners. Most of the guards I met were illiterate, ignorant, and sadistic to one degree or another. All were racists. The boredom of their jobs caused the sicker minds among them to "sport with the prisoners." They would ride their horses over men or sic their dogs on them for the least excuse. I could go into stories right and left about how the bastards enjoyed humiliating us. But one thing occurred day in and day out, just as sure as the sun rose and set: the guards showed us who was boss and that we damn well better pay due reverence to them. They determined our fate.

Every convict who went through a Southern prison in the late 1940s knows what I'm talking about. Of course, sanitary conditions had improved by then. Of course, men were no longer going to sleep so hungry that they tried to eat in their sleep. Of course, the treatment of the sick was a hundred times better than it was before the Second World War. Of course, negligence and open cruelty by the guards and officials had almost disappeared. But when it came to disciplinary methods, it was like being back in the 1920s. Brutality rose among the guards as the quality of the men recruited to be guards fell.

The prejudices and behavior of the guards hardened as they wielded more and more power and authority but as they did so, we were deformed more and more. The hatred generated in us can't ever be fully described. I tried not to let my spirit break. I know I kept my honor but imagine what it was like for others, perhaps weaker in spirit. Imagine being half naked and half fed, being made to get down on your knees and take a beating as if you were nothing. Imagine being made the subject of direct and indirect ridicule every day. A lot of guys preferred death. I came near to that feeling but every instinct I had spoke for life, and I fought.

One of the first convicts I got to know after returning to Raiford from the road camp was James Francis Hill, who had recently been shot in another road gang trying to take a shotgun away from a guard. I knew he had a bad reputation among the prisoners and guards and figured he would make a good partner inside. Later, when we got out, he would be someone I could depend upon if we went robbing together.

Hill told me in confidence that his best friend had betrayed their plan of escape two weeks earlier on the road gang by not following through with his role. Hill explained that he had been able one day to work his way close to an armed guard. Then, without waiting for his friend, he lunged and started tugging with the guard's shotgun, but as they wrestled, the guard pulled the trigger and the buckshot caught Hill in the left forearm, leaving his wrist bleeding and a little twisted out of shape. (A few years later in Atlanta Penitentiary I spoke to Hill's "best friend," Jack White, a career criminal. White denied Hill's accusation and claimed that Hill's plan was pure suicide and it almost got the two of them killed.)

Hill, who was in Raiford for a twelve-year armed robbery stretch, was a real psycho. Yet, if he liked you, he would stop at nothing for you, not even killing another inmate over something trivial. But because he was paranoid, he was very dangerous to deal with. I knew he was from Framingham, Massachusetts, but did not learn until an FBI agent told me later that Hill had once been confined to a mental institution in that state.

If Hill had been shot and killed by that Raiford guard, it automatically would have been labeled justifiable homicide. Prisoners had no rights, a fact that was made clear by the captain the first moment you arrived in the state prison. Raiford officials had few problems in those days running the institutions and its road camps. Over 99 percent of the inmates toed the line, although a good 30 percent of the men, like me, had various psychological problems. Often, I have thought that the tough guys who cause trouble in our prison systems today do so because they know they can get away with it. Under the old system the arrogant ones would have been the most obedient. It used to irritate me to listen to most of the work gang at camp say in unison, "Yes sir, boss!" and this is why the tough animals in prison today don't impress me. I have seen their kind put to the test and, believe me, only one in a hundred is made of the real material.

At Raiford, and later at Atlanta and Alcatraz, I noticed that the toughest cons didn't go around advertising their toughness, and I was sometimes surprised how tough they really were under their masks. A lot of guys today know that the system is hog-tied by the state and federal courts and they take advantage of any weakness they can. Essentially, they are cowards. I have seen every type of man that the prisons hold and how they operate. I watched one old guy at Raiford tell some of their kind to go get a knife and fight him, and he would spot them the knife without taking one for himself. Every single one of them backed down. But if they had the advantage over weaker prisoners, they would come on like gangbusters. Isn't this the way many businessmen operate?

During my stay at Raiford I tried to stay in good shape through hard work and a little boxing in the yard, where we had a roped-off area for a ring. Several good boxers were incarcerated there, including a black middle-weight. I had matches with all of them, and they were all classy guys, especially "Baby Louis," a black fighter who licked me and even heavy-weights from the nearby navy base. But even though I worked out a lot with these buddies, I was never on the official boxing team.

At that time in the early 1950s, the women prisoners were still housed in a section near the Raiford recreation yard, and the boxing matches and ball games we participated in were only about two hundred feet from them. There was never any problem with the guys trying to get over to the women, because we all knew what to expect from the officials. During our weekly movies, the women sat across the aisle from us, and other than wistful looks we gave each other, there was no communication. Today the women prisoners have their own prison near Ocala.

Many of us at Raiford milled around the east gate every weekday after lunch, waiting to return to work inside the institution. One noontime while watching a crap game, a white buddy of mine, Amos Walker, who had been in reform school with me, accidentally stepped on the toe of another white guy who had just shined his shoes. The big, muscular guy started cursing Amos. My buddy said, "I didn't know I was on your goddamn shoe. I'm sorry." But the big man continued to run off at the mouth. So, I stepped in and said, "Fuck your shiny shoe!" This infuriated the convict. He turned towards me, saying, "I don't think the two of you can whip my ass." He was beginning to swing his right arm to strike, but James Francis Hill stepped over, put his arms around Amos and me, and said, "If my two friends can't, then the three of us can." The big guy backed off and said no more. Hill had a bad reputation all over the Florida prison system. We became better friends after that and made plans to team up once we were back on the streets. We pledged to help Amos escape when we got out, because our friend was loaded down with time.

Six months before my release from Raiford, Charlie Bashlor, a sixteen-year-old kid from Detroit, shot and killed the vice president of a Jacksonville bank and received a life sentence to be served at Raiford. When I met Charlie, we hit it off like brothers. He explained that he had no intention of killing the banker, he only wanted to get away. The banker had worked with delinquent boys and felt he could handle Charlie. So, he had tried to take Charlie's gun even after Charlie pulled the trigger twice and it had misfired. But the third time the gun discharged and a bullet hit the banker in the forehead.

Charlie and I spent a lot of time together at Raiford. Since I had a two-man cell by myself, I tried to get him moved in with me, but the cell house officer refused and kept him in a cell with ten other inmates. Although he made a few other friends, we talked a couple of times a day. Years later, in 1991, I saw Charlie in the news a couple of times, once for trying to escape. In the 1990s, I worked in a garage and handled the car repair work for Mr. Foster, who was a supervisor at Raiford. He enjoyed talking to me while I worked on his car. One day I told him how unjust the system was by releasing garbage while keeping guys like Charlie incarcerated and treating them inhumanely for not breaking down or giving in. He said, "Well, you know, your friend may not be the same guy you knew in 1951."

Maybe so. But I still maintain that Charlie stayed in prison because he never once let his spirit sway. He would never agree to be a "yes" man. Today I see guys make parole after five or six years on vicious rape and murder charges and I know that our prison systems are not as great as so many believe. Charlie was a good kid when I knew him, and after decades in prison he is still there for an accidental murder.

I worked in the tobacco factory, stripping tobacco leaves during my last six months at Raiford. The man who worked next to me was a distinguished looking judge who had murdered his wife, claiming that robbers did it. He almost got away with it, but a detective did some good police work and found a flaw in his story, so he was convicted. At Raiford the judge made friends with an inmate and spent a lot of money on him at the canteen. Meanwhile, he was buying protection.

When I was released from Raiford in April 1952, after serving my two-year sentence (excluding seven months in the road gang), a records officer by the name of L.A. Dugger (his son is Florida's Director of Prisons today) walked me to the gate and gave me a $10 bill. He said he sincerely hoped I would straighten out. He believed I had the ability and intelligence to do anything I set my mind to. "You don't need to live the kind of life you've led," he said. He added, "A taxi is due anytime from Stark to deliver the morning papers. Would you like to wait and get a ride to town?" I said, "No, it's okay." I was so anxious to get away from Raiford that I took off walking towards Stark, some twelve miles away. A black man, also just released, joined me. About a mile down the road, the taxi driver pulled over to give us a lift to town but when the driver noticed that the man with me was black, he wouldn't let him get in the taxi. So, I said I would walk too.

About twenty minutes later, a man in a pickup truck stopped and allowed both of us to ride in the back. He dropped us off at a Greyhound bus station. As my black companion walked up to the ticket counter, I noticed a bunch of white guys who looked like rednecks, sitting around a Coke stand and staring at us. The cab driver who I turned down had apparently driven by and told them to be on the lookout for us, since I was a troublemaker. But I could not have cared less about their opinion, because I knew I was right and felt better inside for it.

I bought a bus ticket to Jacksonville, and when I arrived, I had $8.50 left. My mother said that if I wanted, I could stay with her and her boyfriend Davis until I got my feet on the ground. Since I had no money, no job, and no prospects for anything at the moment, I accepted and thanked her. I still didn't like Davis because he had made my mother give away her second batch of kids, but he tried to be friendly, although it was probably out of fear.

Jobs were hard to come by in the spring of 1952, especially for an ex-con. I tried the unemployment office first, and some supervisor there heard me answering some questions to a friendly receptionist about where I had been in prison. He called me over to talk but it turned out he was just nosy, and I left with nothing. After looking for work every morning, I started hanging out at Clyde's Saloon on Bay Street in the afternoons. At the time, it was the oldest bar in the South. The neighborhood was cluttered with pawnshops, cafes, cheap bars, and pool halls. Clyde's Saloon was where most of the action was on Bay Street, and guys from Raiford were always hanging out there. Soon enough I was mingling with all the ex-cons. Two of the former prisoners who I met worked at a nearby ice cream factory. Since they were about to quit their steady jobs and leave town, I applied for their job. After a brief interview, the owner, who was partial to former convicts, hired me.

It was cold, working in the factory's deep freeze. My job was to lift boxes of ice cream off a pulley belt and place them on nearby shelves. No matter how much clothing I put on, I still shivered all day. Even the special suit and coat the company offered didn't help. I still had to go outside every half hour to allow my face to warm up. A few weeks later, I was able to switch to the evening shift, loading trucks outside the deep freeze. There was no way I was going to die in order to keep a job in an icebox.

Every night a few cops would stop by in their patrol car and shout, "Bring me a couple of Eskimo Pies from the damaged bin." Anyone, even kids, could help themselves to free ice cream from the damaged bin. On one particular night, a kid who had just been released from the Marianna reform school was hanging around the dock. He heard the cops and walked over to the damaged bin, took out two Eskimo Pies, unwrapped them, and, without the cops seeing him, pulled down his pants and slowly rubbed the pies against his peter. Then, as he smiled at me, he wrapped them up and walked down and handed them to the cops.

The two patrolmen asked him what took so long as they sat in their car eating the ice cream. A bunch of us workers looked down from the dock, having a good laugh. One cop saw us, climbed out of the patrol car, and asked, "What's so goddamn funny?" One of the workers who was also an ex-con said, "You officers act like you're really hungry." The cop answered, "We are, and if we want any bullshit out of you guys, we'll come up there and beat it out." We all roared with laughter. If they had known what we thought was so funny, they would probably have pulled their guns on us.

I continued working at the ice cream factory for about a month, but I became restless. I didn't particularly enjoy living with my mother and her boyfriend, and I didn't particularly like loading ice cream at night. I took off for Miami, where I landed a job as a busboy at the Casablanca Hotel on the beach. The job meant I could have all the free boxing time I wanted in the hotel gym. I was out of training and wanted to get myself back in condition. Back then, you could earn $25 for four rounds of professional fighting. Some guys fought as often as twice a week. In the Fifth Street gym I met Chris Dundee, who arranged fights at the Miami Beach Auditorium. Through him I met his brother, Angelo Dundee. Angelo would canvas gyms, looking for fighters to fill preliminary cards. He was young then and looked nothing like he did later. Once I was in shape, I returned to Miami so that I could get better professional training. I began working out at the Magic City Gym on Southwest Sixth Street where Rocky Graziano worked out whenever he was in town.

Most of the Miami fighters held down regular jobs. Billy Lauderdale, my favorite boxing buddy, was learning to be a carpenter. Later, he entered dental college. He invested all the money he picked up boxing in land deals with his father. Years later when land was high, he borrowed money from the bank to build inexpensive houses and made it big. By 1972, Billy was a millionaire businessman. Billy Lima, my other stablemate and a good feather-weight who fought world champion Willie Pep twice in 1952, is driving a Tampa city bus now and Billy Kilgore, who fought on television a lot, is driving a jitney-taxi at the Miami Airport.

One of the heavy-weights I trained with at Miami City was Gordon Pouliot, a city cop. One day in the dressing room, my switchblade knife fell out of my pants on the floor. He picked it up and handed it to me, asking, "What do you want with this thing?" He told me it was against the law to carry it and if another cop caught me with it, he would book me. "Just get rid of it," he said. He later joined the US Border Patrol and today, while in retirement, he trains fighters. I often see him on ESPN cable fights, working his fighters' corners. I saw him spar with Rocky Graziano in the gym one day, and the two went at it pretty well. Rocky himself had been in reform school and was a regular guy in the gym, with no phony airs. He mingled easily with ex-cons.

By autumn of 1952, I was fighting for Jimmy Murdock in semi-pro fights at the Beaver Street Area for $25 a bout. One day I was talking to a fight trainer named Al and he gave me the name and address of Jerry White, a trainer and manager of fighters in Miami. So, I went back to Miami and met Jerry and he started training me as a professional boxer. He had me scheduled to fight Petey Ridgeway, a feather-weight who said he would come up to my weight if I couldn't make his but he came by the gym to watch me work out one day and changed his mind. So, Jerry lined me up for an amateur fight at the Opalocka Optimist Club, and we were paid cash instead of prizes, which was illegal but cash always attracts more fighters.

The last fight I had before launching my crime wave was scheduled against Billy Yoham, who now appears in the ESPN Cable Network fights as a referee. But Billy had to cancel for some reason, and I fought a Mexican from San Bernardino, California who was stationed near Tampa with the Air Force. Today Billy Yoham is a doctor. His brother Skippy and I worked out together in the gym every day and became good friends. Boxing gave me a feeling of being something besides a thug, a hood, and an ex-con. But because I could never stick with anything for long, I soon went back to being a thug.

I was training for my first pro fight when I started dating my landlady's daughter, Nancy Westbrook, a young woman of sixteen who had just dropped out of high school. I was doing real well with her, with my boxing, and life in general until one Sunday morning I received a long-distance telephone call from James Hill. He had just been released from Raiford after doing twelve years for armed robbery and an additional year and a half for trying to take the shotgun away from a guard. Hill wanted us to become a crime team as we had promised each other back in prison.

I said, "Come on down," but wasn't too happy about it. Actually, I had forgotten all about him, but he flew down the next day and we met in my room. He had a suitcase full of guns with him, and I picked out a German luger from a pile of eight guns. I had to admit that holding the piece felt good. We immediately began pulling a series of stick-ups, the first of which was a supermarket. We got away with about $225 in cash. Then we went after a loan company. Hill hated all loan companies and called them "fucking bloodsuckers." In Raiford he vowed he would make this one particular loan company pay for causing his wife to dump him. While we held a bunch of people at gunpoint, he started shouting wild things about the officers there and how one guy fucked his wife and stole money from him and other crazy things.

After that stick-up, the Miami newspapers referred to Hill as a "three-gun maniac" because he carried a pistol in each hand and one in his belt.

The FBI and Miami police issued bulletins describing him as extremely dangerous. But we didn't hurt anyone or get away with more than five or six hundred dollars in that job. In fact, in the four jobs we pulled together we got less than $900, and we just fired our guns eight or ten times to get people's attention.

We left Miami and headed north, stopping off at Nancy's place for an hour so I could tell her I didn't want her to waste her life on me. She was real loyal and said she would wait, no matter what happened. But I was in deep, serious trouble now and left her without looking back. Hill had another score to settle in Jacksonville. He and I drove up and down Bay Street, looking for a sex fiend named James Smith. Smith was a typical jailhouse asshole who picked his spots to bully and when finally challenged would back down. He worked in the Raiford tobacco factory when I did and pulled a knife a couple of times on guys who had done nothing but he never once used it.

Smith knew better than to pull anything like that on me. He knew that I knew he was a coward who only wanted to impress people. One day a 19-year-old named Red who weighed about 190 pounds told him in front of everybody that he was a phony motherfucker and to pull his knife. Smith said, "You know I wouldn't pull a knife on you, Red." Red said, "I know you wouldn't, because you queers don't have the guts." And Smith didn't try to argue the point. All the sex criminals I have seen in institutions, without exception, turned out to be cowards.

Hill was going to take James Smith for a long, long ride: so long, in fact, that he wouldn't return. But fortunately for Smith, we couldn't find him. We finally ran into another Raiford ex-con known as "Georgia Day" on Bay Street. Hill told the man that he owed Smith some money and wanted to pay him back before he left town. Georgia Boy said, "Yeah, I can show you where he lives." He got into the car with us and as we drove along Hill said that we had to keep cool and find the right place to pick him up. Georgia Boy was quiet for a long time, then asked to stop at a service station restroom. No sooner had he turned the corner of the station than he took off across an empty field. Hill cursed and wanted to go after him. But I said, "Aw, to hell with it." Smith will never know how close he came to getting killed. If he had died at the time, it would have saved a woman he later raped and left for dead in Confederate Park.

On our drive west through the Florida panhandle, Hill and I had a lot of time to talk. We didn't do much laughing, because we knew we were already being hunted. And if you were armed and hunted in the South in those days, it generally meant you died in some stupid shoot-out in some black mudhole filled with dead water. We talked mostly about George Heroux, Boss Casey, and the general life prisoners lived in road gangs. When George Heroux was on the streets of Miami, he was so clean-cut and good looking, he caused people to stop in their tracks and stare. When he was spread out on the front pages of all of Florida's newspapers, the boxers at the gym couldn't believe it. They knew Heroux as a friendly and easygoing kid who liked to watch the fighters spar. He played cards with all of us and he was very open and friendly. No one disliked him.

"They filed so many charges against him," I commented, "that the judge asked the prosecutor why he didn't charge him with speeding and reckless driving, too, when he turned that car over." Hill was quiet, reflecting. Then he said, "He told me that the goddamn prosecutor answered he was still thinking about filing those charges, too. George got 25 years for kidnaping, plus some more for taking the guns away from that chief of police and his two cops. Then the goddamn government gave him another 45 years for three bank robberies. And later, that same goddamn prosecutor said for the second time that George belonged in Alcatraz, this time for the rest of his life, for killing that piece of trash, the deputy warden, who had been provoking George all along."

We talked for hours. And the more we talked, the angrier we got. "Remember how bad they were at Raiford, hanging you up to the bars with handcuffs?" I asked. "I even saw the bastards hang one poor guy by his thumbs in the Raiford flattop, where the dead house was. They never did me that way because I never gave them enough reason. But some of my friends like Charlie Bashlor were done that way."

"Remember how the guards in the county jail would talk to us?" Hill asked. "I heard one tell a friend of mine who said he needed to use the telephone bad in order to get in touch with someone who could get him out. 'Well, old buddy,' the prick said, 'the only thing I can tell you is to draw a picture of your ass on the wall and crawl through the hole. You might find a friend in there!' The fucking cracker thought he was funny. He's not gonna think it's funny when Reese gets out and starts tracking his whereabouts."

"Remember the guard we called Sneaky Pete, the one who beat up on Heroux so bad?"

"Yeah," Hill answered.

"Well, I heard later he had put lead in the end of his walking stick."

We drove on in silence. Then Hill snarled, "That motherfucker wouldn't give you the sweat off his balls if you were dying of thirst. How did George really get the gun into Raiford?" he asked.

"Well, the way he told me, his wife hid the gun in her panties when she entered the prison. Then she went to the women's restroom in the visiting park and hid it in a toilet. An old con, 'Peppers,' who had the run of the prison, got it and brought it through the west gate and wrapped it in a package. George then took the transformer out of his old 1930s-style radio, put the gun in its place, and put the radio back together. When he was placed on "F" floor, a light detention unit, he asked Captain Wainright to bring him his radio. The captain picked up his radio personally and placed it in his hands, never knowing it contained the gun he would later be shot with. Heroux's wife, Ruth, was only 23 and a really beautiful girl. She had a race jockey at Hialeah buy the gun for her and it was later traced back to him and he got a ten-year sentence for buying the death gun. Ruth finally confessed and got a ten-year sentence, too. Heroux's rap partner, Gerhardt Puff, had just been executed in Sing Sing for killing an FBI agent, and that may have pushed Heroux over the edge. I don't know. The papers played up the courage Puff showed the night he was executed. He ate a whole fried chicken and a pint of strawberry ice cream and smoked a cigar. Then he walked to his death with a big smile and asked, 'Who gives a flying fuck?' I personally never liked Puff, because I suspected he cheated George on his share of the money they stole together. Heroux told me that he and Puff used to argue a lot over money, and I just got the feeling the arguments were over who deserved what. The landlady who owned the duplex Heroux was arrested at confirmed my suspicion in the papers after Godwin's killing. I've seen guys like Puff all my life ..."

I was mad as we talked that day, and I'm still mad. Today inmates have color television sets, telephones, and air conditioning. There are no chain gangs. As I've said, if there still were chain gangs for the more ornery, they would be too tired to make any trouble. They would be saying, "Yes sir, boss," and jumping when he told them to jump. Very few guys are tough enough to withstand that kind of treatment. No one is beaten in prison today the way the walking bosses beat us with their sticks. No guard today almost kills you then says, "All right, old buddy, let's get up and try it again."

As Hill drove that night, I quietly thought about my life. Things had been going so well and now I really fucked up. I could see that Hill and most of the other guys I knew on Bay Street were immature, but I couldn't see that immaturity in myself. I could always see the faults of others, but not my own. I certainly wasn't proud of myself at that moment but when you're hurting emotionally, you sometimes do crazy things. And I knew I was being stupid and probably speeding to my death at that very moment. I couldn't foresee what was waiting up ahead, but I knew it wasn't going to be good.

CHAPTER TWO
WILD CRIME SPREE

"Your three-day escapade through Florida, Georgia, and Tennessee was the height of insanity."
—US Commissioner T.V. Cashen, US District Court, Jacksonville,
October 29, 1952

As we entered Alabama early the next morning, we began talking about our friend Amos Walker who was then in a Raiford road camp. I had known Amos a long time; we had been in reform school together and he was also a good friend of Clarence Anglin. I remember he was in Raiford for a twenty-year stretch, but I don't remember what his crime was or why he was sent to the road gang.

Back then it took thirteen years to do a twenty-year sentence. Hill and I talked about what a good welterweight boxer Amos was and how he wouldn't hesitate to tangle with anybody. The more we talked, the stronger our conviction grew that we could spring him.

After driving on a bit, Hill pulled the car off the highway and made a U-turn. "What the hell. Let's go get him," he said simply. We had just driven hundreds of miles away from a manhunt going on throughout northern Florida, and now we were headed right back into it. I just shrugged my shoulders. No one was going to out-reason Hill.

Late that same day, we pulled up to our old Raiford road camp, where I had spent so much time in the sweat box. Because Hill had never been in that camp, he climbed out of the car and walked into the captain's office. He introduced himself as Amos's friend who had been sent by the Walker family to talk over some property problems. Hill asked politely if he could drive out to where Amos was working and talk to him for a few minutes. He also hoped to leave his friend a couple of cartons of cigarettes. The captain said he saw nothing wrong with that, and he told Hill how to get to Amos's work site, about fifteen miles away.

I drove down the highway with Hill and turned onto a secondary road to where the road gang was finishing up for the afternoon. As I pulled up to the first of two shotgun-carrying guards with the road gang between them, Hill jumped out of the car with his Luger hidden in one hand behind his back, saying, "Sir, there is a bad wreck just down the road, and we need some help." Amos, who was putting his tools into a pickup, saw Hill and froze as if he couldn't believe his eyes. Hill walked closer to the guard, pointing in the opposite direction. As the guard looked past him and me sitting quietly in the car, Hill swung the Luger around and struck the guard's head. Then he spun the shocked guard around to serve as a shield and told the second guard to drop his shotgun. He had done this in a few seconds, surprising even me with his skill. The second guard started to raise his shotgun, but Hill pointed the Luger at the hostage guard's head. The guard, who was bleeding heavily said, "Boss, you better do what he says. He means business." The second guard dropped his shotgun.

Hill called to Amos, who was standing next to the tool truck in stunned silence. The other prisoners also remained silent and stood rooted to the ground. Hill motioned to Amos, who ran to the car and climbed in. "What the hell are you guys doing?" he asked me with a confused expression on his face. Hill released the guard after taking the two shotguns, and we were on our way. A few miles down the road, Amos said we were too reckless for him and asked to go his own way. We dropped him off at a side road and sped away toward Georgia. I never have seen him since. Whether he walked back to the road gang or on to freedom all by himself, I just don't know.

The next day, when Hill and I arrived in Georgia. he said we needed to switch cars. A few minutes later on the highway we spotted a nice yellow Chrysler in front of us and Hill said, "That's what we want." As we passed the Chrysler, I pointed to the Chrysler's rear wheel and shouted to the driver, "Your tire is going flat!" He was foolish enough to pull over with us right behind him. Soon enough, he found himself kidnapped. He turned out to be Canadian and had mostly Canadian currency. We drove him off the highway down a little used dirt road, tied his hands behind him with wrapping twine, and left him to walk back to the nearest town. We then drove for the rest of the day, stopping only to eat a hamburger or pee.

As we passed a supermarket about to close for the night, we decided to take it. We parked, climbed out, and entered the building. Almost no one was present since it was so late. The manager walked up and said, "Yes, sir. Can I help you?" Hill said, "Did you send for the boogeyman?" The guy started to smile, but Hill said, "Turn around and walk back to your office. Keep your hands by your side." We tied the frightened man and a few customers, with the same wrapping twine and left. The cash register turned over more than $300.

We took turns driving all night. Around daylight, while I was at the wheel. we passed a new 1951 Buick Roadmaster sitting all by itself on the side of the road. I spun a U-turn and drove back to pull in behind the green Buick. A big fellow about 45 years old was behind the wheel, fast asleep. Hill opened the door and shook the guy awake. He told the man to get out, that we needed to use his car. The motorist explained that his Buick was broken down. Hill tried starting it but couldn't get it to turn over, so we had to leave in our Chrysler. We also had to take the guy along with us, since we had tried to steal his car. Hill went through the man's wallet and found about $400. "Shit! What kind of work do you do?" Hill demanded. "I'm a steel worker." Then Hill laughed and said, "I'm a steal worker, too." The guy laughed. He thought it was funny too.

A few miles down the road we saw a rest stop with only two cars in it and Hill asked me to pull in, since we still needed to change cars. We dumped the Chrysler and the three of us walked up to one of the parked cars and found three Marines asleep in it. Hill woke them up and made them get out at gunpoint but then I spotted another car nearby. In it, a guy and a girl were asleep, or pretending to be. I tapped on the window with my pistol. The guy looked up and I shouted, "Get the hell away from here!" I could hear his girlfriend ask him what was going on. He answered, "Some fucking asshole with a gun wants us to get out." He turned back to me and started cursing. Half-amused and half-angered, I busted out his window with the butt of my gun to show him who was the boss in that situation. Hill fired a shot in our direction to get the guy's attention. He calmed down fast enough.

Hill came over, still holding the three marines and the Buick owner at gunpoint, and demanded the guy's wallet. He started going through it and found some rubbers. He said, "Ya'll been messing around, huh?" It embarrassed the woman and Hill said, 'There isn't anything wrong with that. Me and Hoppy like to fuck, too." He made a weird laughing sound that scared the couple. He had made the same sound in the loan company when he ranted about how the loan company caused him to lose his wife. Since then, the police and media had referred to him as a "three-gun maniac." Hill was a maniac, all right. It was just luck we didn't kill some of these people we were kidnapping, right and left.

Our situation was getting crazier by the minute. We now had six people on our hands. I hadn't bargained for this, but Hill wasn't fazed. Hell, he seemed to be having a good time. He put the girl in the front seat of the marine's car between himself and me and said we'd stop somewhere to get some tape to tie all of them up with. So off we drove--five men crammed into the back seat and three of us in the front. At the next town we came to, I pulled in the parking lot behind a drug store and walked inside to buy two rolls of dressing tape. I also bought some gauze so that the pharmacist wouldn't become suspicious. When I returned to the car, the young woman started begging us to let one of the marines change places with her so that she could sit in the backseat next to her boyfriend. Without questioning it, we did but before we could get out of town, the two lovers jumped out of the car at a stoplight. As they scrambled to get away between the other cars stopped at the light, both stumbled and fell. Hill angrily jumped out of the passenger's side, waving his gun and screaming, "Goddamn you, get back in the car!" I shouted, "Fuck them, let's go before a cop shows up!" Hill climbed back in the car and we took off without them.

The street I was on ended at a service station, but a side street continued to the right at a sharp angle. I was doing about 60 when I turned to the right and I felt the car starting to slide but I managed to get it under control even though I hit a curb. As I zoomed away, several guys at the station started yelling and hooting.

In Sparta, Tennessee, the next day, we stopped at a drive-in restaurant. When the curb-girl came up to the driver's window and asked what we wanted, Hill leaned over and told her he wanted to eat her pussy. The girl left immediately and told the manager, who then sent another girl to ask us to leave. Hill said, "Well, we ought to rob the motherfucker anyway." I said, "No, too many people around, plus we got these guys in the backseat." As I started to back out, I scratched the fender of the car next to us. The young driver screamed at me, called me stupid, and we started arguing. A big buddy of his walked over. At that point Hill got out with the Luger visible in his belt and said, "There's nothing wrong with this piece of shit. If I were you, I would get in it and drive away while you're still in good health." They saw his pistol and said no more. We then drove off. Hill told me we should have robbed the place to get even, as well as get something to eat for all six of us. He said that sometimes you have to take chances or you'll never make it big. I answered, "You can't take chances when you're crowded with so many bodies all around you."

When we got a couple of miles outside Sparta, I pulled off onto a dirt road and into some thick woods. By now the couple who had jumped out at the red light had notified the police and we knew there were road blocks waiting for us. We hid the car in a clump of bushes and took off with the three marines as hostages, leaving the bewildered Buick owner by himself. Since I was in top shape from my boxing exercises, making my way through the woods was no problem. Even Hill was in good shape from working on the chain gang. Besides, neither of us smoked. Of course, the marines were used to the pace and they didn't slow us down as we made our way through the rugged mountains.

It wasn't long before we came up to a farm house. We were way back in the Cumberland Mountains now, and that little house and barn were very isolated. The nearest other farm was about three miles away. As we approached the farm house, I noticed a police airplane circling around the area. As it drifted off, we made a dash to the house and banged on the door. No one was home, so we went inside. Hill said we had to be careful, since the police could be hiding and shoot us from an ambush. We remained in the kitchen for about ten minutes. Then an older man walked up the steps and opened the back door. He smiled and said, "Hello boys," as if he knew us personally. Hill asked him a couple of times if there was anybody else around, but the farmer didn't answer. Hill put his pistol under the farmer's chin and screamed, "If you don't show some respect and start answering, you're gonna lose part of your face." His shrieking voice sounded so crazy that it even scared the three marines. I stepped up and said the old man was too scared to talk. Hill backed off, looking through the kitchen windows to see if he could spot anyone else, then ordered the farmer to fix us all something to eat.

After a half hour or so, we all piled into the farmer's brand-new Pontiac—Hill, the farmer, the three marines, and me. A few miles down the highway, as Hill drove, we approached a roadblock: two police cars, one on each side of the road. They were checking license plates, so we decided to run it. As we sped between the parked police cars, the highway patrolmen shot at our tires. Hill wasn't impressed in the least, even though six shots were fired at the tires. But four penetrated the trunk, one came through the rear window of the car, and one hit the oil pan. We weren't sure where in the oil pan it really hit, but after about three miles we noticed oil leaking and the motor starting to freeze up.

We dodged down a dirt road a fair bit, abandoned the now useless car, and had the farmer wave down a neighboring family who happened to emerge from a side road, headed for town. The farmer asked the driver to give the six of us a ride to town, since his car had broken down. They said they would be happy to oblige if we could somehow make room for everyone. We decided that the man and his wife would sit in front, the man's mother and granddaughter would sit in the back with me and Hill, and we would say "Adios" to the farmer and three marines. The family in the car didn't seem to like our leaving the four behind, so I emphasized I would be returning soon enough with a mechanic to fix the car.

We drove off, listening to country music on the car radio. The music was interrupted by a bulletin that said the local and state police had been chasing extremely dangerous kidnappers all day in the Cumberland Mountains. I glanced at the driver's face, and his expression said it all.

Hill immediately pulled his gun, pointed it at the man's head, and said, "Not only that, we're a coupla killers, too." At that moment, the man, who was apparently no coward, spun the car around and, with one hand on the wheel, lurched for Hill's gun. But Hill pulled it back and fired a shot past his head and through the side window, ordering him to pull over. The elderly lady next to me kept saying, "I knew it, I knew it, I knew it." I tried to calm her down by telling her we wouldn't hurt her and the family, but she kept repeating it, like a stuck record.

When the driver pulled the car over, he handed the keys to his wife and she promptly threw them in the bushes. I walked over and pulled her hair, shouting, "Where are the goddamn keys?" She said she didn't know. So, Hill stepped between her and her husband and said, "Okay, I'm going to make you a goddamn widow woman." He then ordered the husband to get into a small ditch and fired a bullet near his hand. The man, who was as big as a wrestler, had showed no fear until that moment. Hill shouted, "See, it's a real gun; it fires real bullets, and I'll blow your damn head off!" The wife sobbed, "Oh, God, don't hurt him. You can have the car. I threw them right there," she said, pointing to the clump of bushes. I went over and started running my hands around in the leaves and luckily, I found the keys right away. But while I did this, the little girl started running as fast as she could down the highway. She was off like a deer, and we couldn't stop her. Meanwhile, a car or two had slowed down to see what all the commotion was about, but no one dared to stop. I said to the family now huddled together by the side of the highway, "You ain't been too helpful," and climbed into their car. Hill fired a shot in the dirt in front of them as if to warn them not to get to the police too soon. We took off with the rear of the car fishtailing.

We passed a bunch of slower cars on the highway and were well on our way. It was getting dark, so we began to feel safe. But suddenly in the rearview mirror, Hill spotted a flashing red light in the distance. "Here they come," he said. I immediately cut the lights and pulled down a side road that we were approaching. The police car passed and headed on down the highway. We breathed a sigh of relief and decided the best thing to do was to get back on the highway and continue in the direction we were headed. If we fell in with the normal flow of traffic, we might be safe.

We cruised for several miles at about 35 miles per hour and soon a car came up behind us. It stayed close and wouldn't pass even when I dropped to 20 mph. Hill had a gun ready and probably would have opened up if the car turned out to be a police car but eventually it passed us. Hill and I howled with laughter as we saw an old woman at the wheel, shaking her finger at us for going too slow on a major paved road. As we arrived on the outskirts of a small city, I saw in the distance another road block. If I made a U-turn, the police would surely know why. I told Hill to lean down and I would just drive slowly through, since the cops were looking for a new white Pontiac and we were driving a green Ford. We both breathed a sigh of relief as I was waved through without a second look.

Once I was through the road block, I pulled off onto a back road in order to avoid any more road blocks. The forest was quiet and dark, and we decided it was a good place to hide. It wasn't long before we were sound asleep. Anyone could have approached us, and there was little we would have been able to do.

At the first sign of daybreak, I awoke and saw a pickup a hundred yards in front of us. I woke Hill and said the pickup could represent part of the posse chasing us. So, we decided I would check it out and he would cover me. No one was to be seen anywhere around. When I approached the pickup, all I found was a burned-out hulk. An old empty barn was nearby, so Hill and I entered and sat for a while, hungry and cold. We sat discussing our options, wondering how we could escape the area, when I saw a man coming down the dirt road with a shotgun. The way he was walking with the gun and the way he had his eyes cast downward suggested he didn't know we were present.

When the man opened the barn door, Hill started laughing. The guy froze, with a stunned look on his face. He dropped his gun when he saw Hill's Luger pointed at him. Hill asked, "Are you part of the posse looking for us?" "No," he answered slowly, "Me and my partner have just been squirrel hunting." So, the three of us waited for his partner to come along. When he did finally show up an hour later, we caught him by surprise, too. The hunters made fried squirrel and potatoes for us, and Hill paid them for the meal. He said, "You two are poor country people, no better than us." As we looked outside the barn door, we could see an airplane starting to circle again. We told one of the squirrel shooters to go out, get the green Ford, and drive it into the barn. Hill started to get impatient and angry because the man was too hesitant. He fired several shots into the side of the car, screaming at the top of his lungs, 'Move that motherfucker!" Then he ordered the other guy to climb into the trunk, but the second frightened man also hesitated. Enraged, Hill then pumped his gun into the trunk. "Goddamn it! Get in!" he screamed, pointing the gun at the fellow's head.

At that point, I had a few words with Hill. I reminded him the man had told us he was a disabled veteran and probably couldn't handle bending over. Hill understood and said, "Well, we better get the hell out of here, or we're gonna find ourselves trapped." Since we both had on relatively good clothes which made us look out of place in those woods, we took the squirrel hunters' coats to make us look like farmers. We left one of the men tied up in the barn and took the second guy with us. We told him to drive and act normal if we were stopped or met anyone.

A while later we pulled into a country store and filled up with gas. Hill told the attendant we were on our way hunting. We then stayed on secondary roads to avoid roadblocks, but we ran into one anyway. We managed to bypass it in the dark. Then Hill and I started to talk about the disabled veteran we left behind, and soon were in an argument over the way he treated the man. He didn't say much after that, but later, when I went to sleep in the back seat, he awoke me by jamming a pistol in my side. He said, "Hoppy, let's have your pistol. Hand it over and be careful doing it." Then, he said, "Now, get out of this car!" After I climbed out, he snarled, "Don't ever think about getting even. Just be glad you're getting off with your life." Then he drove off with the man we had kidnapped.

I didn't know where I was, so I just started walking and found myself inside a small town within an hour or so. I found an all-night cafe and ordered breakfast. On the juke box, Hank Thompson sang, "Waiting in the Lobby of Your Heart." I don't think I ever felt lonelier in my entire life. I was lonely for me, for my grandmother, for my girlfriend in Miami, and for my freedom but I sure was in trouble now. And I was dizzy. Even today, every time I hear that song, I think of that moment in Scottsboro, Alabama.

Although it was about 3:00 a.m., there were three or four other people in that cafe. One of them who had just come in told the cook, "I just heard on the news that those two kidnappers ran a roadblock near here a coupla hours ago and are believed to still be in the area." I continued eating and acted unconcerned but I figured that going to a motel or hotel at this hour would draw suspicion. I paid the tab and walked out of the neighborhood. I found some woods nearby and went to sleep.

Later that morning I woke up, brushed myself off, and went to a hotel, where I checked in. I took a bath and then went out to buy a new set of clothes. I thought I might get a high school type jacket, since the police bulletins announced that we were city-dressed. As I paid for the clothes, I kept glancing through the windows, half expecting a police car to pull up. The radio was full of bulletins warning the public that we were in the area and giving our descriptions. I returned to the hotel and remained in the lobby, watching television with several old guys. An hour or so later a car pulled up with two men in it that had FBI written all over them, so I eased out as they came in and looked around.

I walked over to another hotel and checked in under the name of Billy Lauderdale, a stablemate of mine in Miami. I was convinced they were on my trail, because now the police and FBI had my name and a picture. That night I went to a movie to kill time, and two FBI agents, I learned later, raided my room and waited for me to return. I never did.

Hill had taken my pistol, but I still had a large switchblade knife. I forced a guy in a supermarket parking lot to drive me out of town. I dropped him on a lonely road, took his car, and headed for Birmingham. Later, a state trooper told me in court that he had been assigned to wait on top of Signal Mountain that day with a machine gun to watch out for me. He had orders to shoot on sight, and besides, he said, he wasn't going to take any chances. We drove right past him without being noticed.

When I got to Birmingham, I parked the car in a nice neighborhood of old two-story homes. I started walking away when a huge Great Dane came up to me. As I stood there patting his head, a Birmingham police car slowly rounded a corner and came up the street. I sat down on a brick wall in front of the house the Great Dane had emerged from. As I petted the dog, the police car slowly drove by.

It was Sunday morning and I kept walking. As I passed a large church, I figured that would be a good place to hide out. I went in and sat through an entire service, then lingered back as the churchgoers left. I was sitting all alone when an elderly lady came in and sat nearby. We got to talking to each other. She asked me to sit with her in the service coming up and then go home and have a Sunday dinner with her. As much as it would have hidden me for a while, I told her I was on my way to see relatives but she insisted on giving me her phone number in case I changed my mind.

I went to the bus station and boarded a bus for New Orleans. On the trip over, one of the passengers was reading the New Orleans Picayune. The front page was facing me, and on it were blown-up mug shots of me and Hill from Raiford. At one of the stops along the route I got a Florida paper that had the headline, "FBI Stalks Maniac Gunman and Bandit Pal." The story described how federal and local authorities were searching the back alleys of Atlanta, thinking they had boxed us in.

Thirty miles out of New Orleans the bus ran into thick fog, and the city itself was foggier than Alcatraz on a bad day. I located a buddy from Raiford who offered me a place to hide but I decided to go back to

Jacksonville and settle an old score. I was going to go after the walking boss who once kicked me severely while I was down and two shotgun guards covered me. I knew I probably would get life in prison for my part in what Hill did but I felt that if I got even with this one bastard it wouldn't hurt me all that much. What else did I have to lose?

I was in Jacksonville less than two hours when two FBI agents spotted me. It sure made their day. They came up to me, and one of them asked, "Are you Charlie Hopkins?" One of them was studying a wanted poster with my photograph on it as he held it in his hand, looking back and forth at me and the photo. I answered, "Yeah." In a way I was glad that it was all over. At the police station, no one bothered to advise me of my rights. In fact, no one cared about anyone's rights in those days unless you were important or very high up politically. Law enforcement figured you didn't deserve any rights, since you wouldn't be there in the first place if you were innocent. In my case, FBI agents at first tried to talk rough to me but they soon saw that it didn't impress me in the least. So, they sent out for sandwiches and then, while eating them, told me how I had caused my grandmother's death.

According to them, Grandma saw my picture in the Jacksonville newspaper and, because she couldn't read, she walked over to my uncle's house and asked, "Isn't that Charles?" When he saw the mugshot he answered, "Yeah." She then said, "Well, go ahead and read the story to me." When my uncle finished reading the article about my crime spree and arrest, Grandma had a heart seizure and fell over dead.

Six agents had their picture taken with me. Every time I turned around; photographers were waiting for me. While in jail waiting for the trial, I started getting letters and photographs from girls I had never met. The letters came from all over the country. Then there were letters from churchgoers across the country who wanted to save my soul. I never answered anyone. One day an FBI agent was talking to me in the jail booking department and, as I walked away, I passed a guy from my bullpen. We spoke for a few minutes. When my friend got back to his cell, one of the agents asked him, "Do you know Charlie?" My friend said,

"Yeah. We are in the same bullpen." The agent answered, 'Well, Hopkins is a nice guy, but mean."

The words cut deep, and to this day I still think about them. "Am I mean?" I pondered the question over and over as I awaited trial. Sure, I had participated in the wild kidnapping of twenty people and helped rob a couple of supermarkets and savings and loan banks. Yeah, Hill and I stole three automobiles and a pickup and led the FBI and police authorities on a three-state chase. But none of the hostages were harmed, and all were released after a short period. Was I mean? I just didn't know. Here I was, sitting in a cell, nineteen years old, and I couldn't figure out if I was really as mean as the FBI agent said I was. Funny how when you're in a life-and-death situation, you focus on totally irrelevant things.

My only hope for any kind of leniency now was the testimony of the disabled veteran who could say how Hill and I got into a heated argument when Hill shot at him through the trunk of the car and missed. I had shouted at Hill that the guy had scars from fighting the Japanese in the South Pacific and that if he meant to kill him in cold blood he might as well kill me, too. But I was the only one who knew that. After we got to Alabama, Hill pulled his gun on me and told me to get out of the car. I was the only one who knew he had said. "Don't even think about getting even with me. Just be glad you're getting off with your life."

CHAPTER THREE

A THIEF AMONG THIEVES

"At Atlanta we used to hear, 'For a thief to steal from a thief only makes God laugh.' Well, it made us laugh, too, as we stole from those cons who could stand stealing from."

—Charlie Hopkins

"Thieving from a thief who is more of a thief than a thief is not thieving."

—Sicilian proverb

When I arrived in Chattanooga where I was to be tried, I was already well known to the jail inmates because of the exaggerated press accounts about my kidnap-robbery spree. The Chattanooga jail was so large that the prisoners ate in the mess hall, as if they were in a federal or state penitentiary. At lunch it was different. If you were at work or in a cell, you got a baloney sandwich, and that was it. I remember one guy saying to a guard a few days after I arrived. "Hey, you think you can afford this? When we going to eat?" The guard shouted back, "Listen, jackass, you better eat that sandwich before I take it away."

The sheriff of Sparta, Tennessee attended my court appearance in Chattanooga, and when he visited me in my cell, he told me that the young lovers who had jumped out in town at that stoplight weren't too honest and up front with him. He believed me when I said we never took any money from them. They only had a few dollars between them, but they told the police that we lifted about $700 from them, hoping they would get some back. The sheriff said the girl later admitted to him that we never took anything from them, not even the rubbers Hill teased the guy about.

My court-appointed lawyer, Wilkes T. Thrasher, was from a well-to-do Chattanooga family who knew a lot of federal judges as family friends.

He told me he would try to get me a sentence I could pull and still not go through all the other courts that wanted to try me. I listened to his advice and pled guilty. The lawyer described to the judge the kind of life I had. He explained my story would make good reading someday, but not now. He stressed that there was respect for life even among hardened thieves, demonstrated by my concern for the disabled veteran.

If 1 Charge Fails, There Are 19 More

—AP Wirephoto

JACKSONVILLE, Fla.—Charles E. Hopkins, 21, center, caught here and charged with kidnaping 20 persons, is led to jail by two agents of the Federal Bureau of investigation.

The judge said, "I have been dealing with people like this for a long time, and some of them can be pretty foxy." "Well, Your Honor," my lawyer said, "foxy or not, I believe this boy is sincere. He's a good boxer who got off on a wrong foot. Just recently he lost a 10-round decision to Billy Lima, who lost to former world champion Willie Pep. When FBI agents searched the boy, they found in one of the pockets a pair of miniature boxing gloves attached to a gold belt buckle. An inscription on the buckle indicated he had been runner-up in a mid-state Tennessee Golden Gloves competition. Mr. Hopkins was only thirteen when he was put in the Marianna Reform School. There's no denying, your honor, that he participated in that reign of terror. But Mr. Hill, who was ten years older than this boy, was the leader, and as you know, the court-appointed psychiatrists have declared he can't be tried because he is mentally incompetent and has a warped mind beyond cure. At least show leniency to this boy."

But the judge sentenced me to seventeen years for kidnapping and crossing state lines with stolen motor vehicles. The date was November 17, 1952, and although I would be confined and disciplined, I would become a "professional" convict among thousands of other professional convicts. I thanked Mr. Thrasher, who really tried to help me. He was understanding, kind, and compassionate. These qualities helped get Wilkes elected to Congress in 1954. Because I respected him, I gave him what I gave no other man in those dark days: a handshake and a smile. Then they led me away.

After sentencing I was moved to a jail in Knoxville and placed in a big tank full of other federal prisoners until the Bureau of Prisons decided where to incarcerate me permanently. A few times the Knoxville jailers allowed some newspaper reporters to visit me, but I wouldn't talk to them.

The Bureau of Prisons finally decided to send me to the federal penitentiary in Lewisburg, Pennsylvania. As soon as I arrived there, the lieutenant in charge of new arrivals had me escorted down to a big empty room. With just the two of us standing there, he started telling me how well known I was, that some of the inmates there already knew I was coming and had respect for me, and that a few were already agitating trouble for me by spreading rumors that I ratted on Hill. He cautioned me to be on guard, especially since the inmates knew about my reputation as a boxer. "They'll try to stir up fights for you."

I got off to a bad start with the guards when one of them who was sorting out my personal belongings to determine what I could keep and what had to go home told me I couldn't keep all the pictures I had of myself and my different girlfriends. I told him, "This is a bunch of bullshit." That afternoon I wrote a letter to my girlfriend and my mother. Another guard returned them to me. He said, "You're talking about things you're doing here that you're not supposed to. And as for your letter to your girlfriend, what does '*Yo te amo*' mean? You're not supposed to write in code." I said, '*Yo te amo*' in Spanish means 'I love you.'" With that, I wrote a letter to the warden and told him not to let any more guards open my outgoing or incoming mail. I wrote, "Whatever guard does it in the future is a punk and a motherfucker, and I don't want a weak-minded punk like that reading my letters." I explained to him how mad I was at the guard for taking all my girlfriend's pictures and sending them home because I was in them. The warden called me in and told me that they didn't want me there in Lewisburg to start with and had requested I be sent on to Atlanta. But the Bureau of Prisons ordered him to give me a chance.

The lieutenant's prediction about some guys agitating for trouble against me was correct. Several attempts were made to pick fights with me. I refused most. But one big black guy on a construction job I was assigned to made some insulting remarks about my ancestry and I hit him in the face with a two by four, sending him flying. I didn't need this kind of shit, so I asked the deputy warden for a transfer to Atlanta. I explained that I couldn't do my time with a bunch of punks trying to prove how tough they were. He was kind enough to sympathize and again emphasized that no one on the staff had wanted me there in the first place. He said the Lewisburg warden had just recommended that I be sent to Atlanta but he didn't have much hope, since the Bureau of Prisons was standing firm in giving me a chance at Lewisburg because of my youth and because of the concern I had shown for the disabled veteran Hill tried to shoot through the trunk of the car. The Bureau honestly believed that there was some good in me.

In some ways Lewisburg was all right. I met a few inmates there I liked. Alger Hiss was one. He was Assistant Secretary of State for Foreign Affairs and was with Franklin Roosevelt at the Geneva Convention. He was now a clerk in the prison and very cordial to me. Another friend I made was a Boston gangster named Jack Abonis, who was in the isolation unit awaiting transfer to Alcatraz. He told me he had been following me in the papers and felt Hill was crazy. I was placed in that same isolation unit when I arrived but after a few weeks was allowed to enter the general population on the orders of the Bureau of Prisons.

No sooner had I arrived at Atlanta than I had a run in with a black guy in the orientation unit. He tagged me a racist redneck because I referred to him as a coon. But when I was growing up in and around Jacksonville, "coon" was a figure of speech, a term of endearment. Anyway, when I used it, I meant it in a friendly and kidding sort of way. Anyone who knew me knew I was no racist redneck. At the classification board, the warden told me that he didn't intend to put up with any bullshit from me. "I don't care what you call the niggers just so long as you don't stab any of them," he said. "I'm in no mood for any riots caused by a white man," he warned me as he allowed me into the main population.

But I wasn't in the mainstream population more than two weeks before an older white guy who was the head of recreation tried to take a baseball cap away from me. Naturally, I wouldn't let him. I beat him unmercifully. Although he was in the hospital a few weeks, he wouldn't rat on me, although I knew the guards knew who did it. Then, Johnny Johnson, a white boy from Georgia, started breaking into inmates' lockers with me. There was not much in them but a few cigarettes and a little candy. No locker contained money because inmates weren't allowed to keep cash. But word got out that we were the guilty ones. The guy who roomed with Johnny in his cell told my cellmate that if he knew we did it, he would fuck us up bad. So, after the cell door closed that night, Johnny said to the guy so others on the tier could hear that he wanted anybody who thought that we were robbing their lockers to stand up but the roommate said he just wanted to forget it and hoped it didn't happen again.

The issue wouldn't let up. There were thieves among thieves, and the thieves wanted to know who the thieves were. On the way to the recreation yard one night, some guy in front of us said that a couple of plumbers were the culprits but would say no more. Johnny and I looked at each other and smiled. Hell, the pickings were too good to care or worry. The fact was, Johnny had an inmate burglar make us a key out of a toothbrush handle that would open tumbler locks. With that key we broke into hundreds of lockers. The guards had a good laugh about it for months. But Johnny and I had decided that the only inmates we would rob would be the guys who were phonies, or rich on the streets, or thought they were somehow special. We wouldn't steal from our friends or those we knew to be poor. And we stole from white and black alike. Skin color makes no difference when you're profiting.

I stayed on red tag a lot at Atlanta, which meant I stayed in my cell except to eat or take a shower. Clyde Sturgis was also on red tag. Since he bunked a few cells away, we had plenty of time to shoot the breeze. A few years before, he had robbed a bank in Kansas City with his girlfriend and another couple. The gang got away with more than $50,000. But the other couple was found shot dead in a parked car shortly thereafter. The authorities could never prove that Clyde was the one who did the killing, so Sturgis got a light twenty-year sentence. His girlfriend was sent to Alderson, Virginia, and wasn't allowed to write him because they had been rap partners. Because he was a good-looking guy, a guard got tight with him, turning him into a homosexual.

The guard didn't mind sending letters for him to his girlfriend. The girlfriend would then write back, sending the letters to the guard's home. He then delivered the letters to Clyde. But Sturgis was dumb enough to keep her letters around his cell instead of flushing them down the toilet. When the letters were found with no censor stamp on them during a routine search, Clyde was put in the hole alone until he told them who the homosexual guard was.

Sturgis broke and told officials who the guard was, but the guy was never charged. He was fired and left the prison system. Having charges brought against a guard for being homosexual was the height of disgrace for a prison. The bad publicity was to be avoided at all costs. Sturgis was transferred immediately, because once he ratted on someone, even a guard, he was marked by both inmates and fellow guards.

I liked Clyde. He never confided in me that he killed the couple, and he never made any homosexual advances to me—he knew better. Once we were off red tag, we ran together for a while. He was with me when a guard on the yard tried to take a baseball cap away from me. I told the guard to go get fucked. Later, Sturgis told me that the deputy warden talked to him about staying away from me because I was nothing but trouble. Just before the officials shipped him off to another federal prison, he told me that a New York Mafia crime family had set up the bank job for him and the couple and that they would get a percentage of the take. Sturgis beat them out of their share, since he was caught before he could deliver it. Now, he was afraid that organized crime would sooner or later catch up with him. I don't know what ever became of him.

George Littlefield, a friend of mine, was also on red tag a lot. George came to Atlanta about a year before I did with a twenty-three-year sentence for robbing a Safeway in Washington, DC. We became fast friends. One day during my first month at Atlanta, some big guy who was a rat gave him a hard time about something I can't remember. When I learned about it, I took care of him. He was six foot six, but I managed to even it up a little. Littlefield was one of the few guys I considered a friend. He was loyal to his friends and scared of nobody. A guy named Scott whom I ran around with sometimes was a dead ringer for Burt Reynolds and built like a wrestler. Well, for some stupid reason, Littlefield told Scott he was going to throw him off the fifth tier. After arguing the point for a while, Scott backed down. I don't think Littlefield could have actually done it, but be would have tried.

Another guy about who used to come around the tiers passing out ice water during the summers also tried to give Littlefield a hard time. One day when I was on red tag, I caught him filling his water pail. I walked up to him and asked why he was giving my friend such a hard time. He stood up and started cursing me. Suddenly, he kicked out and caught me on my side. I then caught him in the face with some good shots. A friend of mine, Johnny Iozza, who was nearby playing cards, got up and put in a few good licks too. My anger flaring, I went to the cell of a rat and beat him up too, for good measure. From there I tried to find another inmate, a former Miami cop named Nickolas, who had brutalized some friends of mine when he was a cop. But Nickolas wasn't in his cell or the cellhouse. So, I returned to my own cell and tried to pretend I was cleaning it when the guards came to put me in the hole.

When I was hauled in front of the deputy warden, I claimed I hadn't touched anyone. He said, "The hell you haven't! You broke the man's jaw in two places! The whole side of his face is red and swollen: This is a big guy. Did your buddy Iozza hit him too? Hopkins, you're nothing but a bully." They threw me into a strip cell.

That night I placed my mattress over the toilet and jumped up and down on it to force all the water out of the line. That way I could talk to guys in other isolation cells just as if we were on the telephone. By this means of communication I learned that, while I had been punching out one of Littlefield's problems that morning, some guy who was supposed to be a real bad-ass started cursing Littlefield during a soft ball game. Then the prick came at him with a bat but George acted like he was going to throw him a left hook and the guy ducked to the left, dropping the bat. Littlefield picked up the bat and hit him on the forehead with it and almost killed the guy. Then, according to my friend, he threw the bat down and walked off before the guards could see what happened. He asked another guy to watch his back on the way in from the yard, and one of the friends of the bad-ass came around me to catch up with Littlefield. But Littlefield spun around and the guy who was almost on him said he liked Littlefield and he didn't want to get into it. Somebody ratted, and they picked up Littlefield while I was on my way to isolation. The rumor was that he would be sent out of Atlanta to Springfield.

In Atlanta some of my buddies and I went to church to get out of our isolation cells and be together for a while. The preacher, who was missing one hand, wasn't sincere. One Sunday he started talking about how cold-hearted some guys were and how they wouldn't shed a tear if their loved ones died. Because we all knew he was talking about me, one of my buddies said, "Shut up, you one armed bandit!" I can't remember the Protestant minister's name, but he had been there a long time before I got there. The reason he said this was that when my mother died in 1953, my aunt wrote to tell me, and she wasn't on my approved list, which at that time was as strict as a national security clearance is today. So, the mail room clerk sent the letter to my parole officer, and he turned it over to the minister. The minister called me to the parole office and gave me a cold look as if I had done something wrong. Then he asked, "Do you know Thelma Wages?" I replied, "Yes, that's my aunt." He said, "Did you know your mother died?" He was as cold and unconcerned as if he had been talking about a cow dying out in the barn. He carried out his Sunday service more like a chore that had to be done and always referred to inmates as "losers." Of course, not all inmates are losers but he seemed to detest the very people he was supposed to help.

When I was released from isolation, I celled in 519, which was an end cell on Atlanta's fifth tier. One day we were sitting there talking when I noticed a guard's leg and shoe propped on the railing behind the cell. The guy was just listening. So, I said, "What do you think of motherfuckers who wear argyle socks?" A guy I knew from Raiford said, "Hell, I threw one off a tier one time." I said, "I think it takes a faggot to wear socks like that, and they are always peeping toms and eavesdroppers." One guy said, "Yeah, I heard they like to live with their mother and not get married." Then a guy called Okie said, "I wish I had a mother that would let me live with her. I'd fuck her, wouldn't you?"

Hearing this, the guard took off without saying anything, but a few days later Captain Lynch gave me a dirty look in the dining room. I gave him one back. As I left the dining room, he had a lieutenant pull me out of line and take me to his office off the main hallway. About five guards made a circle around me and the lieutenant told me what a sorry bastard I was and how they would beat the hell out of me to get my attention. The group of guards were led by one named John Blatchferd who kept trying to provoke me. Blatchferd kept saying he could be just as tough as I wanted to be. After the interrogation, I was thrown into a strip cell.

Around 8:00 one night in early June 1955, the deputy warden at Atlanta walked up to my strip cell. I was surprised, because this was unusual for that time of night. I just stood there naked, wondering what he wanted. He just looked at me for a moment There was nothing in the cell except a mattress in the corner and a few blankets.

"Hopkins," he said in a strange voice, "come along. You're going to shave and shower." Then he motioned to a guard at the end of the tier to open the cell front and let me out. "What the hell is this all about?" I wondered. I didn't know what to expect. Even though I figured they were taking me someplace, I wasn't worried. At least they weren't going to execute me … or were they?

A guard escorted me down to the showers. When I finished, I was handed an electric shaver and freshly ironed gray pants and a white, starched long sleeved shirt. The guard said nothing and I said nothing. Then I was brought to a small isolation cell in the reception-guidance building behind the penitentiary where inmates arrived and were processed. I was told to take a nap with my clothes on. "So, I'm going to be transferred," I thought. "Not back to Raiford, that's for sure. You don't go from federal penitentiary to state prison. No, I'm probably headed for Leavenworth.",

Just before daylight I was awakened and, along with a few other guys—including to my surprise and joy, Billy Duncan and Johnny Iozza, my best friends at Atlanta—loaded onto a bus that had been pulled up to the back-door exit. We were told to remain silent, but one of the inmates whispered to me and Billy and Johnny that we were headed for Kansas. That meant Leavenworth. I shrugged my shoulders, since I didn't particularly care all that much, although it meant losing a few good buddies in Atlanta.

Billy and Johnny sat behind me as we rode most of the day, shackled and chained to our bus seats. Al Heflin sat next to me. He was a partner of

Sammy Hornbeck and Leon Goldstein. Leon died in a police shootout, and Sammy was executed for killing a cop in that same shootout. No one said much as we watched the scenery go by. Cars passed us, and some of those people, realizing who we were because of the heavily barred windows, honked and waved at us. For lunch, the guards passed out some tasteless sandwiches the cooks had prepared the day before. That afternoon Billy, Johnny, and I talked and talked. It was as if we knew we were going to be split up, but we didn't care. They were my best friends in Atlanta, and I was glad we were at least together this afternoon.

Billy was a big, heavy-set kid who was my age, doing fifteen years for bank robbery. His uncle had been on the FBI's "Ten Most Wanted" list in the early 1950s. Billy's uncle was one of the men who had been brutalized by the ex-cop Nicholas I mentioned earlier. After my fight with the two other no-good cons and my search for Nicholas, I told Billy I couldn't find him. Billy had said, "I'll see you tonight. I'm going to get him on the yard and give him a taste of what he gave my uncle. So, I'll see you by supper time."

I wasn't present when he walked up to Nicholas in the yard and demanded, "Do you remember Little Red Duncan?" Nicholas supposedly shifted his cigar around in his mouth and said, "Yeah, I know him. What about him?" Billy then popped him on the jaw, knocking him back against an embankment that surrounds the yard. He hit him with lefts and rights until Nicholas slid to the ground Then he started stomping him. After Nicholas lay unconscious, Billy walked away and mingled with all the other inmates in the yard, who just acted as if nothing happened.

When Nicholas finally came to, he got up and made his way slowly to the lieutenant at the top of the steps. He was standing there with blood running out of his nose and ears, trying to say something. Then he collapsed in a heap. Nicholas died a few hours later, and someone fingered Billy. Billy's partner was Jack Waites, who overheard a hospital orderly telling someone in the mess hall about Billy. Jack, who was worried about his friend, asked the guy how Billy was doing in isolation, but the hospital orderly ignored him. So, after we had left Atlanta, Jack asked to go on sick call, caught the orderly in the hospital ward all by himself, and beat him until he was senseless.

I hoped wherever we went, Billy would be with me. Late that afternoon when we stopped at some bus stop in Tennessee, the lieutenant in charge of the transfer casually told us that Billy was being dropped off at the federal facility at Terra Haute and that I was on my way to Alcatraz.

Alcatraz! That surprised me. "You're going there for assault and because you're an incorrigible."

That didn't surprise me at all, because it was true. But Alcatraz! I really wasn't all that impressed or scared by the reputation of the place. I just didn't give a damn. I had not been warned by the staff at Atlanta that I had been recommended for transfer, so the decision to move me must have been sudden. I sure hated to leave George Littlefield without a goodbye. Plus, there were half a dozen old scores I would have loved to settle before leaving. As I now thought about it, the main thing that most guys feared about going to Alcatraz was not because it had the reputation of being a hellhole of repression, it was because of the isolation. I already had a clear picture of the place from the guys who had been there and returned to Atlanta.

Billy was angry because we were going to be split up. He told me that he was so mad that he was going to fuck somebody up when he got to Terra Haute. Heflin, who was next to me, overheard the remark and commented, "If your buddy wants to fuck somebody up, I'll give him a name." The name he mentioned was Goldstein's brother. "If you wind up at Terra Haute, kill that fucking son of a bitch," he said. "He was the one who ratted us out in the bank robbery. That led to the death of his own brother. It cost Hornbeck his life, too." Billy turned to Heflin and asked, "Tell me what the motherfucker looks like."

Later on, when Billy was transferred from Terra Haute to Alcatraz, he told me that when he finally found Goldstein's brother in the Terra Haute recreation yard, the guy turned out to be bigger than he was. Billy, who had only arrived a few days before and didn't know anybody, walked up to him in a yard full of the guy's friends and asked, "Do you remember

Heflin?" When Goldstein's brother started to answer, Billy grabbed the man and began stabbing him but because the weapon was a simple prison butter knife, it bent after the first few thrusts. Billy let go of him and tried to straighten the blade with his heel. Goldstein's brother staggered back about thirty feet, looking at Billy as if he couldn't believe it. By then, guards ran up and Billy cursed his luck. My best friend got five more years, plus a ticket to the Rock.

After a one-night layover at Terre Haute, we got going early the next morning for Leavenworth. On this part of the trip we were placed in individual seats on the prison bus with our hands chained to our waist and leg irons on. I got up and started ambling up the aisle to sit with Johnny Iozza, but the guard shouted, "Charlie, get back to your seat!" I shouted, "Well, fuck you!" But Johnny said, "No, don't argue with him." I moved back to my seat. I sat all alone for the rest of the trip, just watching the scenery roll by.

When we got to Leavenworth, the lieutenant in charge was a man named Bradley, the guard I had made fun of for wearing argyle socks. He said, "Well, you finally made it, didn't you, Hopkins?" A big husky guard named Buford said. "You think you're tough, huh? Well, I can be just as tough as you." Then he got a little rough with me, using a tongue depressor. He ordered me to open up my mouth so he could look in. I knew he was hoping I would hit him so that four or five others could pile on me but I wasn't that stupid.

Those guards didn't bother anybody else. I suppose they had been put up to it by Bradley. The brass all hated me because my reputation had preceded me. I used to provoke certain lieutenants or captains I thought were arrogant or racist, the kind of bastards who were too full of their own shit. So, I figured that it was human nature for Bradley and his cohorts to want to get back at me. Also, he was pals with Captain Lynch, the captain of the guards at Atlanta, who I especially went after every chance I got.

They were all probably hoping I would try to escape or kill one of them so they could shoot me. Even though I behaved myself and said nothing, I was the only one who didn't get any tobacco at Leavenworth.

But I got a few smokes from Big Red Smith, who would wind up killing three police detectives in a Los Angeles Sears department store in 1964.

Big Red had originally stabbed a guy in Lewisburg Penitentiary and had been transferred to Atlanta. There, he and I became friends. But he had a run-in with Mr. Cough, the deputy warden, and he was again being transferred, this time to the Rock. I liked Big Red a lot. He was an intelligent person who had taken care of inventory and purchasing in the Atlanta prison industries.

He was called Big Red because of his bright red hair, not his size. He was about twenty-three years old, five feet, eight inches tall, and weighed 165 pounds. He was a nice-looking white guy and got along well with all the black inmates. But, as I say, after he was released and killed four detectives in that shoot-out in LA, the police bulletins warned cops throughout the county that he was a dead shot. When the LA police searched his apartment, they found some pictures of him in the nude with a pistol in each hand. The gun he used to kill the cops with was one he pulled out of his girlfriend's purse. In spite of what happened. I always felt that Big Red wasn't a bad person. In that shoot-out, he just felt like he had done enough time and wasn't going back to prison.

At the time, Leavenworth had a goon squad that was known throughout the federal prison system for roughing guys up. During the week I spent at Leavenworth, I was kept in the isolation block. There, I watched a guy named Gillette, who was also waiting to go to Alcatraz, carve grasshoppers and other bugs out of discarded toothbrush handles with a paperclip and a razorblade. Because he was a whiz at sculpting, guards would give Gillette extra food for his little toothbrush handle grasshoppers.

I have always felt that Gillette was the inmate who made the dummy heads used by Frank Manis and the Anglin brothers in the 1962 Alcatraz escape. There was no question that this old con was an ace at everything he did. One day he pulled a fast one on me and Pineapple Joe. He made a Butterfinger candy bar out of wood and painted it to look like chocolate. Then he put a real Butterfinger wrapper around it, which be he had saved from Christmas. He then gave it to me and I bit right into it because I was so hungry for chocolate but I came up with a mouthful of wood. I told Pineapple Joe how he had a good laugh at my expense, and Joe said, "'That motherfucker got me, too. The candy looked real, didn't it?"

When the day came, twenty of us climbed aboard a train for San Francisco and Alcatraz Island. We were chained in pairs. The guy I was chained to was Charlie Stegal. He was an inmate who tried to escape from Atlanta by hiding out in a storm drain that led to an open field.* Heflin sat behind us, and Johnny Iozza behind him. As the train pulled out, Heflin leaned forward and said, "I sure hope your buddy gets that motherfucking brother of Goldstein. Sammy is sitting on death row and will soon fry now because of him." "I half-turned and said, "Billy will get him if he finds him. You can bet your life on that." He smiled. "Yeah, I believe he will."

I don't remember where we got off the train and stepped aboard the bus that would take us over the Oakland–San Francisco Bay Bridge. All I remember is that men holding rifles were standing around everywhere on the bus. We laughed at all the attention we were getting, and Heflin commented that we must be more valuable than America's whole gold reserve.

CHAPTER FOUR

"LOOK AT THAT BIG MOTHERFUCKER!!"

"Alcatraz is not a penitentiary ... Alcatraz is Alcatraz ..."
—E. J. Miller, Associate Warden at Alcatraz in 1940

It was a bright clear morning as the prison bus started crossing the Bay amid the rush-hour commuter traffic. We all knew we would be able to catch a glimpse of the Rock from the bridge, and we were more interested in seeing it than the San Francisco skyline. But we couldn't spot it until we passed through the Treasure Island tunnel, and suddenly there it was, off to our right, looming out of the bay. The morning sun on its cream-colored exterior made it look more like a Monte Carlo casino than a notorious penitentiary. No one said a word except Johnny Iozza, who sat in front of me and exclaimed more to himself than the rest of us, "Look at that big motherfucker!"

No matter what you called the federal prison, whether Hellcatraz, the Rock of Despair, or America's Devil's Island, it was brutal-looking and ugly. Like some old derelict, the Rock just seemed to be stuck there, dead in the water. And it was a big motherfucker, just like Johnny said.

Iozza turned and winked at me. "Tile bigger the pen, the better the men," he laughed. Johnny was 6'2" and weighed 230 pounds. He was a professional fighter with nine fights under his belt, and was undefeated, with six wins by knock-out. He whipped Harold Mitchell, a guy who had fought Rocky Marciano. During our train ride, Johnny said that he wanted it known he would take on the baddest guy on the Rock so other Alcatraz inmates would then leave him alone. Well, as it turned out, a few days later, when we knew the routine in Alcatraz, an inmate named Bishop repeated what Iozza said to Allen West, a con whom he knew from Atlanta. West told Joe Schultz, probably the toughest inmate in the joint, and Schultz, who always loved a good fight, challenged Johnny in the mess hall, thinking he was just another big guy. Joe Schultz backed down soon enough, the only time I ever saw him do that.

Johnny was an ex-marine and was doing five years for taking his brother-in-law's mortgaged car out of state without permission from the bank. Johnny told me he was just covering for his brother-in-law. I could tell Iozza wasn't the criminal type. He was a nice guy with a baby face and was sent to Alcatraz probably because he had helped me in that one beating and was known to hang around with me at Atlanta. Johnny wasn't afraid of anybody and would especially go after a con he thought was a bully. This was why deputy warden Cough said Johnny and me were no-good bullies. But Johnny really didn't help me in any of the fights I had. He was nearby when I hit the big water carrier. Sure, Johnny popped him a shot or two to even it up a little. But the officials were afraid he would seriously hurt someone in a fight and considered him a bully, which he was not.

For example, a 250-pound Atlanta lieutenant we called "Hog Jaw" Wallace noticed us go through the chow line twice one night at dinner time and pulled us out of line on the way out. Johnny didn't appreciate the way Hog Jaw asked us about it and said, "Yeah, we ate twice. So, what about it?" Because of that remark, Hog Jaw complained to the deputy warden that Johnny was a bully. Cough called me in and gave me hell, but he never addressed Johnny like that, because he knew danger when he saw it. He also probably saw too that Iozza wasn't a real criminal. He was just a twenty-three-year-old guy whom you couldn't insult without a fight.

Johnny was very loyal and would never use people to help himself. As far as I was concerned, he was better than a lot of people in high places, including the guards and their superiors. None of us had much to say that morning as we boarded the prison launch at Fort Mason in San Francisco for the short ride over to the island. Even though the sun was shining, it was damp and cold, and the waters were so choppy that the boat seemed to hold back. Was this some kind of omen?

When we finally pulled alongside the Alcatraz dock, I stared up at the foreboding cell house. Looking up at the prison on top of a solid rock island sure made a newcomer feel insignificant. I wondered if the prison was really as terrible as some of the inmates at Atlanta had claimed. A lot of guys coming back from a two- or three-year stretch liked to boast how they survived the unsurvivable. You really couldn't be sure if what they claimed was a bunch of bullshit or not.

We stepped onto the dock and were lined up. I looked up at an armed guard in a nearby steel watchtower who was leaning on the railing, rifle in hand, studying us. Myth had it that there was an arsenal of rifles, machine guns, gas projectiles, grenades, and semiautomatic pistols in all the Alcatraz towers. As we waited for whatever was next, some guards' wives led some kids behind us to the boat, ready to return to Fort Mason. The kids were on their way to school on the mainland. Then, a large empty dump truck came crawling down the one road on the island to the dock.

We were ordered into the back of the truck and began the short slow ride up the hill to the prison. Two inmates on trash detail off the side of the road stopped their work to watch us pass by. Farther up, five inmate gardeners were strung out along the road attending to the bright orange and yellow nasturtiums. They, too, paused to look. No one waved or said anything.

I wasn't afraid or apprehensive as the truck made its last turn on the road that ran alongside the cell house. I figured I'd get the same rough treatment from the guards as I got at Leavenworth, but so what? The truck stopped at a basement door and we waited for about five minutes, standing in the dump truck bed, for the inside guards to open up. No one spoke, not the Leavenworth guards who had accompanied us cross-country, not us, not even the seagulls that were perched on the fence, staring down at us.

Standing there in the back of the truck, I was able to take one last look all around this side of the island, believing I wouldn't catch another sight like this for a long, long time. There below me was the dark blue water; it looked heavy and dangerous. A number of small white fishing crafts were dead in the water, off in the distance. Monstrous and lonely Angel Island lay off to the north. And the five or six East Bay cities seemed still far off in the eastern distance. I had to admit, this little bit of scenery from one corner of the island was awesome. I wondered what the scenery was like from the other side of the cell house, especially from the recreation yard, where I hoped I'd be spending a lot of time.

Lieutenant Mahan then opened the back door of the basement from the inside and walked out with several guards. He spotted one of the Leavenworth guards who had sat in the bus's gun cage, a son of a bitch who had given us dirty looks all the way to California. Apparently, they were good friends, because they shook hands, talked, and laughed a lot.

After we climbed down from the dump truck and entered a small waiting room next to the shower room, the door was slammed shut and Heflin and I kinda glanced at each other, a smile crossing our lips. So, we were now inside Alcatraz! Sure, all America knew that Alcatraz Island Prison housed such notorious gangsters as Al "Scarface" Capone, "Machine Gun" Kelly, and the survivors of his gang, Alvin "Creepy" Karpis, Doc Barker, Roy Gardner, the daring mail-train bandit, and hundreds of others. But I would bet none of these old-timers could match in toughness any one of us arriving that day.

The chains were removed from our wrists and ankles and we were led from the anteroom down a corridor to a room near the showers. There we were strip-searched before we took a shower, and an MTA (medical technician assistant) wearing a rubber glove stuck his finger in everybody's ass, looking for contraband. This happened in every prison, and it was always an ugly moment for me. I was often tempted to turn around and slug the MTA. They did this even though each inmate had gone through the same procedure when he left Leavenworth in chains. After the search, we were put directly on the prison coach, under heavy guard with no contact with anyone. Either this search was done as another form of subtle punishment, or else it was just another stupid rule.

As Johnny's turn came up after mine, he said disgustedly, "This is a bunch of bullshit, man!" Lieutenant Mahan said, "You're getting off to a bad start. You're going to be dealing with easygoing guards and bad ones. So, you can make it as hard on yourself as you want it to be."

Afterwards we were issued clothes, shaving gear, a small mirror, and a piece of cardboard to cut the glare from the bulb in our cell. This was all an inmate was allowed to keep in his cell other than books and an artist's paint kit, if you had the cash to purchase it. Anything else was considered contraband, and possession of contraband was a punishable offense.

Lieutenant Mahan, who was civil enough towards us new arrivals, and who later proved to be one of the more decent officers in the penitentiary, told us that after we settled into our cells, he would let us into the mess hall for a late morning breakfast. The guard who escorted me up to my cell on the ground floor of the section in the cell house everyone called Broadway only spoke when he showed me how to put the cardboard shade over the light bulb. Then he left.

As I looked around, I noticed a lot of black guys standing at their cell door fronts across the broad aisle, watching and speaking to the other black guys they knew. The black inmates were celled in one section, one man to a cell, like everybody else in Alcatraz. I knew several cons from Atlanta on Alcatraz, like Joe Belizone, Allen West, Pork Chops, and George Campbell, so I knew I would feel more at home than the other arrivals who had to make all new friends.

I wasn't in my cell more than five minutes when a black guy named Jimmy Groves who celled across and up one tier from me called down and asked about a friend of his who had been transferred from Alcatraz to Atlanta. "Hey you down there. You know "Yard Bird" at Atlanta? How's he doing?"

I could tell he and other black inmates were hungry for news. For days afterwards, they bombarded me with questions about other black friends, once they saw I was friendly enough and not a racist. They also wanted to know about things going on outside, because at the time, they had no radios and only half-a-dozen prison-approved magazines that contained little news and no politics. The white inmates who did hear a few things from visitors, guards, and each other sure weren't passing it on to the black cons. Later, I heard one redneck comment, "Keep the niggers in the dark. It's best that way. They don't care anyway." The guards seemed to feel the same way. What I couldn't figure out was that if the main pastime in the penitentiary was reading, chess, and talking, why not at least educate with the reading and talking? Why did the censors have to chop up the Time and Life magazines? If everyone had intelligent reading, especially current events and politics, everybody would be talking, which would help keep their minds off their misery. Tensions would fall. If inmates are hungry for news, feed them news. What's the big deal? Some of the black guys lost themselves playing chess, at least. I got to where I could read a book even with six or eight guys, two to a game, hollering out chess moves to each other from their cells across the aisle from me. I learned over the years in confinement to tune all distractions out. To this day, however, I can't read unless something distracting, like television and radio, is going on. The cons who couldn't read, or didn't like to, or who weren't provided proper and interesting books and magazines did hard time, and you could recognize them in the mess hall, yard, or industries.

Around 11:30 a.m. we new arrivals were taken into the dining room for the late breakfast Mahan had promised. If we wanted, we could have scrambled eggs, toast, and coffee before the main population came in for lunch, an hour or so later. I sat next to Johnny Iozza and asked, "Where did you disappear to when we all went to the shower?" He got mad and red in the face and shouted, "That motherfucker stuck his finger in my ass, and I had to shit! So, the goons made me wait until you all showered before they let me go into the shitter. Then they let me shower." I fell out laughing, almost landing on the floor but no one else at our table dared laugh, because as I mentioned Johnny weighed 230 pounds, and they weren't about to experiment with his temperament by laughing at him.

It's funny how you remember first impressions and, believe me, that first afternoon and evening were full of impressions. A day doesn't go by today that some fragment of Alcatraz life doesn't surface, either in a dream or when I'm wide awake. Those little things that first day and in the weeks, months, and years that followed add up to fifteen hundred days of little things, and those fifteen hundred days full of little things would add up to the rest of a life filled with memories I don't want to remember.

What were the little things? I have in mind snapshots: endless glances up and down Broadway: inmates sweeping and humming; inmates carrying towels, squeegees, and buckets; endless cleaning, scrubbing, polishing, scraping, and painting; guards with clipboards; loud buzzers; the opening, closing, banging, and clicking of doors; the flushing of toilets; the library and hospital being opened each day; the dining room and kitchen being cleaned up after meals; laundry being collected from cell to cell; inmates being searched on their way out to the recreation yard; shouting throughout the cellhouse; loud singing and the playing of small musical instruments; the close-ups of those I liked and hated; the dinner trays being passed to those in isolation or solitary confinement; the buzzing motors in the industries; to say nothing of the other endless, routine prison duties.

And later, when I had outside duties as a gardener, how will I ever erase from my memory the Frisco waterfront; the two great bridges; the orange ball of the sun coming up over the East Bay hills; morning and evening lights of commuters on the bridges; the white sailing boats and fishing vessels; freighters passing by; the waves breaking against the unbreakable rocks of the shore; the circling seagulls; the wind and salt air blowing over me?

That afternoon all twenty of us new arrivals remained in lockup, adjusting to our new institution. The guards who walked down Broadway past my cell to the mess hall or yard on their various assignments neither glanced at me nor said anything. I soon learned that almost all the Alcatraz guards were reserved and said nothing to you unless it was about official business. But I also learned that there were a couple of guards who seemed to enjoy a chance to hassle you over little things, like having your shirt collar buttoned, or sitting down and not standing at the cell front for the count.

For dinner that night, while the main population went to their usual meals in the prison's mess hall, we newcomers got a sandwich and an apple to hold us over until morning. That was all. No drink, no dessert, no coffee, nothing. One of the guards just walked by and tossed a sandwich and the apple on the bed. I figured it was just one more way for the guards, who we called the "hacks" to say, "We're in charge here. You are nothing. We are everything." I shouted, "Fuck you for your generosity!" as he passed but the goon didn't react.

CHARLIE HOPKINS CELL ON ALCATRAZ, NEXT TO THAT OF "CREEPY" AL KARPIS

That night I fell asleep as usual. As soon as my head hit the pillow, I was out like a light. But unusually for me, I awoke by 10:00 or 10:30 p.m. I only slept an hour or so and awoke suddenly. I lay there wide awake, listening to all the sounds. Lights were out, but not the sounds. There were the usual sounds I knew from Atlanta, like flushing toilets and inmates talking to each other when they weren't supposed to. But here were new sounds, like the wind blowing through the Golden Gate across the bay and slamming into the cellhouse. Somehow, I enjoyed it. I didn't feel depressed, because as far as I was concerned my life was over. But that first night, I felt a strange peace—no anger, no hostility, no resentment. I was at peace here, listening to everything and anything. It was a new experience.

The next morning, I was admitted into the main population to have breakfast with the other inmates. I looked around to see if I could recognize anybody I knew. No luck but this was only the first line. Two more would follow our meal. As we were lined up to return to our cells, I spotted Allen West, an inmate I had known both at Raiford and Atlanta. There is no way I can describe how much contempt and hatred I had for this miserable, phony, son-of-a-bitch cocksucker. He was a good friend of Joe Belizone, a tough ex-marine I met at Lewisburg Federal Prison.

I couldn't figure out why Joe took up time with West. I tried to tell Joe that he was nothing more than a two-bit would-be gangster who lived off the reputations of other guys. Furthermore, I explained that he had been a homosexual rat at Raiford, and there were guys at Atlanta who wanted to kill him. But Joe didn't seem to mind that West was a degenerate who, whenever he could, hung around passive young homos. Now, in the dining room, as West caught me studying him, he looked away.

That evening, after an idle afternoon in my cell, I was eating at a dining table with a bunch of guys including Joe Schultz. It just so happened that he and Johnny Iozza sat across from each other. To us it appeared they didn't know one another. At first, Schultz pretended Johnny was just another big guy but he knew he was face-to-face with a professional boxer. After finishing his meal in silence, Schultz looked over at Johnny as he was continuing to eat, minding his own business. Schultz suddenly said, "Hey you, did you lose something at this table?" as if to ask, "What the fuck are you doing sitting here?"

Surprised, Johnny looked up at him across the table and calmly said, "No, I didn't lose anything here. Did you?" Schultz said, "Yeah, motherfucker. That spot you're sitting on." Johnny stood up slowly and said, "That's fight talk, man." Joe slowly smiled and said, "Yeah, champ. I already heard about you and your boast on the train. You're supposed to be bad but you're not half as bad as me, believe me. I'll get it on with you anytime. You name it." Johnny sat down and continued eating as if nothing had happened but I knew Iozza was fuming and thinking when he might get this guy.

After that, all of us at the table ate in silence. I knew things would explode sooner or later, probably right after Johnny got his belly full. A few minutes later Schultz got up to get some more bread from a cart next to our table. Johnny, who was finished eating and now was picking his teeth with a fingernail he had torn off, started ragging Schultz about how bad he was supposed to be. Schultz couldn't believe his ears. A newcomer didn't behave this way in the Alcatraz mess hall. Schultz, insulted and angry, started shouting at Johnny, saying he would either soon be in the hospital or dead on a prison stretcher. By that time a guard was standing behind them, forcing each to sit down. But that little affair wouldn't be the last Johnny would have with Schultz.

Because my cell was near the first six cells in front of Broadway designated as the sick call area, I was able to talk to a few guys who lined up there the next morning. Mike, a young kid I knew from Atlanta, walked by, and I said, "Hey, Mike!" He was glad to see me, and we talked a bit. But then Joe Schultz came up and Mike told me he was his best friend. I said. "Mike, are you sure he ain't your brother?" Schultz looked at me and answered, "Yeah, I'm his brother. Want to make something out of it?" I looked at Schultz and thought to myself, "This mean son-of-a-bitch looks just like Hercules." In the mess hall I mostly saw him sitting. Now, I was face to face with him, even though we had the barred cell front separating us. He was only five feet ten inches tall, but he had a tremendous build. His arms were as long and hairy as those of a gorilla, and his muscles were certainly in the same proportion as those of an ape. I would hear Warden Madigan say he was the biggest and toughest little man he ever saw. I laughed and said, "No, I don't want to make anything out of it. You're gonna have your hands full as it is."

Two days later in the basement shower room, Johnny Iozza made his way to the steps that led down from the main cell house floor to see if Schultz was in the line of men coming down to take their turn in the shower. "I want to slug with him so bad I can't shit. I want to try to give him a concussion before the guards break us up."

The basement shower room had a small partition between each shower, which gave an inmate a little privacy from the others, but not from the guards. In 1956, these partitions would all be torn out and the space made into one big shower room. After that the inmates had no privacy whatsoever. With that innovation a lot of knifings and killings stopped. Now, as Johnny waited to get Schultz, a con who arrived with me from Atlanta got mad at the guards for watching him shower and he shouted as loud as he could that all guards were nothing more than a bunch of "noodle gazers."

Johnny tried to linger around the stairs as much as he could without being noticed but one of the lieutenants spotted him and finally told us both to hurry up and get into the shower and stop fooling around. I saw Joe Belizone toweling himself off near the benches and went over to ask him why Schultz was not there. Joe said Schultz was in D-Block, the isolation section. I asked why, and he answered, "Because he stole food awhile back and hasn't gone to court yet. They picked him up last night."

"Yeah," I said sarcastically, "The way I figure it, the hacks got wind that Johnny was going to bash him and wanted to prevent hospital costs to the government. If he wasn't in D-Block he would be getting his ass kicked right about now."

Joe laughed, "I don't know about that, Charlie. Schultz is a pretty rough guy."

"Johnny is no jailhouse brawler. He's a pro. Tomorrow I'll show you his picture in my ring record book."

When I went over and told Iozza, Johnny was pissed. "Hell, I didn't want the guy to go to the hole. I wanted to put the hole in him."

We weren't sure whether it was stealing food that got him thrown into isolation or whether he asked to go there but he would be released sooner or later, and Johnny would rectify the insult. The next day in the yard, everybody was passing around the ring record book I brought out to prove Johnny was a pro. In fact, that record book circulated for days throughout the cell house, with everybody checking the record. While this was going on, I met with some of my Atlanta friends in the yard to talk about bringing Johnny and Schultz together to make peace. Dago John came up, and someone asked him if he could do anything. He said, "I doubt if Joe will listen to me. I don't carry much weight with him." Then this black man walked up and some of the guys said in a real respectful way, "Hi, Bumpy." I didn't know who he was, but I liked the way he handled himself, even before we spoke to each other.

Black inmates normally don't come busting into a group of white inmates talking business, but this guy was as calm and self-assured as if he had been dealing with and controlling whites all his life. I also sensed a deep integrity, a kind of sensitivity in him. I didn't doubt this man was violent, but there was something else that caught my attention. Later that night, when I was thinking about him, I realized that what he had was a basic dignity about him. Later, Joe Carnes, a Rock old-timer whom I celled next to, would tell me that it wasn't dignity that caught my eye that afternoon when I met Bumpy; it was an integrity of being.

Bumpy was cool. He said simply, "I will talk with Schultz. He will listen to me." That's all he said, and he walked away. Bumpy didn't head for all the other blacks who deliberately segregated themselves in one corner of the recreation yard. He just walked around, talking to everybody: black, white, Hispanic, you name it. Bumpy didn't seem black or white. He was himself, relaxed and at peace. I liked him the way he was, and I felt we would be friends.

ELLSWORTH "BUMPY" JOHNSON

A week or so later, while I was in the yard, I saw Joe Schultz walk down the steps from the cell house. It was his first day out of isolation. He sought out George Campbell, who was standing a short distance away.

They talked awhile then walked toward the little group I was in. When Joe saw me, he walked right up and said to me, "I don't like that big motherfucking friend of yours."

Everybody stopped talking and I said, "Well Schultz, if you knew him, you would like him like I like him." Since Johnny was on idle status, he was probably in his cell at this moment.

Schultz said he had seen Johnny's fight record in isolation that morning and added, "If he whips me or sticks a blade in my ass today, he will have to do it again tomorrow." I said, "Well, Johnny has already told me that he didn't want to fight my friends. I told him you were a friend of a couple of my friends. They say around here that you're a bully, but I don't see it that way. You might bully other bullies or guys with attitude problems but my friend Johnny doesn't want to fight my friend's friends. Some guys have to prove themselves all the time, but I don't think you're one of those guys." He stood there in silence looking at his shoes, then said, "Aw, the shit with it," and walked away. With that simple gesture, the war was called off. Schultz and Johnny became good friends.

CHAPTER FIVE
CRAZY HOUSE

"In lunatic asylums it is a well-known fact that patients are far more dangerous when suffering from fear than when moved by rage or hatred."

—C. G. Jung

The days passed quickly while I was on idle status. You would think otherwise. But for me, being alone was kind of therapeutic. A lot of guys couldn't stand the loneliness of those hours, but I cherished them. One morning Warden Madigan came down Broadway with three well-dressed visitors who had VIP written all over them. He stopped mid-way up Broadway toward the mess hall, and I could see him waving his arm around the cellhouse saying something to the effect of, "Alcatraz allows the government to give cheap, efficient, and secure incarceration. You gentlemen know how important it is that a safe, escape-proof prison be in line with today's costs."

One of the VIPs asked a question, and Madigan answered, "No, I wouldn't say they are all irreclaimable. In fact, I've not been too attracted to the concept that we house the nation's most desperate in one prison. Other countries tried that and it failed in every one. In the old days the presence here of gangsters like Al Capone and Machine Gun Kelly was pure window dressing for the exhibition of our prize malefactors. But other men with equal if not worse records, more daring and notorious escape risks, have been assembled here since we opened in 1934. But we have managed all right and I would say that through the years all of our custodial staffs have done a damn good job. In spite of the volume of danger here, the place has been pretty subdued."

I got a big kick out of listening to this shit. Here was the "official" Bureau of Prison's public relations line: Alcatraz was a "pretty subdued" place over the years! I wasn't there in the 1930s and 1940s or part of the 1950s but all I knew was that during the first month I was in Alcatraz I saw more hate and passion with the potential of flaming into killing frenzy than I had seen or heard about at any other institution.

Everybody in America, whether you were a criminal or an ordinary Joe Blow, heard that Alcatraz was a place where brutal beatings and other forms of inhuman treatment were handed out. And everyone knew it was the government's toughest prison and had such things as dungeons. But no one ever heard what a lot of convicts had been saying since 1934, "Alcatraz itself ought to be put on trial before the public—not us cons."

One of the first stories I was told was a favorite among the old cons. It was told and retold by guys like Alvin Karpis, Whitey Franklin, Jimmy Groves, Blackie Audette, Joe Carnes, and others. If I heard it once, I heard it a thousand times. I heard it at breakfast, lunch, and dinner, at work and at play in the yard. Everybody told it, and I never tired of hearing it.

The story dealt with Henri Young, a bank robber from the Pacific Northwest. When he entered Alcatraz in the summer of 1937 at the age of 23, he was facing a 70-year sentence. But by 1941, more than half of his five years on the island had been spent in solitary confinement. When he was released into the population, he was filled with hate and bitterness. The guards felt he was one of the most troublesome men they had ever seen. The first time he ate with the guys in the mess hall in late November 1941, after all that time in isolation, he spotted a man at the next table that made his blood run cold. The man he saw was Rufus McCain: bank robber, kidnapper, and all-around bad man. McCain, who was 32 years old, was probably the most hated man of all the incorrigibles on the Rock. He was from Durant, Oklahoma, and was serving 99 years for kidnapping and escape. By all standards, McCain was vicious—but not for long.

As Young tried to eat, he stared at McCain. He didn't recognize the guys sitting around his bitter enemy. They had come to the island after he had been thrown into a solitary cell. Why did Young hate McCain so much? Why did he want vengeance? Well, McCain had gone yellow, cringing before the guards when Young's escape plan, of which McCain was a part, failed. As McCain stared back, Young put a dull mess hall knife to his throat and tauntingly ran it back and forth, as if to say, "This is what you're going to get."

In the mess hall the next morning, Young ate in his group of several inmates. McCain saw him, turned, and hissed the worst epithet one man can utter to another: "Motherfucker." Young, trying with all his power to maintain his composure and dignity before the other cons and yard guards, was so full of hate he almost fainted. A friend had to pull him back.

A few hours later that morning in the industries, Young left his workplace and caught McCain busy at work in the tailor shop. Young attacked McCain's throat with a razor blade fixed to a toothbrush with black tape. In a few seconds, McCain's head hung all the way down to his belly. No one prior had seen so much blood on the floor at one time in many years.

What really made the Alcatraz inmates laugh, then and now, was that when that bastard E.J. Miller, the associate warden, asked Young, "Why did you do it?" Young looked at him and shrugged his shoulders. "I didn't know I did. Did I do it?"

"You cut his throat from ear to ear. You killed McCain. Admit it!" demanded Miller.

"What do you mean I killed McCain?" Young asked. His eyes got really glassy and he said, "I won't deny it and I won't admit it But, really, I don't believe I killed him."

Well, Young went to trial, and little did anyone foresee that soon, Alcatraz itself would actually be put on trial for cruelty, inhumanity, and brutality. When Young was brought before United States Judge Michael I. Roche and asked for his plea, he listened with a puzzled look on his face and quietly pleaded not guilty. The judge said he would appoint two attorneys to defend him. Young was grateful but then asked politely, "Your honor, if I may, can I ask that whoever you appoint as my attorneys be as young as possible?"

James McInnis and Sol A. Abrams were appointed. The prosecuting US Attorney, Frank J. Hennessy, was certain he had an airtight case. Other than maybe pleading insanity, Young had no case. MacInnis and Abrams went to work. They came up with scientific terms like "irresistible impulse," "dual personality," "a strange psycho-physiological state," and "psychological unconsciousness." The theory the two attorneys developed was that the terrors and cruelties of Alcatraz had so unbalanced Young that he became a split personality, unaccountable for his actions. And they were going to prove this actually happened.

On March 15, 1941, the trial began in the federal courthouse in downtown San Francisco. In the opening remarks by the two defense attorneys, MacInnis and Abrams told the jury, mostly composed of women, of Young's long periods in solitary confinement and isolation cells. They said Henri was "punch drunk" when the deadly razor cut McCain's jugular vein. They argued that Young was addled by all the beatings he received from the guards as a part of the Rock's way of life.

Throughout the next few days, the two brilliant attorneys carefully stripped away the mask that Uncle Sam had carefully placed on the most notorious prison in the world. And word had it that Young played his part to the hilt. He was dressed in a conservative business suit, he looked fresh and polished, and he paid absolute attention, listening to every word. He seemed confident and unworried by the fact that he was on trial for murder.

Twenty-three Alcatraz convicts took the stand for the defense that month and all told the jury what no outside person had heard up to that point: the sordid details of existence on the infamous Rock. First, everybody said the same thing about McCain: he was not only a kidnapper and killer but a degenerate too. At Alcatraz he made homosexual advances toward younger inmates. Second, when Warden James A. Johnston was called, he spent two days going through every detail of life in the penitentiary. Abrams and McInnis made him cough up the specifics about solitary confinement: how the cells were only five by nine feet and unlighted, how convicts slept without beds, without mattresses, and sometimes without blankets.

He had to say how men in solitary used to get one meal every three days, but that by 1940 they were getting meals every other day with soup on alternate days. But Johnston didn't know a lot of things either. For example, he was shocked to learn that one of his guards had on various occasions forced Young to drink milk mixed with gasoline.

Young's convict record on the Rock showed that he had been thrown into solitary confinement almost continuously for a series of violations that ranged from throwing water on guards to banging his pillow on the cell front bars. When the two attorneys asked why pillow banging was a serious enough offense to warrant solitary confinement, the ruler of Alcatraz, Johnston, said that prisoners often kept up a terrific racket by hammering the concrete floors with feather pillows. Abrams asked the warden why Young would be making noise in the first place. Was Henri rebelling against some prison injustice? Johnston answered, "Well, you may assume some men do not like Alcatraz."

When the attorney asked the warden about the effects of solitary confinement on the mental states of prisoners, the number of convicts who had gone insane on Alcatraz, and the extent to which corporal punishment was used, the prosecutor objected and was sustained. When J.E. Miller, the associate warden, took the stand, he answered a lot of questions. He told the jury, for example, that prison regulations did not allow a man to be kept in solitary for more than nineteen days at a stretch, although some served eighteen days, were taken out for a day or two, then sent back to serve another eighteen days.

When the inmates selected by the defense came to court, they were brought two at a time, manacled. The government took no chances on a break. They took every precaution. A dozen armed deputy marshals and prison guards were positioned all around. Proper signals had to be given to get in. The whole works were thrown in to safeguard "the incorrigibles from this country's Devil's Island."

"Disregard the responses," the judge told the jury. But the judge couldn't erase the mental impressions made on the jurors. The stories told by the inmates were true. Any con who survived Alcatraz in the 1930s will tell you so. For example, William Dunnock, a 34-year-old bank robber, told the jury how he had been flung into solitary after the guards beat him and broke his nose. Associate Warden Miller's name came up often. It seems he especially enjoyed kicking the inmates. One inmate, Whitely Lewis, had been slugged so severely by him and other guards that he went insane. Inmate John Stadig's mind snapped under prison rigors, Sailor Quake committed suicide, and Walter Bearden, even though he was tubercular, was made to stay in the prison's dark, damp underground cell until he began bleeding in his lungs. Not only that that, he was denied medical attention—then he died.

Inmate after inmate testified how the associate warden would throw a man into the hands of guards with the order, "Beat this man's brains out" if he didn't do or say as Miller wanted. When the attorneys brought Miller back to the stand for further questioning, he denied everything. But Abrams and McInnis got hold of prison records showing that Young was thrown into solitary after leading prisoners in singing, "We'll hang old Meathead [Miller] to a sour apple tree." The only thing Miller would admit was that he occasionally placed someone in solitary so that he would emerge with "a better outlook on life."

"Well," the attorneys told the jury, "you can see how it's Alcatraz that should be put on trial, not Henri Young. The truth is that the effects of Alcatraz on Henri's mind, his mental condition, made him commit the murder. Twenty men have gone insane at Alcatraz since 1934. Alcatraz is guilty, not Young. Alcatraz should be sentenced, not Young. Young must be acquitted." Naturally, the prosecutor said the defense was being given too much leeway in offering irrelevant testimony. Hennessy especially objected to the way the defense's witnesses were "snapping" their answers before he could raise any objections.

Then the key witness for Young took the stand. He was William Mahan, one of the most infamous convicts at Alcatraz at the time. He was one of the kidnappers of little Georg Weyerhauser in Tacoma in 1935. Now, at the age of 39, he had a 60-year sentence hanging on him. Mahan testified, "McCain was always boasting about the brutal things he had done and what he was going to do. Once I was a janitor in his cellblock. McCain had a dustpan in his cell. He refused to give it back to me. I let him keep it for about two hours. Then I went to get it. I saw that a piece of metal had been taken off. It was a piece of iron that was gone—now it was sharp on both sides..."

"What did you do then?" asked MacInnis.

"I asked for it back. He told me he was going to kill Young. I told him if he used that piece of iron as a knife it would involve me, but he said he was going to kill him anyway."

Harmon M. Waley, Mahan's partner, who was serving 45 years on Alcatraz, corroborated Mahan's story that McCain boasted he would kill Young as soon as Henri was released from solitary. He also described how he had been sick and asked the prison doctor for help. When the doctor refused, Waley made a remark to him and was then thrown in the dungeon for three days, in spite of the fact that he had a fever. "I was beaten up. I was half crazy. And I was put in a straitjacket."

The next morning, MacInnis, in his opening remarks, told the court that each man who had gone back to Alcatraz was being subjected to "duress and intimidation" once the inmate returned to the island. Several convicts informed MacInnis that they had been warned by guards "to lay off Alcatraz." Harold Brest, serving life and an additional 55-year sentence for kidnapping in Pennsylvania, took the stand that morning and testified that on the morning of the murder, he heard McCain shout obscenities at Young. "He made a rotten reference to Henri's mother. For that reason, he killed McCain. I would have done the same thing."

Carl Hood, a young man who killed another inmate at Leavenworth, took the stand and said that he, too, heard McCain refer to Young as performing an abnormal sexual act with his mother. MacInnis asked what the reference was. Hood wouldn't answer. He just looked solemnly at the attorney. Then he slowly said, "It's the foulest name in the English language. It's the worst name one man can call another man."

"Well, what is it?"

"All I'm going to say is that the word is so vile that it's grounds for murder—on Alcatraz, at least."

"Were you there when he called Young this heinous name?"

"Yes, I was. I was talking to McCain when Young walked by after getting out of solitary. He said, 'There's the motherfucker now!' McCain yelled, 'Scat, you motherfucker!'"

The epithet brought blushes to the courtroom. Both the men and the women looked at their shoes. The judge was embarrassed.

"What was Young's reaction?" MacInnis asked.

"He gave McCain a funny look and walked away."

Two hours later, McCain lay dying on the floor and Young was standing over him, a homemade weapon dripping blood in his hand. They had hated each other so much that only one of them would leave the island alive.

To drive home the point that Young was a victim of the Alcatraz system, the defense attorneys called more inmate witnesses. One said he had been beaten with a blackjack by a male nurse in the prison hospital. Another said he was beaten with a metal pan.

As the trial went on, it became clear that Young's attorneys were sending a message to Washington that conditions on Alcatraz were "unbelievably inhuman" and demanded an immediate investigation. The statement was sent to Attorney General Jackson, J. Edgar Hoover of the FBI, and James V. Bennett, the Director of the Bureau of Prisons. Well, you can imagine how pissed Bennett and Warden Johnston were. Bennett said the jury had been misled because Young was "the worst and most dangerous criminal with whom Alcatraz officials have ever dealt."

Johnston said it was an old trick for defense attorneys to throw in irrelevant material to confuse jurors: "The defense avoids having its defendant tried and instead tries to put on trial those who put the defendant on trial!" Johnston went on to admit that Alcatraz was designed as a prison of "maximum security" and "minimum privilege," a place to hold machine-gun bandits, kidnappers, escape artists, and recalcitrant prisoners who flouted the rules of other prisons and obstructed the government's program of protecting society and rehabilitating criminals.

"I do not wish to imply that Alcatraz is a pleasant place or an attractive place. But it is a clean place, a sanitary place, a place where food is, I am sorry to say, better than that which many families in the lower and even middle-income brackets receive." And he was especially emphatic in saying, "I have issued strict orders that no guard is ever to take upon himself the disciplining of any convict. He is never to use corporal punishment as a matter of discipline. Corporal punishment is prohibited in all our federal institutions."

Young, meanwhile, received an additional three years with his original 15-year sentence. That was the maximum that could be imposed after the jury's verdict of involuntary manslaughter. Judge Roche was angry and said, insofar as he could, that Young and the two attorneys had hoodwinked the jury. "You planned a cold-blooded, deliberate murder. You took a man's life without provocation. I've sentenced men to the gallows for less."

Young smiled and happily returned to Alcatraz to finish the remainder of his fifteen years and then begin three more. The worst word in the history of the universe had cost him another thousand days. But that motherfucker McCain was dead in a grave. It was worth it.

I heard this story within a few days of my arrival at Alcatraz and, as I've said, I've never tired of listening to it. I'm not saying there was a lot of excessive harshness or cruelty in those early days, because I wasn't there to witness it. And I sure as heck don't want to enter into any debates with former Alcatraz guards who are still alive today to tell me the beatings and harassment just weren't so. All I know is what I heard when I came to the island, and reliable convicts don't lie much among themselves. This story of Young and how he put Alcatraz on trial helped put the place into perspective for me and it told me what I might expect. Every time I think of it, I shake my head in disbelief: Alcatraz was brought to its knees— indirectly—by one word. And it seems like today if you *don't* call someone a motherfucker it's an insult.

Henri Young may have maneuvered a scheme to put Alcatraz itself on trial, but my goal was to sleep. For a while, I behaved as if in a trance. I was entirely unsympathetic and unfriendly toward everything and everyone. It wasn't because I was having a problem adjusting to Alcatraz, it was just that I was in the process of dying inside. I thought little and felt nothing. With the exception of talking to a few friends, I had no reactions at all. Not even the thought of the long monotonous years ahead jarred me into any feeling.

The lack of hard news and real companionship was what bothered most guys and, as I mentioned, the boredom it created caused a lot of behavior problems. You could get more information out of a guard when you were in D-Block than from the official news sources. This was mainly because they got bored too, spending eight hours a day in D with no one but the inmates to talk to. I used to talk to the ones who were willing to talk to me about a lot of subjects, and some would tell me stories about things they did when they were young.

I remember one guard telling me about seeing his childhood buddy coming through the prison system years before, and he often reflected how his own life could have easily gone bad. I can't remember the guard's name, but he was a big red-headed guy, and he also told me that all the Alcatraz guards were trained to never, ever trust an inmate. He said the officials also taught them that some men would end up in jail, no matter what kind of raising they had, since that was what fate had in store for them. I told him it was a good idea not to trust inmates, because I didn't trust them, either. If you and a guard spent time in the main cellhouse talking like that to each other, it looked bad from both angles. But in lock-up it wasn't frowned upon by either the cons or the hacks.

Officer Baker at Alcatraz was as quiet as some of the inmates were and never talked to me about himself. He did his job very well, but he also was flexible. If he liked you, he would ignore petty rules that were bullshit to start with. Some guards couldn't do this. All they knew was what the rule book said and they followed it to the letter. I'll never understand why Joe Cretzer shot Baker in the 1946 crash-out attempt, unless he just flipped out. But I remember Carnes telling me that after Cretzer shot the guards, he looked at Officer Sundstrom who was sitting in a corner, and then turned and walked away. He said Cretzer liked Sundstrom. I liked Sundstrom, too, because he was a nice guy and never showed any hostility towards inmates. He took my mug shot, and I asked him about sending one to my aunt. A couple of days later he stopped by my cell and told me he had cut the logo off and mailed one to my aunt. After my release, I asked her about it, and she said she never received it but she always has had a little problem telling the truth. Then again, the associate warden J.D. Latimer, who we called Skinhead, may have stopped Sundstrom's letter without Sundstrom knowing it.

One guard named Jamison worked the cell house a lot, and he appeared to hate the inmates he had to work with. I heard one inmate we called Cricket curse him out good one night. You could hear him shouting at Jamison all over the cell house. Bill Long was a guard who went by the book and couldn't bend a rule if his life depended on it. He was 6'4" and weighed about 220. Iozza used to beg him to open his door in D-block so they could fight. Johnny cursed him, taunted him, demanded to fuck his mother, and called him "pussy" over and over but Long still wouldn't open the door, even while he was passing out mattresses in the strip cells. He always had two other guards standing next to him. John would say over and over, "Hey, Long, you must be pussy, 'cause jam don't shake like that." or "Hey, Long, you ain't nothing but a hound dog."

While the other two guards were laughing, Long unlocked the utility corridor, slipped up to Johnny's ventilator, and kicked the screen hard while Johnny had his face against it, yelling at him. Johnny went crazy then and started asking what Long's mother's cunt was like, since word was all over the prison that Long was eating it. The officials finally transferred John to Springfield.

The daily routine on Alcatraz in the mid-1950s was to get up about daylight, stand at your door when the bell sounded for count, eat breakfast, go to work for anywhere from an hour and a half to three and a half hours, eat lunch, go to sick call on Broadway, return to work for a couple of hours, return to your cell, eat supper, return to your cell, either read or listen to the radio from 7:00 p.m. until about 9:30 p.m., and take a shower and a couple of times a week. That was it in the 1950s and there were no exceptions for time, place, or persons concerning this procedure. One other routine that never changed was Lieutenant Mitchell and his cigar. I never saw him without a cigar in the corner of his mouth.

Several guys I knew who had been in prison for long periods had turned homosexual, but I wouldn't mention their names, because that was their business and they were good people. The way they gave oral sex, which was the only chance they had, was to work as a cellhouse orderly or in the library and stop in front of a cell. Their partner would stand on the bars high enough so that the orderly could stand up and the guard couldn't see anything, even when he turned the corner.

Sometimes it happened that way on shower night by timing it right. Shower night was the only time you didn't return in a group. Some guy called Yard Bird started a rumor, when he got back to Atlanta, that Karpis was homosexual, but it was a dirty lie. Some guys were jealous of people who had done things with a gun that they didn't have the guts to do and would try to run them down. When I first arrived on the Rock I asked a guy I worked with about what Yard Bird said in Atlanta, and he said, "You better watch whoever told you that, for he is a no-good motherfucker and he may be testing you to see how you will react."

Karpis never showed any indication to me that he would mess with a man in any manner. He minded his own business and left other people alone. He had a few friends and they were all he associated with. I was one, Pappy Kyle was his best friend, and Bigsey Gilford and Jack Bishop were the other two. Bigsey, I'm sure, would mess with another man, because I had to tell him a couple of times about trying to hug me and being too friendly. Karpis never touched anybody. He sneaked up behind me one time, acting like he was a stranger, but he was just horsing around.

When Joe Schultz later got to Springfield, he had all kinds of pretty homos who looked like girls after him, and he tried to satisfy them all. He got written up once for kissing a guy inside a stairwell, and he told me the report said he was "osculating with Lamoree," a little sissy from 10-E who looked just like a girl. Joe broke off with one of the sissies once and told me he was going to make "her" pay him alimony. A buddy of mine and I were sitting on the yard talking one day, and a couple of sissies from 10-

E stopped by. Stan, my buddy, liked one of them, so he said, "Let's me and you walk around." The sissy only weighed ninety pounds, while Stan was 6'1" and weighed 220. But in ten minutes he was back, telling me that the little sissy told him how jealous she was, and if she caught him running around on her, she would cut his balls off. He said, "I ain't getting involved with that crazy bitch."

There was one young Mexican in 10-E nicknamed Sabotage who looked like a pretty girl to me, but I never messed with him, because I didn't want that kind of stuff put on my record. The Birdman was in Building Eight at Springfield, which was for medical patients, and he got caught in a closet with a young boy. The talk was that the boy was fucking the Birdman. The officials never did anything to him because, I guess, they felt he had been isolated long enough.

We had a television set on each ward in Springfield and a list of programs were drawn up each week and posted on the ward. The guard had a key to the TV, and he changed channels to control what we saw. We saw a lot of westerns, one of which was Have Gun, Will Travel. Some of the guys had cards printed up that said, "Have Dick, Will Travel," and they passed them out to the sissies in 10-E. I think the librarian there was gay, because he always had several of them hanging around his desk and he saved the best magazines for the sissies.

In Raiford they kept the homos on G floor cell twelve, at least the ones who were obvious. The guys who had money on the outside could pay the deputy and avoid being sent to a road camp or assigned to a road crew. They could also get a soft job, a two-man cell, and whoever they wanted for cell mates. Some guys lived it up. One gay guy had a military disability check and another had a state check as a retired school teacher, and they both lived it up. I saw a few fights at Raiford over sex, but the only killing there was when Bill Hadeley killed a rat in a sixteen-man cell after the doors were locked. He stabbed him to death and got a life sentence. They had more killings at road camps than in Raiford, because that is where the tougher guys went. George Heroux was kept in Raiford for security, because on the road camps you could get a gun slipped in and they knew what he would do with a gun.

When I was in the reform school, we had several gay boys in my cottage and, since the cottage master's apartment was on the first floor, they would go in the bathroom after lights were out. We were counted once an hour by some elderly guy who went from building to building, all night long. Just before I was released a new man named Durden was hired to be the relief cottage master for my building. He was also in charge of the yard crew of which I was the foreman, and I noticed he was obsessed with talking to me about a buddy of mine named Jessie, who had just been released, and what our relationship was.

He gave me better grades for my work than I was entitled to, but it helped get me released. About a year after my release I met a kid named Rozier, and he said they had caught Durden fucking a kid named Swilley. I knew then why he kept talking to me about Jessie. Rozier said all the State of Florida did was fire Durden, because they didn't want any publicity. Most of the kids there had parents who didn't want to be bothered with them. That's why I say they should be cut like a hog so taxpayers don't have to raise their kids for them.

The Bureau of Prisons put out a pamphlet on how good Alcatraz was in the 1950s. It said that each prisoner was given a physical, an aptitude test, and shown educational films. This certainly wasn't correct unless they started it after I left there in 1960, which I doubt, since they closed the place in 1963. For example, in the '50s, you got to see two movies a month, and they were either westerns, war pictures, comedies, or love stories. Only about six magazines were allowed and they were Time, Life, Sports Illustrated, The Ring, Field and Stream, Popular Mechanics, and Look. Several writs were filed in federal court over things like this but denied on the grounds that the court had no jurisdiction over the warden's rules and regulations.

This little pamphlet also said the inmates at Alcatraz had plenty of nutritious food to eat. The only stipulation was that whatever food you took for yourself you had to eat. You couldn't leave any on your plate, or you were in trouble.

Some of the guys I knew couldn't adjust to the cooking very well and ate little. Personally, I never had a problem with prison cooking, because I had been used to that type of food since age ten. Sometimes the chow was better than what I ate at home, depending on what home and what jail I was in. The food at Raiford was so terrible you would certainly have to adjust. But the food on Alcatraz was the best of any institution I had been in. Of course, a lot of guys complained anyway.

CHAPTER SIX

CELLHOUSE BUDDIES

Hallucinations and delusions, delusions and hallucinations ...
No matter how you say it, it's still prison psychosis ...
And Death is counting up our days. counting them one by one,
counting them one by one, counting them one by one ...
The day is getting dark now, the day is getting dark now ...
                                        —Ellsworth "Bumpy" Johnson

When I was still at Atlanta, some anonymous rat wrote the deputy
warden about me and Johnny Iozza:

Dear Sir:

*Inmate Hopkins and Iozza are strong-arming other inmates. I don't
care about the other guys, but when they hit my friends, it's going too far.
They caught the boy in the checkroom tunnel and slapped him when he
resisted their homosexual advances. They both claim to be prizefighters
and think they are the toughest guys in the institution. I am going to use a
blade on them the next time they proposition my friend. They have already
beat up several guys just to prove how tough they are. Some of the boys
won't come to you, but something has to be done. Hopkins is a sneaky,
cunning punk who will smile at your face and attack you from the back. I
also have heard he made a hook in the machine shop and him and Buck
Morris was supposed to set a tower on fire in an attempt to get the gun
from the guard.*

This letter, which was unsigned, appeared in my 981-page file, which
I obtained in early 1992 from the FBI under the Freedom of Information
Act. I don't recall if anything ever came of this, because in those days I
was just plain wacko. I know I wasn't interested in any homosexuality.

Today, as I think about the letter, I believe I know who wrote it, because the guy asked Billy Duncan to talk to me and Johnny about leaving his homosexual buddy alone. He told Billy he was ready to use a blade on me.

The problem may have started one morning when Johnny and I were leaning against a wall in the library talking, and a young, husky guy walked past. He paused, looking Johnny over, and asked, "Have you got something you want from me?" Johnny stood straight up and said, "Yeah, I want some of your fucking fat ass!" What Johnny meant was that he wanted to whip the guy's ass, not have sex with him, because Johnny hated all homos. Furthermore, he was worse than I was when it came to other people staring at you and, besides, Johnny loved to fight, for any reason at all.

He especially loved to fight big guys, since they couldn't get out of his way and all he had to do was bang them on the head or jaw. Well, once the husky guy saw that Johnny meant business, he backed off, said nothing, and went about his way. The guy who wrote the deputy warden was lying about our approaching his friend in the checkroom tunnel. Hell, that is the last place you wanted to start any kind of trouble, since the area was always thick with guards. All the guy was doing was trying to make trouble for me and Johnny. We hung around together a lot, and when I was transferred to Alcatraz, Johnny was, too. I don't think he really belonged there, but because he associated with me, he got the same treatment I did.

Just before Thanksgiving Day after we got to the Rock, Johnny Iozza stood up during lunch and looked around the mess hall for an inmate named Simcox, who just happened to be sitting across from him. Johnny didn't know Simcox, but he had heard some bad things about him and wanted to see what he looked like but at that very moment Simcox gave Iozza a dirty look and jabbed his tray with his fork. Johnny looked down at him in an annoyed way and asked, "What the fuck is your problem, boy?" Simcox just sneered back at him, then said, "I heard all about you, and not much of it is good."

Because Simcox was 6'3" and weighed 215 pounds, he felt he could get away with talking to Johnny that way. To me, at that moment, Simcox appeared to be nothing more than a good specimen of Hitler's master race. Later, I learned that Simcox began a six-month sentence in Korea for some little thing like fighting but in the stockade, he stabbed an MP and got an additional twenty years. When he got to Leavenworth, he stabbed an inmate there and was sentenced to twenty more years. I liked him from the start, even though he started giving Johnny a bad time. He carried himself well.

But after lunch that day, a black inmate named Bebop passed Johnny a knife in the yard and warned him to have it on him the next time he ran into Simcox. No sooner had he said it than Simcox and about six of his friends formed a circle around me and Johnny. This didn't faze Johnny at all. In fact, he laughed. I wasn't too concerned about it either, because I knew I could handle at least two or three all by myself. One of Simcox's friends said to Johnny, "You want to fight me, man?"

Iozza smiled directly at Simcox and answered, "I don't fight ants. I want the big guy." Simcox looked Johnny over, and at that moment he didn't seem to be so cocksure of himself as he was at lunch. Simcox said, "Well, my friends just want to make sure I'm looked after, just like you and him look out for each other."

Johnny answered, "Hoppy here is my best friend, and since he's kind of skinny, he needs a little looking after but I don't need anybody looking out for me. I've just about had it with you motherfuckers looking for chickenshit jailhouse fights." Simcox didn't answer. But a few minutes later he went after another guy in the yard, and a lieutenant who spotted him said, "You want to fight so goddamn bad; you can fight yourself in isolation," and escorted him to D-block.

In December 1955, a cycle of stabbings and killings started that lasted several months and even made the *Congressional Record* in April 1956. Senator William Langer of North Dakota referred to the rash of violence as "an uprising on bloody Alcatraz." We were allowed to read the *Congressional Record* article in which the author hoped the revelations would bring about much-needed change in the prison. One of the first of those bloody killings occurred on Christmas Day, and it made a guy called Cricket lose his appetite so that I got to eat his fried chicken.

Cricket's real name was Carricker, AZ#1204. The main reason Cricket threw up was because I told him that Simcox intended to kill him, too, that day. But Webb, a close friend of Simcox's, liked Cricket and talked Simcox out of it. Cricket was only nineteen years old, had a big mouth, and was doing 23 years for robbing a Safeway store in Washington, DC. He was George Littlefield's rap partner, and I tried to help Cricket out, too, because Littlefield had been my best friend in Atlanta. George told me in Atlanta how Cricket almost strangled his lawyer in front of the judge for losing his case. He later stabbed a black guy in Lewisburg and was sent to Atlanta before I arrived, then on to Alcatraz.

Cricket sent Simcox a note in D-block, apologizing for running his mouth so much. He wrote, "Simcox, I can't fight a lick, so I make up for it with my mouth." At Alcatraz Cricket was whipped a couple of times and was later transferred to Leavenworth. He even used to run his mouth off at Karpis for looking at him, shouting, "You're a cheap, 50-year old gangster and I'm 21!" He was so foulmouthed he was cute but by that time Schultz and Joe Carnes started watching out for Cricket and therefore he got away with a lot. I have to admit, I liked him too.

The reason Cricket lost his appetite on that Christmas Day in 1955 goes back a few weeks, when an incident occurred between Dog, a white inmate, and Clarence "Joe" Carnes, a Choctaw Indian from Oklahoma. Carnes had participated in the 1946 "blast-out" escape attempt from Alcatraz and had spent seven years in isolation and solitary confinement because of it. Now, he was one of the most respected inmates on the Rock.

Well, just after Thanksgiving, Dog and Carnes got into an argument over a stupid cushion seat. Carnes who rarely lost his cool, called Dog a "nigger-lover" because he was tight with a black homo named Jessie, who, according to a lot of white inmates, looked like an ape. In fact, most of the white inmates quit talking to Dog because of his association with Jessie. I never heard Carnes refer to a black as "nigger" except for that one time but I'm sure it was because both Bumpy Johnson and Jimmy Groves had taught him and me that there was a tremendous difference in meaning when you called someone "nigger."

Bumpy used to say, "There are niggers and there are blacks, just like there are whites and white trash." Jimmy, who had killed three white inmates over the years, always backed me and Carnes, even against some of the black inmates, as Bumpy did. So, when Carnes called Dog a "nigger-lover," it wasn't meant in a racial way. It simply meant that he loved the trash of the black population.

Well, Simcox told me that he was going to stab Dog to death for how he insulted Carnes, that "nobody does his friends that way," and, while he was at it, he was going to kill Cricket. If he couldn't get Cricket, he would then go after Shortgrass Webb, a friend of Cricket's. I tried to talk Simcox out of the murders. He finally agreed to give up Cricket but was absolutely adamant about Shortgrass. "That motherfucker has been having an affair with Georgia Boy. Everybody knows it," claimed Simcox. "Georgia Boy" was a black homo from Atlanta.

On the day Simcox was supposed to knife Shortgrass, he didn't leave his cell, because he had been tipped off by Red Smith, who liked him. Not coming down to the yard that day saved Shortgrass's life. Simcox told me on the yard to be careful and take care of myself. Then he started walking back and forth with Joe Schultz by the long steps where Dog was sitting with another fellow. Simcox stopped and started talking with Dog. As they were saying something to each other, Dog started taking his Navy pea coat off. At that moment, Simcox whipped out a knife and stabbed him through his left jaw. Blood gushed out of his mouth. Then Simcox stabbed him so hard under his left rib with an upward swoop that it knocked Dog down.

As Dog tried to recover, Simcox stabbed him in the side of the neck, then again under his right rib cage. Somehow, even after all of this, Dog managed to stumble away, with Simcox running right after him. Just as Simcox was about to strike him again, Lieutenant Mahan jumped in front of Simcox, who dropped the knife, turned, and walked away. Mahan ordered two guards to carry Dog up the steps, since no inmate on the yard would help. Mahan pinched Dog's neck with his fingers to stop the blood, and that maneuver saved Dog's life. We had fried chicken that day and, as I said, I ate Cricket's because he was so sickened by what he saw, realizing that it could have been him, that he had no appetite.

I only remember one guy who everybody ignored, and he was a Japanese war criminal. We called him Tommy because we couldn't pronounce his real name. Tommy was spotted in a Los Angeles department store in 1948 by an ex-GI who was tortured in a Tokyo prisoner of war camp. Tommy had been the interpreter who grilled him. When he recognized Tommy, he tried to kill him with his bare hands on the spot and told the police why. Tommy was a pastel artist and did a portrait of his grandmother that was so detailed it looked like a photograph. Frazier, who was an ex-marine, and who had been stationed in Japan, was the only one who talked to Tommy.

Robinson was an inmate who became famous at Atlanta because he made Joe Costello, the feared mafia chieftain, get his own clothes in the prison laundry. Robinson killed a guy one day and told Tommy that the only reason he didn't stab him, too, was because of Red Lovett, who celled next to Tommy. Red spent a lot of time with Tommy, and they ate together. Tommy stayed close to Red for protection and had a health habit of drinking a glass of hot water each morning before breakfast. He got Red to doing it too. There was a sink at one corner behind the steam table, and that was where Tommy and Red went together and got their hot water before they ate. Red was a good guy and got a lot of respect from the other guys. He shot two FBI agents who tried to arrest him in a restaurant, and one of them died. He told me that he grabbed his gun and opened fire without even thinking. He celled near me and Joe Carnes, and Carnes told me a lot about him.

Once, during the spring of 1956, Carnes got hold of an institution list of every inmate who had ever been on Alcatraz. It listed who had been killed and by whom. If a con had been killed by another inmate, it only referred to the inmate's number. I never asked Joe how he got the list, because if something came up, I would be a suspect for having known. But if I didn't know, I didn't have anything to tell. Joe also had a section of a manuscript on the history of the federal prison system, written by Robert Stroud, the "Birdman of Alcatraz." Stroud also listed and wrote about every inmate who had been on the island. If the manuscript had been published it would have sold well, since it was interesting and entertaining. Joe said the bureau confiscated Stroud's sections.

At that time an inmate had no rights at all, and the federal courts would return a writ and claim the courts had no right to interfere with the warden's policies and rules. The Birdman would compose writs just to harass the warden. And so did Beefstew, who submitted excellent writs. But sometimes he got carried away and referred to FBI agents or the Alcatraz guards as Gestapo agents. Larry Trumble was always laughing at Beefstew for saying things like that. Beefstew was a solid con who was as anti-establishment as they came and fought the prison personnel and bureau with writs on anything and everything. He even wrote one for Joe Cretzer in the early 1940s, before the famous 1946 blast-out attempt. Beefstew was always in a good mood and smiled a lot, even in D-block. I never saw a guy spend so much time alone like that and not have it affect his personality in some way. He was in his forties and would chalk up seventeen years on the Rock.

Beefstew never worked a day while he was on Alcatraz, and every now and then he would be placed in D-block for it. I remember being in D-block on May 2, 1956, and Beefstew said, "This time ten years ago, this place was rocking from bombs, and Cretzer was tearing up some ass." The administration didn't really care if Beefstew or anyone else worked or not, but the hacks had to show Beefstew he wasn't the boss. So, they threw him in isolation from time to time.

In the spring of 1956, I became a cell house orderly and had to polish the cell house floors every day with paste wax. No one had ever gotten the mess hall's floor as shiny as I did. It was spit and polish, and I was proud of my work. Jimmy Groves went around dusting off bars and anything else that needed dusting. Jimmy and I were allowed out of our cells a couple of hours every morning to do this work. Things were constantly being painted. I painted my floor a bright red, and Joe Schultz tried to out-do me by painting the lower part of his walls purple. Lieutenant Ardway told him it was too passionate and he had to paint it another color. I heard an Indian in the cell next to Schultz say, "Tell me all about how fucking passionate you are, Joe. And while you're at it, let me see a picture of your wife so I can fuck her in my sleep." Joe said, "Hell no, I don't want you falling in love with my wife." Anybody else making a comment like this would have died. Joe told me his wife called him "Bugs" in her letters.

A lot of guys like me never wrote anyone and preferred it that way. Others needed the contact. I told my girlfriend after my arrest to find somebody else for her own good. I even quit writing my mother, because it only reminded me of things I couldn't have, and it made things harder. The things I missed the most at that time in Alcatraz were being able to go to a place like Robert's Drug Store in Miami and sit at the counter like I used to do and have a girl's companionship. I missed being able to get up in the middle of the night when I couldn't sleep and go somewhere, anywhere, or just sit in a bar and listen to country music coming out of the juke box.

I never was much of a drinker, but I liked bars, a little beer, and talking to a woman. I used to hear the fog horn at night on the Rock and it reminded me a lot of Hank Williams and some of his songs, like "Lonesome Whistle" and "I'm So Lonesome I Could Cry." It really was lonely on the Rock late at night. For a long time after I left Alcatraz, I missed the fog horn. Even today I still feed sea gulls when I can, since they were like mascots to me. Schultz liked birds and animals and so did most of the other guys. Anybody caught throwing rocks or attempting to hurt the birds would be knifed.

A lot of the guys on the Rock said they saw nothing wrong with religion, that it had done them a lot of good, even though they didn't believe in it. Others cursed it. A good psychiatrist could have had a field day with some of my friends. I would like to see what a psychiatrist would have had to say about Simcox. By this time, he and I had become good pals and he told me how he killed two enemy soldiers in a fox hole in Korea who had him pinned down. When his company commander praised him, Simcox said, "I didn't do it for you guys." When asked why not, he said, "I did it because I like to kill." He told me he got cut off from his platoon once in enemy territory and spent the night alone. And every time the bushes rattled; he would throw a hand grenade into them. He loved the military, and I said, "Guys like you make the best soldiers."

When Simcox was isolated in D-block, I would split the cover of a book, fill it with tobacco and paper matches split in half to make them thin enough to pass undetected as well as go farther, and then glue the book back together. He would order that particular book from the library and Carnes would deliver it. Later when I began working in the library, I found books with Al Capone's AZ #85 still in them as sign outs. That meant they hadn't been read much, since the checkout sheet in back of the book showed only 12 or 15 checkouts out of 30 slots.

One of the most popular books in the Alcatraz library at the time was *From Here to Eternity*. Simcox's favorite book was *The Hoods*, which we received in the library early in 1956.* I read it first, because when it came in the mail I was working in the library. I then passed it to Simcox. He read the book a couple of times because it had a character called "Noodles the Shive" whom he could relate to. Noodles was always knifing somebody in a fight. His other favorite book, as well as mine, was *Knock on Any Door*. The story was about a kid who grows up in the slums and goes through reform schools and prisons until he ends up killing a policeman. His motto was, "Live Fast, Die Young, and Leave a Good-Looking Corpse." Simcox felt the same way. He held no regrets for his own life or anyone else's unless you were a friend of his. Simcox told me one day that he didn't want a transfer to another prison, since some con would fuck with him and he would wind up having to kill the son of a bitch.

I didn't tell anybody, but when I was alone in my cell, I preferred reading shoot-em-up westerns, of which there were hundreds. There were also plenty of books on jungle expeditions. Simcox and I read them all, passing them back and forth. On the Rock, Simcox and I had a special code, using several letters of the alphabet. Joe Carnes taught us this code.

Johnny Iozza got hold of *On the Waterfront* when it first arrived at Alcatraz and loaned it to me before sending it back to the library. I let Simcox read it, and when Johnny asked me about his book and I said Simcox had it, he got so mad he wouldn't talk to me for a few days. Simcox said he understood why. Simcox and Johnny, who pretended to like each other, were jealous over me. Since I had been Johnny's friend first, he felt I should stick close to him. To me, their quarrel sounded a little childish. Hell, I liked them both equally.

As I mentioned, Johnny Iozza was an ex-marine prizefighter who was sent to Alcatraz because he was hanging around with me in Atlanta. At Atlanta, the deputy warden kept getting reports that we were stealing from other inmates and bullying and extorting cigarettes from them. He thought Johnny broke the big guy's jaw, which I was responsible for but Iozza wasn't the type of guy who belonged on the Rock. I explained how he went to jail only because he covered for his brother-in-law, who faced charges of taking a mortgaged car out of state.

I don't know what part of Italy his parents came from, but he had blond hair and blue eyes. Parts of northern Italy were settled by the Swiss, and Johnny looked part Swiss. He could speak and understand Italian, because I listened to him speak it in Atlanta to some of the Italian gangsters. His mother wrote all her letters to him in Italian, but she was from an old Italian family and could barely speak English. But Johnny wouldn't hang out with the Italian cons. He complained that they liked to do everything the old way and keep to themselves. Johnny didn't go for that nonsense. "They should go back to the old country if that's the way they want to live," he told me. "Many of those old wops and dagoes are Mafia. I'm not into that stuff, because once you join 'em, you die with 'em."

Johnny told me he got kicked out of the Marine Corps because he just couldn't jump up at five in the morning and listen to all that drill bullshit. At Alcatraz, he wouldn't take orders from the guards either and stayed in D-block most of the time. Every day he would razz the guards and inmates alike, and he eventually wound up in Springfield.

When you're young you have more fire, and the loneliness and boredom of prison gets to you much more than it does the older guys. Yet it was usually the older guys who hung it up first. A couple of times the suicides were accidents. I learned about them from the grapevine. The saddest one I heard about was how a guy in an adjoining cell in D-block was supposed to call the guard in time to save his neighbor, who was pretending to hang himself. The guy pretending to hang himself wanted to leave isolation in order to get into the hospital. But the guy who was supposed to say something never said anything, so the con hung there, strangling himself to death before the guard made all his rounds.

In another suicide, a poor guy who was in the hole put an improvised rope around his neck so that when the guard came along passing out food, the inmate would jump from his bed the moment he heard the cell door next to his unlocked. When he heard the click of the cell door next to his, he let his weight come down, hoping that the guard who opened his door next would see him dangling there and rescue him. But the guard changed his mind after opening the cell next to the dangling inmate and went back to his desk to get something he had forgotten.

In the few minutes it took, the inmate lost his life. At least, this is the way we figured it. I knew the guy was gone when I saw his eyes wide open as they carried him past my cell. I never knew any of these men, because they were quiet and kept a low profile.

For about fifteen to twenty years, as I mentioned, a lot of guys who had been incarcerated on Alcatraz had a routine of reading, working, and playing handball and dominoes. This was their whole life—nothing less, nothing more. A few like Joe Schultz couldn't get interested in anything and did real hard time, spending a lot of it in and out of D-block.

Beefstew spent 24 hours a day in his cell writing, leaving it only to go to the dining room and yard on weekends. But he was naturally so jolly that he showed no ill effects from it. I had one character housed a few cells next to mine who I didn't pay much attention to. I don't remember his name, but later on I saw him before a Senate hearing on organized crime during which he was asked about a mob murder he may have committed for $2,500. He said, "No, that hit wasn't mine, because I can't do one that cheap. After paying taxes, I wouldn't have anything left."

Some guys, especially the gangsters, kept so far out of sight on the Rock that you hardly knew they were around. One day Simcox and I had a good laugh about an article that appeared in Time Magazine describing how Frank Costello was before a Senate committee. He was asked by Senator McClellan about an illegal $30,000 transaction he might have made. Costello replied, "I didn't do anything illegal, because I don't need $30,000. I probably have $30,000 in my pocket right now."

There were several desperadoes at Alcatraz that Simcox and I liked to talk to and hear accounts of their achievements and failures. These were guys like Joe Bentz, Red Smith, and Clyde Johnson, who had blazing gunfights with the police but you would never know how tough they were by the way they acted. Red Smith was one of my buddies. We were both twenty-five years old in 1958, and he came to see me when I was in the prison hospital before I was transferred. Six years later, after I was released from the system, I read about him killing four detectives in a Sears department store in LA.

Red's action saddened me, because I knew he was basically good. Apparently, the shootings started over a payroll scheme he had going. When he was waiting for the manager of the department store to approve a counterfeit payroll check he presented, the clerk got suspicious. He said he would have to talk to the manager and asked Red to please wait. Red and his girlfriend sat on a bench beside a revolving glass door. The clerk then sent for security with the code words "Maintenance to the boiler room," meaning "Notify Police!" Four detectives about to go off duty took the call at the police station, thinking it was just routine. When the detectives approached Red after speaking to the manager, Red pulled his gun, hidden in his girlfriend's purse, hoping to disarm the four. The four detectives pulled their guns, and it all ended in a bloody shootout. Red never got a scratch, but four detectives lay dead. He out-shot them all, made it to the parking lot, and drove away without his girlfriend.

Red headed for Chicago, and somewhere along the way he picked up a hitchhiker who had just been released from Leavenworth prison. Ironically, the two knew each other from serving time together at Leavenworth years before. When Red reached Chicago, he made an illegal left turn and a traffic cop stopped him. The cop, who recognized him from an all-points bulletin warning that Red was a dead shot, told Red that since he was a tourist, he would just warn him about the illegal turn.

As Red drove off, the cop radioed for backup support. Red was suspicious, so he parked the car in a night club parking lot, got out, and started walking. But within a few minutes he was surrounded and captured. The judge he appeared before in Chicago for a bond hearing called him an animal. I never heard any more about his fate. I'll always remember Red for his intelligence and being a good sax player. It seems like fate decides things for you sometimes.

When Red talked to me in the hospital, he said the reason we never got along too well at first was because I came on like John Dillinger. I said I didn't think I was the Dillinger type, but that sometimes life made you that way. But by the same token, I explained to him that I don't believe in all the bullshit that somebody will abuse a child to death or rape and murder because they themselves were abused by their parents or suffered "post-traumatic stress." I feel criminals often use terms like that to test the intelligence of the juries.

Simcox and I used to say that you could kill a dozen cops or bystanders in a bank robbery and be totally accepted by the inmates on Alcatraz. But if you were a child killer, we personally would beat the guy to death on the Rock. When Billy Cook, the 22-year-old mass killer, was at Alcatraz, he was shunned because he killed a whole family, including a baby and a dog. There in isolation he lived in fear of the other inmates, since they told him what they thought about the killings, even though he tried to explain that he was out of his mind at the time.

Jimmy Groves shouted at him, "Well, why didn't you kill that goddamn policeman, too?" Billy said he was a friend and came to warn him, so he made it look like he kidnapped the cop. Joe Carnes asked him why he killed the baby and dog and didn't kill the cop, and he whined and made a bunch of excuses. Most of the guys felt like his death would be good riddance. Had he not been in isolation so long, sooner or later he would have been stabbed by someone in a bad mood who had nothing to lose. He wasn't attacked on the Rock that I knew of, although Simcox and I were seriously thinking about it. Billy was glad to get away from the guys on the Rock. He was executed in San Quentin for killing a traveling salesman who picked him up hitchhiking. His last words from the gas chamber were, "I hate everybody."

On the day he was buried, some bleeding-heart lady put a bouquet of roses on his grave and told the news media she would repeat it on the anniversary of his death every year. There are plenty more like her, because women sometimes fall in love with men on death row through the news media. For their own sick reasons, they get a lot of attention because of it. They don't love the guys, because they can't possibly know them. It is scary to know that so many people like her are running around loose and never have been arrested. They are considered law-abiding Christians.

I never held it against Jane Fonda for protesting against the Vietnam War like most people did, but when George Jackson and two more blacks killed a guard by beating him to death in California's Soledad Prison, then threw him off the fifth tier just because he was white, Jane Fonda, who joined an anti-government mob demanding their release, was finished in my book. What a dumb slut she turned out to be. I know I have more morals and self-respect than she does. Still, she and others are supposedly outstanding citizens.

Two of these do-gooders went on to become lawmakers for the State of California and the United States Congress: Tom Hayden and Ron Dellums. I want to throw up every time I hear or read their names. So much for high morals, while I can't even find a decent job.

Jack Twinning was a good example of the type of guy Simcox and I mixed with. He had been sent to Alcatraz because he was "incorrigible" like Simcox and me. In 1958 he finally killed a guy who had been bullying him for a long time. The bully had been pushing him around even before they went to the Rock. One day the bully had an inmate friend tell Jack that he wanted to talk to him. So Moe, the bully's friend, went into the room where Jack worked in the laundry, and after a few words, Jack beat him to death with an iron bar. Jack simply called the killing self-defense, because Moe was out of bounds and looking for trouble. We all applauded.

Twelve years later, Twinning was driving on the expressway near Newhall, California, when some loudmouth in another car started honking and gesturing at him and then sped off when Jack flashed his gun. The driver then notified the state police, and four patrol cars forced Jack off an exit and into the parking lot of a restaurant full of people who had just left church. They all witnessed Jack and the patrolmen engage in a long shootout from behind their cars. Jack had a .44 Magnum, and when the battle was over, the four cops were dead.

Jack took over a nearby house, and when the posse surrounded the house, he told the lady to take her kids and leave, because he didn't want them to get hurt. He kept her husband as a hostage for a couple of hours, and during that time Jack talked to him about the twelve years he spent in prison. After he talked to the police on the phone, he told the man to leave the house, because he didn't want him to get hurt either. As soon as the man closed the front door, Jack blew his own head off with a shotgun. I liked Jack, and I was sorry to learn how he died. I was especially proud of the way he treated the woman and her children. The loudmouth driver who got the patrolmen killed never got a scratch on himself, since he ran off like the chicken he was.

Joe Bentz was also a friend of ours. He robbed supermarkets and a couple of banks across several states, all by himself. He bad two gunfights with the police that I know of, one at an intersection in San Diego with a motorcycle cop, and one in Wyoming, where he left a policeman wounded. Then in 1952, he had a couple of shootouts with the police and was on the FBI's Ten Most Wanted list. Joe was busted after the Sunday paper supplement, Parade Magazine, ran a story about him and he was recognized. He was a quiet guy with an air of strength about him and a look that spelled "Don't fuck with me."

He ate at the table with me and Karpis and would talk if you wanted to. Otherwise he didn't say much. He came to the hospital to see me, too, just before I was transferred. Bentz gave me some of his eggnog, which the doctor had ordered for him. Schultz respected him, although he never said a word to him. I liked the guy even though we never really talked much. He always seemed to have a sense of decency about him.

Johnny Johnson was a career bank robber who had already spent about twelve or 13 years on the Rock when I met him. He was the prison's altar boy for all the Catholic services in the chapel above the prison armory. After his release from Alcatraz in the early 1950s, he killed a guy in Los Angeles and then fled to Baltimore. But he made the mistake of trusting a reporter he made friends with. When Johnny called the reporter to find out where he stood with the law, the reporter immediately notified the FBI and told agents Johnny was supposed to call again after he had gotten some information for him. The FBI tapped the reporter's phone, and when Johnny called from a theater lobby where he was watching a Mickey Spillane movie, *I, the Jury*, the agents traced the call.

The reporter told Johnny to turn himself in and that if he did so, he and his newspaper would try to help him in his defense. Johnny replied, "Even if I beat the murder rap, I will have to return for violation of a conditional release, and I won't ever, under any circumstance, go back to the Rock—not even for one hour!" Within minutes of that statement, the reporter heard a barrage of gunfire. Johnny and an FBI agent lay dead, with the second agent near death himself.

I was in Atlanta at the time, and Walter Winchell interrupted his news broadcast, saying that a desperado recently released from Alcatraz had shot and killed an FBI agent in a roaring gun battle in a Baltimore theater lobby. As the wounded FBI agent was being wheeled into the hospital's operating room, he asked what Johnny's condition was. When told the ex-inmate was dead, the agent said, "May God have mercy on his soul." That FBI agent died a few moments later. He must have been a fine man, because his last thoughts were for God to show mercy to a dead bandit.

When I knew Johnny, he was a decent sort. He spent all his yard time on the Rock playing handball with Benny Rayburn. Benny was a real likable guy who was always in a good mood. He stayed in good physical condition and was liked by everyone. Benny was so good at composing writs that he went to work as a law researcher for the San Diego California Federal Defender's Office. I read a newspaper account of him several years ago.

Red Winhoven was another favorite of mine. Simcox liked him a lot too. Red was a career bank robber who arrived on Alcatraz in the 1930s. He and I shared a lot, and I remember he told me once that he was all for a guy who could walk into a bank and take money away from people who were just as crooked as we were. But he had no respect for someone who committed crimes against women, children, animals, or the elderly.

He said he spent most of his life in prison and had noticed that those inmates who had attacked the helpless always turned out to be cowards in the end. Red was also a handyman and an excellent artist—a painter. On the Rock he operated the movie projector, did the electric and plumbing repairs, and rewired motors. It was well known among some of the inmates that he was the one who found the roof ventilation flue above B-block that Morris and the Anglins used as their way out in June 1962.

Allen West picked up this important piece of information from Red and passed it on to the Anglins. Red made the discovery of the engineering weakness and never got the credit for it. Red had been on death row at San Quentin for two years when the Anglin break occurred. He and Ernie Lopez had robbed an LA bank in July 1960, and the way Simcox and I heard it, a bank employee shot at them in the bank parking lot. Red, in turn, shot the employee to death. Red would spend eleven years on death row at San Quentin before his death of a heart attack in 1971. He was one of the best portrait painters I ever saw.

In 1956, an attorney from the US Department of Justice came through the Rock and saw a portrait of movie star June Havoc in Red's cell. The cell was the one Cretzer shot the guards in during the 1946 crash-out attempt. The attorney had the warden introduce him to Red and offered to buy the painting from him, but Red told him he could have the picture. Red told me that the attorney sent him some money after he got back to Washington, DC. I really felt for him about all those years he spent on death row, because he, too, was a neat guy.

In January or February 1957, I was isolated in D-block for making a knife in the laundry that the hacks learned about from a snitch but never found, because Red Winhoven refused to let Lieutenant Simpson have it. He disposed of it while the lieutenant went to get help. Since he couldn't really prove what I had made, Skinhead charged me with being involved in the Teddy Green and Larry Trumble escape plot, for which they had just been busted. Larry was doing 25 years for bank robbery and was compared to John Dillinger in various newspaper accounts.

He claimed that comparison got him the excessive sentence, and he therefore filed an appeal. Larry looked like Max Schmeling, the German heavy-weight boxing champion in the 1930s, and was a rugged street fighter himself. He could whip any guy, including Schultz and Iozza, in a minute. I first met him in Atlanta and told him he looked like an FBI agent who arrested me. He split a gut, laughing at my remark.

Skinhead claimed I had cracked my toilet at the bottom and resealed it with soap. But Larry had been in my cell before me, and Teddy told me Larry had broken the toilet to hold tools that had been smuggled into the cellhouse before he was moved to a new cell between Teddy and Forrest Tucker, who was in on the escape attempt. Skinhead was bound and determined to get me, even if it meant a trumped-up charge of conspiracy to escape. Joe Bentz was also housed in a cell that was fixed to hold tools and because of it was held in D-block for a week until he was released. A psychiatrist in Springfield later told me that I had gotten away with so much shit that Skinhead's bum raps made up for some of it.

One day a short time later, Teddy Green and I were talking in D-block when we heard gunfire. Then the siren went off, and a few minutes later guards, some without shirts, came running down the outside catwalk of D-block and down into the yard. A few minutes later they shoved a couple of black guys up the steps and into D-block and put them in open-front cells. A few minutes after that, they brought in Joe Schultz. As the guards took him toward the hole in D-block, Joe had a wild look on his face and said in a calm voice to one of the blacks, "I'm not through with you yet, nigger."

The black said, "You put your hands on me and I'll kill you," and Joe said, "You're not leaving this island alive, nigger."

What happened was that Joe got drunk in the kitchen on raisin jack, a drink made of raisins, sugar, yeast, and apples. When he left the mess hall, he stumbled down the steps to the yard, where he leaned against the wall with his hands behind him. At that point, Fuller, a black guy he had backed down a couple of times, came up and tried to stab him. George Campbell, who happened to be standing beside Joe, hit Fuller's arm and deflected the knife, giving Joe a chance to grab Fuller. But several blacks ran over to help Fuller, and a white guy in his fifties—I can't remember his name— knocked two of them out.

Meanwhile, the guard on the wall, who saw what was going on, started firing his rifle in the air. About eight guys were involved in the fight. But only Schultz, Fuller, and two other blacks, named Austin and Hayes, were busted. A black named Campbell, the white guy who knocked him down, and another black were never picked up. Austin was all right, and Schultz told him he had nothing against him but Austin was Fuller's friend and had to help him.

The black who Joe promised to kill was transferred while Joe was in lockup, and before Skinhead would let him out, he made Schultz promise not to bother Fuller. The first morning after his release from isolation, Joe went up to Fuller, who was out on the yard, waiting to go to work. Schultz told him about the promise he made to Skinhead in order to get out and said he would keep it, but he added, "If you ever cross my path again, I will cut both cheeks of your ass off and make shoe leather out of them!"

Then, as soon as he got to the laundry, Schultz walked up to Mitchell, another black, who was 6'4" and weighed about 220. Mitchell was Fuller's best friend, and Schultz told him what he had just told Fuller, adding, "The same thing goes for you." As Joe turned away, Mitchell threw a punch but

Joe was expecting it and ducked. Then he dropped Mitchell flat on his back with a left hook, and Mitchell remained motionless. Another black we called Peaches, who was supposed to be bad, came running over, and Schultz said, "Come on. You want some?" Peaches sat down at a table and didn't say a word. A new guy who watched it told me, "Man, you was right about Schultz, he is a bad dude. He dropped that big guy with a left hook, like Marciano's."

Although Schultz liked to rob banks, he had a good heart and respected all women and children, even those of the guards. He had a daughter of his own on the outside world. Joe kissed a teller at a bank he robbed in LA, and they dubbed him "The Kissing Bandit." He thought it was funny. Joe told me that the way he met his wife was in a department store where she was a clerk. Because he kept looking at her, she asked, "Can I help you?" and he said, "Yeah. Give me your telephone number."

Joe Schultz had a lot of respect for Joe Carnes and let remarks made by Carnes slide when they got into an argument during softball games. One day Schultz was catching and claimed Carnes was giving his signals away. He told Carnes he wasn't trying to bully him, but Carnes had better watch his step. Carnes unleashed a stream of profanity, fierce even for Alcatraz. Anyone else who cursed Joe the way Carnes did would have gotten his jaw broken or a blade in the ribs.

I had a run-in with a black guy who was called Blue because he was so black, he looked like he had a blue tint. One day after that, during the spring of 1956, we were in the mess hall, and another black called Gator turned around and looked at me. I knew it was about my beef with Blue, so I looked at him and said, "The same thing goes for you." When we got back to our cells Carnes got his knife out and told me he would get behind Blue and not to look at him, since it would tip Blue off. But it never got that far, because Blue came up to me and said, "I look at everybody, and nobody is going to stare me down. Why was you staring at me?" I laughed, because it was a good question.

I can't remember Gator's real name, but he was a sexual pervert. One white guy named Cliff came within an inch of stabbing Gator after Gator lured him to the hospital, where he had Bigsey Gilford's job at the time. Gator used the pretext that he would give Cliff a blow job. Cliff, like Johnny Iozza, hated all homos. But he was anxious to be alone with Gator in order to teach him a lesson. "Gator," he said, "I've come up here to slice your fucking pecker off." Gator snickered, "Well, go ahead and try. But I know you don't have a blade on you." Cliff said, "No, but I can get one." That weekend I loaned Cliff my shiv and he stopped Gator on the yard and said, "You still think I can't get a blade?" Gator said, "Oh, you probably got one on you now but I told you I don't want no trouble, and I apologize for offending you."

Schultz owed Gator some cigarettes from betting on boxing, and one day he went to Gator on the yard and said, "Hey, you black motherfucker. I don't intend to pay you what I owe you, unless you want me to pay you off in boxing lessons. You're just about the right size for me to tee off on your jaw."

When I was in the old bug cages before they were remodeled, the hall door was left open most of the time so that the attendant could throw cigarettes to me and the others. Gator was the attendant then, and when Simcox was brought from D-block to the hospital for minor surgery, he told Gator that he should slip some cigarettes to me like a good con would. "But, if you say anything to him like you did Clifford, I'll cut your fucking head off when I get out of D-block." Gator said, "I got no intentions of saying anything." Simcox said, "Well, he's a friend of mine, and you better remember that."

Simcox and I could talk through the wall between the bug cage and the first cell on the ward. It was here that Simcox told how he intended to kill Gauvin for spitting in his face and would need a knife as soon as he got out of isolation in case Gauvin beat him out of D-block. I told Carnes what Simcox said about killing Gauvin for spitting in his face, and Joe made a point of going to D-block so he could talk Simcox out of it. Carnes was a loner, and Simcox and I were the two closest people to him. Joe had very little to say to anybody else. I only saw him laugh about twice, and once was when we were listening to Gunsmoke and a redneck racist called an Indian a dog-eater. Joe had no problem making conversation with Simcox and me.

A funny thing about Carnes: he didn't smoke on the Rock where he had the stress and boredom, but started smoking after his release. He kept his weight down and stayed in good condition doing pushups in his cell and playing handball. Every time I saw him on television after his release in 1976, his face looked puffy. Fate dealt him a sorry hand, and sometimes I curse fate for being so biased.

Simcox and I used to sit in church and talk about the long hair Jesus had in the large framed portrait on the chapel wall. Whenever Simcox would talk about sexually assaulting Jesus, we would all get to laughing. Reverend McCormick, who was Protestant, never knew what we were laughing about, and I'm glad he didn't, because he was a decent man. Simcox would never do anything to offend Reverend McCormick, because he was like a father to him. Schultz tried going to church to find peace of mind. But he started cracking up and kept getting worse, to the point where he didn't trust anyone but me and Cricket. He even turned on Dago John, who was one of his best friends, and nothing could persuade him to change his mind.

He would go into the mess hall, for example, and ask everyone at the table, "What the fuck you guys looking at?" If someone said, "Pass the coffee," he would set the coffee pot in front of his tray and say, "There it is. You reach for it, and I'll break your motherfucking jaw. When I want coffee, I go to the coffee urn. I don't ask you for nothing and don't you tell me to pass the coffee." The officials finally put him in the hospital, and every time someone checked in, he would accuse them of trying to spy on him for the Bureau of Prisons. The only guy Schultz didn't accuse of betrayal was Joe Bentz, because Joe was in the hospital cell next to mine. Joe used to give me some of the eggnogs the doctor prescribed for him, and because of that, Schultz must have figured he was okay.

A lot of celebrities came through the island with the warden in the spring of 1955. Some I saw, and some I didn't. It depended on where you were at the time they were escorted through. Rocky Marciano saw his picture in Joe Schultz's cell and was flattered. He called to Al Weill, his manager, "Al, Al, come here!" Johnny Iozza worked as a sparring partner for Marciano in 1951, and he said Marciano was the only person he felt could whip his ass. He said Marciano had tremendous power. When Marciano fought and we could listen to it on the radio, the whole cell house rocked with thundering noise, and I was one of the guys participating in the noise-making.

When Archie Moore, the black boxer, knocked Marciano down in the second round of their famous fight, Iozza was in D-block and heard the blacks yelling and screaming. He asked the guard, "What happened?" Then a few minutes later Marciano floored Moore, and the noise was so bad you couldn't hear yourself think. Johnny told me his heart sank, because he thought Moore had stopped Marciano again.

When Spider Webb, a black fighter who was the number one middleweight contender, was in San Francisco to fight on television, he took a tour of the island, and the warden stopped at my cell in the hospital and introduced Spider to me. He told Spider I used to be a fighter, too. Little things like that cheered me up from the pain of a bleeding ulcer that I had developed. Schultz took notice, and it seemed to cheer him up, too, because he loved the fight game.

Simcox and I always had a good laugh over Dago John and his attacks on spaghetti. John was a little old Italian guy, and on days we ate spaghetti, we would always let him be the first one in the mess hall, because he ate so much and it took him so long, he always held up his section leaving the mess hall. This meant we were always fifteen or twenty minutes late for eating. Every day he got a menu for the following day, and about seven in the evening he would shout from his cell so everyone in the cell house could hear, "Okay, listen everybody. Tomorrow for breakfast …" and he would then read off the menu. Then he would go to lunch and then dinner. I only remember him missing one menu. That evening someone yelled out to him not to forget, and he shouted back angrily that the "goddamn hacks" never gave him a menu that evening. Later, I hated to see Joe Schultz insult Dago John the way he did, because John was old and a good guy.

Skinhead came through the cellhouse one day and told Joe Schultz that he did a good thing when he beat up Williams, and Joe said, "Well, you didn't tell me that when I beat him up. All you did was put me in the dark hole." Schultz had watched as Williams stabbed a guy in the stomach three or four times, and two FBI agents came in to ask Schultz for information. Joe cursed them out, shouting, "Get the hell away from me!" He didn't want any of us to think he was a rat.

A buddy of mine named Carl Smith was called out of the cell house by the FBI one day, and instead of refusing to talk to the agents and immediately returning to his cell, he chose to ask the agents about something. Carl was doing 25 years for bank robbery. He loved all animals and told me he would especially kill, without blinking an eye, anyone he saw mistreating a cat. Carl was a health fanatic. He ate all the fruit he could get and exercised every day. He told me he was in the county jail with George Heroux, and after he and Heroux were released, he robbed a bank and then paid the bond for Gerhardt Puff.

Carl was certainly no rat but because he was gone about fifteen minutes, McKinney, a white guy we called Mac, who had spent about four years in D-block for beating a guard with a trumpet, called him a rat and spit at him. Smitty, Carl's rap partner, almost beat McKinney to death using baseball bats. McKinney was in the hospital for several months. Because Mac cursed those FBI agents, he was moved to D-block, where he got well. Every day he hassled Carl and Smitty, who were also in isolation. If they passed his cell, Mac would throw urine at them. Smitty was soon sent off to Springfield. Later when I arrived there, he started to say something about Mac. I said, "Mac is good people," and he agreed. Mac was another talented artist, one of the best I have ever met. Red Winhoven said Mac was what was known as a cartoonist. He had a lot of fun on D-block, drawing pornographic pictures of Skinhead and other guards, and we enjoyed throwing them out on the walkways so the guards would find them. Instead of turning them in and making a report, the guards always kept the pictures of Skinhead fucking his wife in unnatural places.

The first song we heard on the radio that year by Elvis Presley was "Heartbreak Hotel," and I became his fan. Karpis and a guy named Lewis, who celled near me, both said Elvis couldn't sing worth shit, that he was a flash in the pan and probably a homo. But one night we listened to him sing "Love Me Tender," and when it was finished Lewis said, "Hey, man, I apologize for what I said about Elvis. He's no sissy. That guy can sing."

We had a record room that an inmate named Duncan ran on weekends, playing records through the intercom in the yard. His choices were all country music with a little Louis Armstrong thrown in. In the record collection was a wartime record called "In the Fuehrer's Face" that was played a lot. I heard an inmate named Frazier tell Duncan he would whip his ass if he ever played it again. So, the next day, Duncan played it 20 times.

We got every new record Elvis cut, and we had all kinds of Jimmy Rogers records from the early thirties. Karpis liked country music and played a guitar pretty well himself. In summer 1956, we started getting a station which played black music, mostly rock, that I listened to a lot. I heard Fats Domino and Little Richard before they made it into the big time. After Little Richard became famous, we heard one night how he had driven to Georgia in a pink Cadillac and was beaten up by some racist cops. Some of the blacks started laughing, and Blue shouted, "That mother done tried to show his Cadillac off and got his head roped."

The blacks on Alcatraz couldn't stand Chester on Gunsmoke. They called him an ass-kisser because of the way he followed Matt Dillon around, whining all the time. I remember that when Elvis first came along, we were discussing his style of singing and Frenchy shouted, "That motherfucker tries to dry hump the microphone!" Frenchy, whose real name was Charles French, was celled in B-136 next to Tommy, the Japanese war criminal. At the time I was in B-140.

Frenchy was the guy who used his mother and fourteen-year-old sister to help him rob banks. His mother drove the getaway car and carried a shotgun, while his sister carried a pistol and went into the bank with him. I read all kinds of stories about him. The FBI said his fourteen-year-old sister was as cool as a young cucumber. Frenchy did a lot of oil portraits and always signed his name and the date on them. He painted one for me of Jake LaMotta, the world middleweight champion. Clyde Johnson and Red Lovett celled near us, too. Some guys thought Red was Tommy's old man because they felt that the Japanese war criminal was a passive homo.

I honestly believe Alcatraz made some guys gay but there weren't any opportunities for them to do anything other than what I've already mentioned. When I later got to Springfield, I saw that they had marriages, and some gays looked like girls and acted like girls, swishing around and cutting their pants to fit skin-tight. Every time you turned a corner in a tunnel, you would find someone kissing. The guards called them "queens" and left them alone.

Of all the dangerous guys I met on the Rock, the one I feared and respected the most was Whitey Franklin. Whitey was fearless, and you could see death in his eyes. If he liked you, he would do a lot for you but he didn't take to too many people, because he was a loner. Whitey told me he was in on the attempt to crash out of Alcatraz in 1946. He was in a strip cell and was going to get out of D-block by attacking the guard in there, but just before the cons took over the cell house, the guard went in to use the toilet for guards, slamming the door shut and locking it. This was all that saved that guard.

Some of the former Alcatraz officials would say today that Whitey is full of shit for saying this but Whitey didn't lie or brag; he wasn't that kind of guy. Remember that all the officials have to go on are the guards' version of any incidents that happened involving them. Also, don't forget that the guards all want to look like they are alert and on the job. Their supervisors cover for them, just like inmates cover for each other. When the bombardment started on D-block, Whitey pulled his blanket over him and went to sleep.

Whitey had an ugly scar on his shoulder near his collar bone from trying to escape. I talked to him a lot about what he did and what he planned to do in the future, and he wasn't ashamed to tell me that he had turned his life around and had no intention of committing any more crimes.

He said, "Hoppy, you can bet all your money on that." This is probably why Bigsey smarted off to Whitey and almost got himself killed, because Bigsey was doing life for kidnapping, he may have resented the fact that Whitey was trying to turn his life around but he changed his tune fast when Whitey confronted him one day by saying, "Well, I didn't come to argue with you. I came to kill you."

Later Warden Madigan, who was a con-wise warden, went to bat for Whitey. Otherwise, Whitey would have died on Alcatraz. Some convicts do change, and Whitey Franklin and I are two good examples. But we were both bad people to cross, because we never forgot or forgave. If someone gave me a good enough reason, I would beat the hell out of him and think no more about it than shooting a snake in the grass. When you get right down to it, that's all some people are.

I used to lie and cheat with the best of the liars and cheaters on Alcatraz, and the cellhouse was full of our type. But no prison official believed we were suffering from a sickness that has to be treated. The thing was, the inmate had to be receptive to the treatment; you couldn't beat it out of us. I have seen some hacks try to cure some of us that way. For example, some of us would borrow cartons of cigarettes, knowing full well we couldn't pay the guy back and knowing the other person would hurt us if they weren't paid back.

Guys like this were sick. Once in Springfield, Schultz and I got into a poker game in the yard, and a guy named Lucas, who I knew was a bad loser from Atlanta, came over and joined the game but promptly lost. Sure enough, he lost a bunch of cigarettes and then, in the mess hall, threw a pot of hot coffee in a young inmate's face. Schultz beat the guy until he had blood running out of his ears.

The guards tried to stop Schultz, but Joe pushed the guards away and continued beating on Lucas. An inmate office worker showed me a report the psychiatrists wrote about the incident, saying that Schultz beat Lucas out of loyalty for his friends and a false sense of justice. I would have to say without exception that Joe Schultz was the most loyal and dependable person I ever met in prison. If anyone wanted to stop him, he had better have had a gun, since a knife wouldn't do it. The man had an enormous amount of physical power.

The last buddy I want to mention was the "Atomic Spy," Morton Sobell. He never bothered anyone and we never bothered him. He was so educated, so intelligent, so superior in intellect, that he practically reeked with knowledge. Since this was so intimidating to those who were stupid, dull, and uneducated, he was allowed to go his own way. He had feminine ways about him, but he was no homo. I think he was so over-smart; his brain didn't have room to breathe.

Surprisingly—or not so surprisingly, maybe—not many of us thought about escape. Oh, sure, we dreamed about it, but our chances of actually making it were about as good as winning a $100 million lottery. I didn't spend any time in my cell conceiving of ways to break out. Simcox and I used to strain our memories, recalling movies or books that focused on prison escapes. The only ones we could think of ended with the escapees being riddled by machine-gun fire. Those that dealt with escaping from Alcatraz ended with the guys all drowned. Simcox's favorite movie was *I Am a Fugitive from a Chain Gang*, which starred Paul Muni. His favorite line in that movie was, "They made an animal out of me."

CHAPTER SEVEN
A KILLING THAT SHOULDN'T HAVE HAPPENED

"Our sentence is not severe. Whatever commandment the culprit has violated is simply written upon his skin by the harrow."

—Franz Kafka, "In the Penal Colony"

Although I saw and said hello to Bumpy Johnson almost daily since I had arrived on the Rock, I really hadn't gotten to know him. We just didn't move in the same circles. But one thing was certain: everybody—and I mean inmates and guards alike—respected the man. He belonged to himself, unlike any man I have ever encountered in or out of prison, and that goes for Joe Carnes, too. Although Bumpy was black, he was not "black." But he sure wasn't white, either. He was somehow above race.

One afternoon in the yard during the summer of 1956, I was involved in an argument about to turn violent with Blue and another black inmate named Walker. Bumpy sauntered over and listened for a few minutes, then said to Blue, "Why don't you take your friend and go take a walk at the other end of the yard?" Blue looked at him with a mixture of anger and fear, like a little boy who's about to be spanked by his dad. Blue lowered his head without another word, and he and Walker walked away. Bumpy said to me, "Some of these niggers are real ignorant. You have to overlook their stupidity. But be on guard, because some of them will knife you in a second. That's why some of the guys, black and white, come into the yard with a hardcover book under their belt. A thick book can stop a sharp knife in the stomach."

At the time I didn't know anything about him or his past. I just thought he was kind of gutsy for wanting to be a peacemaker between Johnny and Schultz, and for the way he mingled with whites without being intimidated. He sure as hell wasn't afraid of any of the blacks I'd met so far. Even Schultz, who was a racist and had a lot of problems with the black inmates at all the penitentiaries he did time in, liked and respected Bumpy. In fact, Joe would stand humbly before Bumpy, listening to his advice. I was appreciative for his warning and felt I had made a friend. If he ever needed me, I would be ready. ·

I asked Bumpy later that day if he had read the *Rubaiyat of Omar Khayyam*. Bumpy said, "It's one of my favorites." I then asked him for his interpretation and why he liked it. He answered, "Tomorrow in the yard I'll explain it all."

Well, the next afternoon he handed me four or five handwritten pages of interpretation, plus a list of other books we had right there in the Alcatraz library that would complement the *Rubaiyat*. We shared our thoughts about it and agreed it was one of the great masterpieces of world literature. Neither of us used ten-gallon words in describing our feelings. We just talked naturally, and because of that we took a more sincere liking to each other. We talked almost every day after that.

One thing was certain: the black inmates listened to Bumpy and did whatever he suggested or ordered them to do. He loved to play chess, and every night I heard him calling out moves to another inmate across the cell house. His shaved head was his trade mark. So was his dark blue navy peacoat, which he wore regardless of the weather. He had penetrating eyes and always appeared to be mad when he was talking to you but that was nothing more than a sign of his deep intensity. He was serious and he was real.

Bumpy never talked about his business on the streets, because it was no one else's business. The only person he confided in, the only man he felt akin to, was Joe Carnes. Joe was chess champion at Alcatraz, and Bumpy was the runner-up. They became the best of friends. Later, when Joe and I celled next to each other, he confided in me Bumpy's entire history. Years later, a black guy I became friends with at Springfield confirmed all the details of Bumpy's background that Joe had told me.

Ellsworth "Bumpy" Johnson ran Harlem in the 1930s and 1940s. He was born in 1906 and died of natural causes in 1968. Joe said he was a "black millionaire" from all his rackets. Because he kept drugs out of

Harlem in the 1930s and cut the throats of pimps, narcotics and prostitutes were kept to a minimum and he became a virtual folk hero to the black population for forty years. Joe said he never had less than $5,000 in bills in his pocket when he strolled the Harlem streets, passing out $50- and $100-dollar bills to the poor and unfortunate.

The Sicilian Mafia respected him, and Lucky Luciano and Frank Costello considered Bumpy a close friend but Bumpy spent more time in prison than in the outside world. Whenever he went to serve his four or five prison terms, he studied history, psychology, and philosophy. He wrote poetry, and one poem, entitled "Alcatraz," was published in 1961 in a scholarly review dedicated to the black freedom movement. Later, a character named Bumpy would be featured in all the famous Shaft movies of the early 1970s.

Joe told me that at the New York State Penitentiary at Dannemora, he was called "the Professor," because he knew a lot about everything. In World War II he even taught classes in the prison yard about why we were fighting Hitler and Tojo. Bumpy, who was the leader of a Harlem group called The Forty Thieves, was tough and never backed away from trouble or danger. Before I got to Alcatraz, according to Carnes, Bumpy actually prevented a riot by black and white inmates with one single word: "No!" Years later at Bumpy's funeral, Warden Blackwell would send a telegram to be read at the eulogy about how much he depended upon Bumpy to keep the peace during his administration.

In the summer of 1956, a lieutenant came around to my cell and asked if I'd like to go to work. I had been in and out of lockup status since I had arrived. Lockup status meant that, with the exception of being permitted to go into the mess hall and out onto the recreation yard and showers, I remained in my cell. It didn't matter all that much to me. But I figured it would be good to circulate a little, so I asked if I could work in the mess hall.

George Campbell, a buddy from Atlanta, worked there, so I figured he and I could team up. George arrived on Alcatraz a few months before I did and had been given the AZ number 1169. My AZ number was 1186. He was in for robbery and murder while in the army and was sentenced to 35 years. George wasn't mean at all and told me the Army threw the book at him for what was really manslaughter. This was because the army threw the book at anybody who didn't behave.

So, I went to work in the dining room but no sooner had I started than there was trouble. At Raiford and Atlanta I never stayed on a job for long. If I could change jobs, I would quit and tell the guards to do what they wanted. I just didn't care. The chief psychiatrist at Springfield would later point this out as a "personality flaw." I told him to call it what he wanted, but many times I was bum-rapped by the hacks. He answered, "Well, you must remember that psychologically healthy people can survive anything. The weak-minded use 'bum-rapped' as an excuse." I never did adjust to a prison, and for that matter, I knew I wouldn't adjust to Alcatraz, either. But I did kind of want that kitchen job so that George and maybe Schultz and I could play around a bit, maybe even make some home brew.

The trouble that promptly found me on my new job was a loudmouth I came close to cutting in two. The first day I was on the mess line dishing out food, an older guy figured he could bully me into giving him more food than I was supposed to. If I did, it meant other guys at the end of the line would have none. When I said I had to save some for the others, he shouted out loud, "Well, fuck you, motherfucker!"

Now, I didn't give a damn about stealing food from the guards or the administration. Hell, Johnny and I used to steal food at Atlanta every day we were there. But we never, ever put another inmate in the middle of doing it. To be called a motherfucker when all you were doing was safeguarding the food of fellow cons got me boiling. Paige, another buddy of mine from Atlanta who was dishing out potatoes next to me, saw that I was going to kill the son of a bitch right then and there. Paige, AZ# 1164, had arrived on Alcatraz the same day as Campbell. Since he was in for twelve and a half years for manslaughter during a fight he got into in the army, he tried to get me a kitchen knife. But when he went back to where all the knives were kept, he saw that they were all locked up. He came back and said, "The only thing I can get you is a butter knife, and it's too soft."

I was more furious than ever. Without the mess hall guards noticing it, I threw my apron down on the food line and walked over to where the bastard was so I could punch his mouth through the back of his face. But he was sitting with a bunch of guys near the back window and the seating was so crowded I couldn't get through. So, I started calling him every dirty name and cuss word I knew.

I don't remember the jerk's name, but he got real red in the face. I told him that I only stole food for my friends and that I chose the time and place to steal. I told him that if I ever stole food for him, I'd roll it in my shit first. I wanted to tell him so many fucking things that a Florida hurricane would be mild in comparison. But a guard saw the trouble and came right over and ordered me to get back to my can. Later, I figured I lucked out for not landing in the hole but one thing was for certain: had the kitchen knives not been locked up, I wouldn't be telling this story today.

Let me pause a second to say this: if you have never experienced the obsession to kill someone out of hate and revenge, you can't possibly read a few words and know what it's all about. First of all, most of us on Alcatraz were already at the boiling point. We were filled with frustration, enormous anger, and depression all mixed into one confused, frightened, bewildered mind. And that simple, uneducated, and shallow mind was trying to negotiate each day as it came. If some fucker shit on you, all that seemed to be left of your personality was dignity and honor. When this asshole thought he could humiliate me, I could only think of cutting his eyes out, and believe me when I say I meant it. Nothing else mattered. I sure as hell didn't care about my own life. Whether I lived or died didn't even enter into my rage. It was as if I was going to destroy, once and for all, every injustice, every cruelty, every bit of neglect and lack of loving and caring that had happened to me. I didn't even know the guy's name. But in him I saw all the blame for the course my life had taken, and I was going to cut it out of him, no matter what.

The next morning while I was planning how to kill him on the yard, a black guy we called Wild Bill told him he had fucked up and that he better make up for the insult. The jerk, after thinking about it, came up to me while I was standing with a few of my friends but in order not to get too near me, he stood off about fifteen feet and in a loud voice for all to hear, he said, "I hear you're quite an upright man, and I'd like to get it right with you." I looked at him and said, "You should already be dead for eighteen hours. Go on about your way. You'll never be a friend of mine." And from that day on he avoided my steam table.

It wasn't long before I became good at stealing food from the Alcatraz steam table. Campbell, Paige, and I would plan it so that I could pick up a whole tray off the steam table when the guard for that mess hall area wasn't looking and slide it on the floor under the bench table nearest where we were serving. In those days the inmates who came in first were seated beginning at the front. The first mess hall table was only eight or ten feet from the steamtable.

Once I shoved the tray full of food under the first table, the inmates there would kick it under to the second table, then the third and fourth tables, until it reached the last table, where George, Paige, and I were supposed to be sitting for our own meals. Getting caught would have meant the hole plus losing the privilege of working in the mess hall. But I took my chances, because the extra food, especially the meat, was always good, and I couldn't get enough of it. The other inmates on the steamtable knew better than to say anything, since they would be gambling with their lives.

While assigned to the Alcatraz kitchen and mess hall detail, I worked with a couple of blacks and got along fine with them. A lot of the other white guys refused to work with people they called "niggers." Schultz was especially friendly with one black kitchen worker named Brown, whom he knew from his Los Angeles jail days. Brown started out with a five-year sentence but, while appealing his case, was released on bond and went searching for and found the one witness against him. He killed the man on the spot. The police and district attorney couldn't prove Brown did it, but the judge in the case gave him forty years on his resentence instead of five. Brown told me that while Schultz was in the LA jail with him, Joe beat up half the guys there, damn near killing some.

In those summer days, I really didn't have a lasting hate or dislike for any of the guys I met at Alcatraz except for one. And that one guy was Allen West, AZ#ll30, who was serving five years for attempted escape. Every day that I saw him in the mess hall or in the lines or on the yard, my blood would begin to boil. I tried to put my finger on why I disliked him so much and decided it was because I saw him for exactly what he was: a smug and smirking hypocrite. Some of the guys said he was "suggestible minded." That is, he would do whatever someone else did; he would follow anyone who led; he would always agree with whoever spoke last. In other words, he was a kiss-ass who sucked up to everybody.

The first time I ever saw West was in the orientation unit at Atlanta, where he was bragging to an inmate, I was standing next to about being Floyd Hill's partner. The guy thought West was talking about James Hill. To clarify whether West was talking about Floyd or James, he asked, "Do you mean James Hill?" West said, "Hell no! That stupid ass does only stupid things." "Well," responded the inmate, "the Hill you're talking about is this guy's partner," he said, pointing to me. Given an excuse, I jumped in and said, "How in the fuck does my buddy concern you?" West looked silly, then uttered, "It doesn't concern me. I was just running my mouth." I looked him over and said, "Yeah, that's about all you can do, since you're nothing but a little runt who needs a clique of tough guys to back you up." He never forgot those words and neither did I.

While I was still at Atlanta, an inmate I knew named Sal Cesario had a problem with a Puerto Rican. West, Porkchop, Cowboy, Cesario, and I left the mess hall after dinner one evening to go to the Puerto Rican's cell on the third tier. When we got up there, West said to the Puerto Rican, "You want trouble, Chico?" The guy answered, "Yeah, I want trouble," and pulled out a knife. Cowboy grabbed a chair—they had those heavy oak chairs there, like in the old cowboy movies—and started jabbing it at the Puerto Rican, who backed down the catwalk, swinging the knife.

Cowboy knocked the knife out of his hand, but somebody passed him another one through the bars. We let him go and went to our cells, but less than thirty minutes later, West, Porkchop, and Cesario were picked up by the hacks. They left Cowboy and me alone, so I figured that whoever ratted must have liked Cowboy and me. Then an inmate clerk told me that West had said to the deputy warden that the trouble was over Cesario, and the warden told him, "You didn't know that Puerto Rican was a killer?"

When I got my files from the National Archives, I saw that I had been recommended for Alcatraz that month, but James Bennett, the director of the Bureau of Prisons, overruled the recommendation because he wanted to give me another chance. This was because I had kept my crime partner from killing some of our hostages during our kidnapping spree. I went to the Rock the next year, anyway.

Anyway, back to Alcatraz. One day in the yard, West walked right up to where I was sitting with some friends and asked, "Why is it you don't like me? I never did anything to you at Atlanta. In fact, I heard you were a pretty good head." I answered, "I hate everything about you but I especially hate your fucking guts for ratting on Sal Cesario. It's all over Atlanta and here that you gave the hacks Sal's name."

Sal Cesario was the brother of Johnny Cesario, a ranked boxer in the early 1950s and a good friend of mine. According to a Leavenworth inmate named Bishop I met in isolation; West had given the Atlanta guards Sal's name as having been the one who stabbed a Puerto Rican. West was shocked by the accusation and said, "So help me, it was Sal who gave the lieutenant my name as the stabber. That's why I'm at Alcatraz. Why in the hell do you think I'm here?"

Some of my friends, like Joe Carnes, Joe Belizone, and Charlie Wolf, liked West, so I guess he must have had some good points. If Carnes and the others thought he was a rat, they wouldn't have talked to him; they would have killed him.

One of my most vivid recollections of working on that steamtable at the Rock three times a day for almost a year was when Black Benny, who worked in the kitchen and alongside me, dishing out food, smashed the head of another black guy with an iron pipe when the guy complained Benny was cheating him out of his share of food. I had known Benny in Atlanta. We were friends and played cards with the same people. One day, I saw Benny take this iron pipe from underneath the sink in the kitchen and carry it out to where we were serving. I saw from his glances at the inmates standing in line to be served that he was looking for somebody to come through.

Another black guy Benny had smashed in the head before came up first and started joking with Benny. I could see by Benny's face that he was ready to explode but the other guy didn't catch on. Benny said, "Go on, before I bust your fucking head." Well, the other fellow thought Benny was joking, so he leaned his head over the steam table and said, "Okay, here's my head. Hit it, you motherfucker." Without blinking once, Benny pulled his pipe and smashed the man's head into the tray of hot lima beans. Later, we teased both guys about it. They were thrown into cells next to each other in isolation because the scene had been so funny. There, they got to laughing about it and became friends again.

I remember clearly the first time I laid eyes on Joe Carnes. One day at lunch I was serving from the steam table and I saw a guy I hadn't seen before come through who looked like Edward G. Robinson. I served him his portions and looked at him a couple of times, because there was something about him I couldn't quite put my finger on. As he walked away, he turned and looked at me like, "What the hell is your problem?" I turned to Shortgrass, next to me, and asked, "Who is that?" Shortgrass looked at the guy walking away and said, "'That's Joe Carnes. He just got out of D-block this morning after seven years in lockup." I said, "Yeah, I heard of him. he was involved in the 1946 break when Cretzer shot all those guards. "How old is he?" Shortgrass said, "About 27, I suppose."

Later, when I quit the mess hall, I had to go to the hole because I didn't want to work anymore. When I came out of there, I was put in a cell next to Carnes, and we became good friends.

During my first year on the Rock I suppose Joe Belizone was my best friend. Even though I had mess hall duty, I was still a little lonely. Outside of work, I had nothing to do but read, because I didn't play chess. I knew a lot of guys at Alcatraz, so I didn't feel out of place like some of the new arrivals who didn't know anyone. A lot of the guys felt like they knew me because I got so much publicity when the FBI was tracking me.

When Belizone and I were transferred from Lewisburg to Atlanta, we laid over in Petersburg, Virginia, and I mentioned to Joe that I was the only one with both hands cuffed. He laughed and said, "Well, they consider you a half-assed bad guy." I had to laugh, too. He added, "No, no, really. You got a lot of publicity, and publicity is hard to live down." When I got to Alcatraz, the publicity didn't matter an iota. The guys on the Rock had certain friends whom they were partial to, and that was it. But there weren't any gangs like there are today in other prisons. All the guys in the cellhouse were like one big gang and helped each other the best we could. That is, except for the snitches and known homos.

When some of the inmates, and I was one of them, got bored or lonely enough, we would do something to go to the hole for a while and break the monotony. After going hungry for a few days, the food tasted better and the little freedom you had felt exhilarating compared to no freedom in D-block. You felt better in every way, because you could smoke again, and it kind of gave you a boost after feeling so low. Joe Carnes did this on a regular basis. That's why we got along so well; we thought alike.

Joe told me that one year, when the Birdman was still in D-block, all the isolation holes were full up, so they started putting three and four guys into a cell. They put the Birdman in a cell with a 45-year-old con, and the Birdman tried to fuck him. We got a big laugh out of it. Joe said, "All old motherfuckers are horny, man, and the Birdman is the horniest motherfucker of all." He said the reason the Birdman was moved to the hospital was because they were repairing D-block and covering the gun cages with wicker wire after the 1946 breakout attempt when Joe Cretzer shot all those guards.

D-block was so damaged from machine gun fire that the workers had to use drills and jackhammers all the time. The noise got on the Birdman's nerves, and he started yelling and cursing at the guards and workers. The warden moved him up to the hospital, and once he got used to the hospital, he liked it and didn't want to go back when the repairs were finished. He told the warden that he would rather stay in the hospital, because he liked the peace and quiet.

Most of the guys didn't have any problem with the guards, because they pretty much left you alone. Of course, some guys hated all of them because of things done to them in other prisons by other guards. I hated almost all the Alcatraz guards at that time, because I was mentally confused and didn't realize it. I remember that Bud Osborne, who was doing life for killing an FBI agent, told me I would spend the rest of my life in and out of jail—that guys like me, "hard heads," never really changed. I thought about it a long time after that, and then one day I walked up to him in the yard and said, "Fuck you, motherfucker. I'm going to prove your stupid, five-cent theory wrong."

Once I was out of the hole for having quit the steam table, I wanted to go to work in the laundry so I could be with some of my buddies. But Skinhead told me that if I didn't want to work in the mess hall, then I wasn't going to work at all. I looked him in the face and said, "Then you might as well put me right back in the hole, you sorry son of a bitch." Needless to say, I went right back in the hole. But Joe Carnes was there for some stupid little reason, and we laughed about our situations.

I enjoyed the hole. I got to know some of the guys who had been in there for years. What the hacks didn't realize was that isolation was no weapon against some of the old cons, because they didn't care if the sun shined or not. We used to feed the little mice that climbed the D-block wall and sat in front of our cells, waiting for pieces of bread. When some of the mice would fight over a little scrap of bread, we would all laugh. Somebody would say, "Look at that son of a bitch throw a left jab." Another would laugh, "Did you see that uppercut?" The D-block hacks didn't bother the mice, because they welcomed anything that attracted our attention and kept us out of trouble.

Joe Carnes tried to make friends with the numerous lizards that came into the D-block area but the lizards were awfully hard to catch. So were the mice. One day Joe was able to catch a small mouse by cupping it with his hands. But while doing so, he accidentally knocked it unconscious, and it died. He felt so bad about it he wanted to cry. He wouldn't think anything about clobbering an inmate unconscious, but he sure grieved for the little mouse. I heard from a guy in D-block that when Joe learned about a guy on the docks cutting a seagull's wings off so it couldn't fly anymore, Joe was ready to kill him when he got back to the main population.

But one day Carnes was able to make friends with one particular mouse. The mouse actually got down and crawled across the floor, up the tiers, and into Joe's cell. Joe fed it, gave it water, and petted it lightly with a toothbrush. No one laughed or got wise with him about his love for that little, helpless mouse. The hacks knew about it, but they didn't really care much, even though they could have gotten into trouble for allowing rodents in the cell house.

Joe kept the mouse in a large match box in which he put cotton so the mouse would be comfortable. Well, one day the mouse scampered out of D-block and was perched on an outside ledge sunning itself. Joe was watching the mouse sun itself when all of a sudden, a seagull swooped down and plucked the mouse off the ledge.

Carnes went berserk. I mean, he literally went crazy with grief and anxiety. I had never seen him this way, nor had anyone else. He was so furious; he wouldn't eat for days. Then one day he told me that from that point on, he was declaring a war on all seagulls. And he did. When we were both released from the hole a second time, I saw him go out on the yard, looking for the nearest seagull he could find. Not one of us dared laugh, because he was so intent. And this war lasted all the time I was on Alcatraz. I don't think Joe ever killed one, because no seagull ever came close enough to him to be hit or caught. But he threw anything he could get his hands on at them while he was on the yard. This otherwise kind man had declared war on all the seagulls in the universe, and as far as he was concerned, it was a fight to the finish.

Carnes's behavior was unexplainable. Maybe long stretches in D-block made him this way. Life was hard in D-block, even though some guys preferred the peace and quiet. I remember when we got too quiet, the D-block guard would worry and ask some of us what was wrong. Even when some of the guys were picking on the blacks, he would keep out of it. I guess he thought that as long as they were hassling other inmates, they weren't too messed up in the head. If one of the blacks was talking, and Mac was in a bad mood, he would say, "Hey, blubbermouth, knock it off," and that would get it going. The blacks would start screaming, and Mac would laugh and shout, "Lie down, you shit-complexioned motherfucker! I bet when I see you out in the population, I knock all that moss off the top of your head." And he did, a couple of times.

He hated a certain snitch in the county jail whom he used to curse for going to a meeting with the FBI. He would curse him night and day. As I said, you just didn't talk to the FBI. Mac told me he slipped some hacksaw blades to some guys in the cell house and the hacks caught him, because the guys he sent the blades to fingered him for helping them. He said the first time he broke out of county jail, it happened to be Sunday night, and he broke into a house to get clothes. The people had left supper on the table while they went to church, so Mac ate all the fried chicken he wanted. Then he shit in the bowl and put it back on the table. I fell out, laughing so hard I cried. I'll never know if he was telling the truth or just kidding me.

One day I heard somebody upstairs above my cell say to someone else that I got along good with crazy people. I knew they were talking about me and my friendship with Nick. Oscar "Nick" Nichols, another born loser, spent most of his time on the Rock and in D-block with guys like me and Carnes, inmates known as "fuck-ups" to the quieter guys.

One day in D-block, we had grits and gravy for lunch. Nick took his food, mixed it with his own feces that he had saved up, and, when the guard in charge of D-block walked by, threw the whole mess in his face. The guard, thinking it was gravy mixed with grits, smiled for a few seconds before he got a whiff of the slop dripping from his face. Then the guard went crazy with rage, and all the while Nick was laughing his head off. The guard got the goon squad over to D, pulled Nick out of his cell, and started to beat him with a nightstick.

But Lieutenant "Double Trouble" Ardway came running up, heard the guard's story, and said, "No, we aren't going to have any of that beating stuff. Just put him in a strip cell. After Ardway walked away, the guard made a move as if he was going to hit Nick with his left, and, when Nick ducked, the guard used his right to clobber Nick to his knees. Schultz, who witnessed the whole incident, yelled for the guard—and the whole goon squad for that matter—to open his cell and try knocking him down.

On the day Nick was finally released from Alcatraz, the guard he had thrown the shit on was waiting for him at the docks in Frisco. The guard asked him if he wanted to finish their little fight. Nick said "No" and apologized to him. The guard shook his hand and wished him luck. But it wasn't to be Nick's lucky day. Within hours of his release, Nick purchased a gun from a Fillmore pawnshop and went into a nearby bar. There he began talking dirty, like he always did. Some guy wanting to be a hero to all the other drunks told Nick to shut up, that there was a lady in the house. Nick asked, "What's a lady doing in this crap hole?" The guy tried to whip Nick's ass, and Nick shot him dead. I liked Nick a lot. But like so many others, including myself at the time, he was a born loser.

Mac was another inmate I liked. Some of the cons felt he was crazy. too. But Mac was a good guy and another one of the best artists I had ever seen. Those artists around Fishermen's Wharf today don't have anything on him. I admit I was the one who got him to draw pornographic pictures of different guards and the deputy warden fucking each other, each other's wives, and elephants. The faces would look like exact photos of the guards, while the rest of the drawings were in cartoon form.

One day, the deputy warden called Mac to his office and called him all kinds of dirty names, then put him in a strip cell for drawing "such obscene material." Mac drew me a wanted poster of John Dillinger from an old magazine and a nice picture of Rocky Graziano with his championship belt on but both were stolen by the guards. I asked the hack who packed my stuff when I was leaving for Springfield about the

Graziano picture and he said, "Yes, it's there in your bag," but when I got to Springfield it wasn't in the bag. The Dillinger picture had been stolen a year before by a guard when I was in the hospital for my ulcer.

Mac and Carnes were my favorite friends while I was in the hole. McKinney's AZ number was #1233, and he was serving a twenty-year army sentence for murder. He was from Kentucky and hated stool pigeons worse than he hated blacks. He hated stool pigeons because after he arrived on Alcatraz, he received an additional five-year sentence for concealing a hacksaw blade in his cell. Somebody ratted on him. When it came to amusing himself, he would go after the blacks. For fun, some guys played chess, read, or masturbated but Mac enjoyed heckling the blacks, and if the blacks didn't respond to his name calling, he would yell, "You yellow purple asshole." You'd think Bumpy Johnson would step in and say something to Mac, but Bumpy just laughed.

One day after Mac got out of D-block, a black named Austin went after him in the mess hall and Mac knocked him about ten feet across the polished floor. Although he was just 24 years old, Mac was a big, strong kid. Even guys who didn't especially care for him, like Bumpy, admitted that basically he was "good people." The only time I saw him get whipped was by a badass black named Sunday. Sunday told me how Mac jumped him after the beating, and he had to whip him a second time. When I told Sunday that I thought Mac was decent enough except for being a fucking racist, Sunday said, "I have nothing against the guy, for he is solid and I don't give a shit that he's a racist. At least he tells you he's a racist, right up front but we just don't get along."

One day in the late summer of 1956, Alvin Karpis slipped me a couple of things to read. "Do you want a good laugh tonight, Hoppy? Read these, then," he smiled. One was an old San Francisco newspaper clipping and the other was a page from the *Congressional Record*. I don't know where he got the newspaper clipping, but we were allowed to receive the *Congressional Record*. The clippings were a part of a collection of articles about the Rock that he was allowed to keep in his cell.

"The newspaper editorial gives you an idea what the people across the country think of us. I like the part about Alcatraz being a desecration of Frisco's noble bay," he said, pointing to the yellowed article.

The newspaper clipping must have been written in 1934 when the first inmates arrived. Karpis was certain the mood of the San Franciscans hadn't changed much. We were outcasts, and the people in the city sure didn't want to see us every morning across the bay when they woke up. I'm sure a lot thought, "Why don't you just execute those hardcore incorrigibles and be done with it?" The clipping read:

THE ALCATRAZ EVIL

"Visitors entering San Francisco Bay from the Pacific, after marveling at the great towers of the Golden Gate Bridge, will have their attention called to the stony superstructures imposed on the rock of Alcatraz and are informed: "There are caged the most desperate Federal prisoners in America." A devil's litany of its inmates will be recited. The pious and appropriate refrain can well be, "Spare us, O Lord."

The Federal Government, in spite of a contrary opinion credited to Sanford Bates, Director of Federal Prisons, is concentrating its most notorious and irreclaimable offenders on the "Rock."

When the idea of adapting Alcatraz Island's military prison to other lawbreakers was first considered last year, *The Examiner* quoted this statement ascribed to Sanford Bates, which appeared in *The New York Times*: "Personally I have not been attracted by the idea (of concentrating the most desperate criminals in one prison.) The experience of France and other foreign countries does not seem to indicate that it is a successful means of treatment."

Yet under direction of Mr. Bates that concentration is going on. The presence there of Al Capone may not be sinister; he may be just window dressing for the exhibit of prize malefactors. But other men with equally ugly records and more notorious daring are being assembled. It might be good drama, but it isn't the sort of drama that fits into the spacious San Francisco life.

Penologists agree that it is not wise to concentrate too many of the most vicious type in one institution. Segregation of immature offenders from the more hardened type is essential, but concentrating all the most vicious, creating an unleavened mob of desperation, seems bad penology. It is a desecration of San Francisco's noble bay to convert a conspicuous and picturesque island into a living plague spot.

Prisons are necessary to this particular stage of civilization, but they are not a subject for pride, and the United States is not so congested that its fairest harbor has to be polluted with a concourse of conspicuous Public Enemies."

The second item Karpis handed me was entitled "How Life Is Easier at Alcatraz." Just the title made me laugh out loud. It was from a speech that William Langer, a senator from North Dakota, gave in the Senate on April 19, 1956. He asked approval for a story that appeared in the *Bismarck Tribune* to be included in the *Congressional Record*. The headline of the article was "While Far from a Bed of Roses, How Life Is Easier at Alcatraz," and the piece was written by Leonard Millman.

This was a bunch of bullshit! Alcatraz was in the midst of the bloodiest violence since it became a prison in 1934, and the authorities were describing what a great place it was. Both articles left me laughing and sick at the same time.

Things are kind of confusing in my head in terms of what all happened during the latter part of 1956. I just remember one day flowing into another, week after week, month after month. I got no letters, no visitors, and my only friends in the world were there in the cell house. One holiday passed after another, and I didn't care much. There was nothing to celebrate, and I wasn't going anyplace for a long, long time. I just became one of the numbers lost in a bunch of other numbers. No one cared if I was #1186AZ, or #186AZ, or #1111186AZ. I was just staying afloat as best I could.

I met Alvin Karpis when we were on the same tier together. This was on the flats on C-side. I was in the third cell from the west end, next to the cell where Joe Cretzer shot the guards. Alvin was about three cells down, so we started eating together. I always ended up in the same location each time after I came out of D-block, so we ate together right up until I left.

Karpis was called Public Enemy No. 1 by the FBI because of his rampage of bank robberies and murder in the 1930s. I knew all about his past because of the comic books I had read as a kid. But he never boasted or told me stories about how he was a bank robber and killer. As far as I was concerned, he could have passed for a college professor. Al always gave me good advice, and he seemed more like a big brother then an eating partner.

In the spring of 1957, I was assigned to work the flower gardens on the hill outside D-block. It was a perfect job for me. Skinhead and most of the custodial staff walked up that way to their positions in the industries, and one day he told me I had done a better job with the flowers and weeds than anybody in a long time. I enjoyed the butterflies and hummingbirds that swarmed around the flowers, and I had a chance to feed the seagulls.

What was even better was that Bumpy and I had a chance to talk for an hour or so every day. While I was working in the flowers, Bumpy would come up the hill early from the industries and wait at the hill steps for the lieutenant to unlock the yard door. I learned a great deal from him, because he was so well informed.

If I had been smart, I would have gotten all the facts on his early life and his pre-Alcatraz days for a book someday. Eventually, a movie will be made on this fascinating man. He wasn't all bad, but he wasn't all good, either. Still, he showed so much class to me, that to this day, I think so much of him that I have his mug shot on my hallway wall. A day doesn't go by that I don't think of him. As far as I was concerned, Bumpy should have been warden of Alcatraz or president of a big corporation.

Once on the flower garden job, I took a shovel and turned over all the dirt between the road and D-block. This section was several hundred feet wide. But a few weeks later, it began to grow in thick with grass. Skinhead told me it was looking good, and if I wanted another job to send him a request. But then I accused Lieutenant Ardway, one of the first guards on the Rock when it opened in 1934, of trying to poison me after we had several confrontations. I ended up in the hospital, and Dr. Wolfson told me he needed me to talk to Dr. Whilsell, because he wanted to transfer me to the US Medical Facility at Springfield. He felt I should have been sent there the previous year.

The only hack I really hated was Skinhead, J.B. Latimer, the associate warden. He must have practiced his techniques in Hitler's Germany. Or, maybe he was the prototype of the sadistic wardens depicted in the prison movies of the 1940s and 1950s. In any case, the son of a bitch belonged in the Deep South, running chain gangs, instead of trying to run us in what was called a "modern" federal penitentiary. Jimmy Groves told me that Skinhead started out as a guard in Springfield and hated everybody, including other guards. One day I cursed him during the count call and he got so mad he dropped his cigarette. Lieutenant Mitchell, who observed the scene, almost swallowed his cigar. He came up to my cell and said, "Hey, hey, back off." Skinhead said, "Put the troublemaker back in the dark hole, and we'll let him rot for a hundred years."

Skinhead especially hated McKinney because, as I mentioned, Mac was always drawing cartoons with Skinhead's face on a fat hack, performing all kinds of sexual acts on the wives of other guards, who were always named. Mac even depicted him fucking a big, fat skunk. I used to think up stuff for Mac to draw, and Mac would then improve on it. As I said, his work was so good that most of it was taken home by the guards who found it. Mac and I laughed that the guards probably used the drawings to get their wives hot and aroused.

In early 1957, I got in trouble with one hack for not getting out of bed for the morning count because my stomach was hurting bad. I forgot the guard's name, because he didn't last long at Alcatraz. He was young, cocky, and stupid. Jimmy Groves, a black guy, who celled in front of me, said, "Cool it. You don't have to get up for the count, because your stomach is hurting!" After the count was over, the pee wee did halfway try to say he was sorry and that he had been wrong and I have to honestly say I did see a number of guards apologize for mistakes. As I think about it, I never saw a hack on the Rock beat up an inmate who didn't swing first. My friend Fry got roughed up in front of the dining room, but that was because he swung first and injured a guard's ankle with a kung-Fu kick.

Jimmy Groves was a stone-cold killer who started out with a small army sentence like Simcox's and ended up killing three different inmates over the next thirty years. The first was a man he stabbed in the military prison at Fort Leavenworth before throwing him off the third tier. Jimmy was among the first load of prisoners to open the Rock in 1934, and he was given the AZ number 158. He was feared by guards and inmates alike.

Even as dangerous as Simcox was, he was leery of Groves. I watched Joe Carnes start an argument with Jimmy, but at the time Joe may have had a death wish. Schultz was the only one who didn't fear Groves. I heard Groves tell Shortgrass that because Schultz thought he was so tough he would like to spit in his face and stick a good sharp blade in his gut.

So, I told Schultz what I overheard, and he caught Jimmy on the yard one day and said, "Groves, I heard you want to stick a knife in me?" Jimmy smiled and said, "Who told you that?" Schultz said, "I'm not going into all that. I asked you if you want to stick a knife in me?" Jimmy smiled and said, "No, I didn't say that." Schultz said, "Okay, forget it."

As soon as Groves got in the cell house, he jumped all over Shortgrass and told him he was two-faced. This proved to Schultz that he did say it. So, that night at dinner, Schultz was serving from the steam table when Groves came through. Schultz started cursing him and said, "Nigger, you want to spit in my face, huh?" Groves opened his shirt at the belt line and said, "Come over on this side. I can't spit that far!" But Schulz waited until the next afternoon on the yard to get him. Joe walked back and forth by the card table where Jimmy was gambling and started cursing and telling Groves to make his play. Jimmy finally stood up and flashed a knife, saying, "You come on!" So, Schultz picked up a baseball bat that was nearby and hit him four or five times across the back, disabling him. Then Joe calmly walked away.

The guards never saw the beating but suspected both of them were involved in causing the fight and put them in D-block for a couple of weeks. A black inmate most likely informed on them. Both were let out of D-block eventually, since each denied what happened. But from then on, Jimmy respected Schultz. To tell the truth, I think Jimmy was getting tired of D-block, since he was 55 years old. He was getting tired of being tough, tired of the stabbings, tired of fighting, tired of it all.

Still, one day after getting out of D-block, Jimmy Groves tried to talk to a guard behind the steam table about a friend of his. But the guard wouldn't listen and started to walk away. Jimmy leaned over the steam table and started beating the guard over the head with his dipper. So, back into isolation Jimmy went, whether he was tired of it all or not. McKinney also whacked a guard he didn't care for. He beat a hack with his trumpet at the Broadway desk because he didn't like the way the guard searched his cell. That's when Mac was sent to D-block, where he wound up spending four years.

A few of the guards, like Bloomquist, were intimidated by the inmates. Probably the guard who was the most afraid was one we referred to as "Toilet Paper Slim," because he threw toilet paper at Simcox while he was stabbing an inmate. You could see the fear in his eyes, and he sure as hell didn't want to be on the cell house floor by himself. We knew it and tried to make his life even more miserable but most guards were not intimidated and would tangle with you in a minute if they needed to. These were men like Lieutenant Mitchell and Lieutenant Mahan, and guards like Guam, Gregory, and Baker.

I didn't sense that any of the guys, with the exception of Skinhead, were sickos, like those four Los Angeles officers who beat the shit out of Rodney King, a black man, in early March 1991. That was the case that prompted national outrage. In a home video, four white cops are shown beating a helpless man 56 times with batons, kicking him, and shooting him with a taser electric stun gun after a nighttime traffic stop. For one thing, those cops had to be racist.

Second, they had to have so much hate and violence pent up that all its fury was unleashed on a helpless man already lying on the ground. I've noticed that a lot of short men become guards, cops, priests, or join the military and rise to high ranks so they can get power, feel power, and hurt and cripple others with power. To me, the shorter the man, the more dangerous he is, because he needs to make up through violence for a height he doesn't have.

Many of the guards at Raiford and on the Florida road gangs were little cocksuckers. The same thing held true at Atlanta and at Alcatraz. The short man was more apt to be explosive. This went for the inmates, too. And, if you looked at the heights of those four LA cops on the videotape, they were all less than 5'8".

But like I say: I never saw an Alcatraz officer swing first at an inmate. Provoke him, yes—like Skinhead and Lieutenant Mitchell. Mitchell acted as if he disliked all the convicts. When a young buddy of mine, Vic Monzula, was being released from Alcatraz, he refused to let another guard stick a finger up his ass and told Mitchell to his face to take his cigar out of his mouth and quit acting like Humphrey Bogart.

Vic demanded to know what in the hell he could be taking out of Alcatraz that was so big and important that he would hide it up his ass. Mitchell said, "You don't let us look, you don't go home." Vic let the guards look. Some of the guys then started referring to Mitchell as "Look-in-the-hole."

Vic Monzula was one of the more likeable guys on Alcatraz. He was an Italian American, my age, and nice looking. In fact, we used to tease him that he probably looked like Sal Mineo when he was a teenager. Some of the inmates sensed even then that Mineo was homosexual, and the reference was sort of a dig at Vic, although Vic, who was straight, didn't catch on. Not until recently did the public learn that Mineo was indeed a homo. Well, one day, Indian Mitch began making sexual advances on Vic in D-block. Mitch was the D-block orderly and had the run of the unit. Vic laughed him off. But Indian Mitch persisted.

Finally, Vic, a few days later, was able to get hold of a razor blade, probably passed to him in a book from the library runner. I used to send Simcox tobacco in a library book when he was locked in D-block, so we all knew how to smuggle contraband in library books.

That afternoon, when Indian Mitch was sweeping the tiers, Vic called him over, saying he had something to tell him. When Mitch walked over, Vic said he would have to whisper in his ear, since he didn't want the guy in the next cell to hear. Smiling, Indian Mitch put his ear to the cell front. In a flash, Vic laid the homo's face open with the razor blade.

Vic was never tried for the cutting, because Indian Mitch wouldn't testify against him. Not only did Vic tell me what happened, but so did Indian Mitch, whom I got along with. "Hell, it was my own fault for trying to suck a con's cock who doesn't want it sucked," he said. When he was released, Indian Mitch demanded that he wear an Indian blanket as part of his dress. The officials laughed it off. But, like me, Indian Mitch was a real fuckup, and us fuckups got along well. It was like being in a fraternity.

In the early part of 1957, I kept to myself and pretty much kept to the prison routine. A lot of things were going on and, if I were left out of them, I didn't poke my nose into business that didn't concern me. I followed the old convict adage of never ratting, never allowing anyone to beat you up, and never trying to impress anyone, convict or guard.

Some things that happened were kind of funny, however. For instance, several of us, including Schultz, talked about escaping. We meant it as a joke. But the minute we mentioned it; Schultz started taking cold showers to get his body adjusted to the cold bay water. For months while we laughed about escape, trying like in a game to figure an angle that both guards and other inmates had missed, struggling to find an engineering flaw that the prison authorities and construction engineers had not foreseen, Schultz showered in cold water. And even when we gave up because not one of us could see a way out except dead under a prison blanket, Schultz kept showering in cold water. Even when we insisted that all the talk of escape had been for fun, he kept showering in cold water.

Little did we know that less than five years later, that hypocrite Allen West would figure the ventilation duct above B cellblock could be reached, paving the way for the only successful escape from the prison. But by that time, I was long gone.

I purchased an oil painting kit but never was any good at painting. Like most guys, I read a lot. I noticed some guys ordered books every day, and I knew they couldn't be reading them all. I mentioned it to Carnes, and Joe said a lot of them checked them out just to do something in order to break the monotony. Sometimes the place could get pretty lonely, even with 200 other people around you. Some of them just dreamed of revenge.

I remember one time when Huebert Juelich and I were watching the guard walk back and forth on the dining room catwalk as we ate, and he said, "If I ever get one of them in a crack, I will show them as much mercy as I would show that wall." And I could tell by the look in his eyes that he meant it.

I remember his case well. He had killed a US Marshal who was transporting him to the Atlanta Federal Penitentiary. He hid a hair pin in a Milky Way candy bar and used it to pick his handcuffs. Then he reached over the front seat and grabbed the marshal's pistol. He said the marshal pulled the car over and said, "Take it easy. You can have the car."

When he reached for the car door with his left hand, Juelich thought he was reaching for a stash-out gun and shot him out of panic. He really didn't intend to. He was kept in the hole in the Atlanta pen for two years until he was tried. Juelich then appealed a death sentence, and the guards gave him a real bad time during that additional year. It made him a lot more mean. We went to the Rock on the same shipment, and when I left there he still hadn't been in any type of trouble. He went to work, read a lot, and walked back and forth on the yard. I liked him and saw him as someone you could trust.

When Pork Chops got transferred, I mentioned that I asked the deputy warden for his job, taking care of the flowers on the road and hill facing the Golden Gate Bridge, and got it. I had a feeling Skinhead was hoping that once I got the job I would run, so he could shoot me, but I just wanted a change of scenery.

Karpis told me I didn't need a job as isolated as that one, and he was right. I started to get lonely, even though I enjoyed the flowers and seagulls. Several times a day a tourist boat circled the island, and I could hear the guide mentioning Capone, Kelly, and Karpis on the loudspeaker. The flower garden on the west side of D-block was where the marines dug in and fired on the cellhouse during the 1946 siege. I dug up a machine gun shell one day, but a hack stole it from my cell as a souvenir.

In the first two years, there was one thing I demanded from others, and this was loyalty in return for loyalty from me. A man in prison hasn't got much to give his friends, but loyalty is one valuable gift, and his word is another. Many of the guards understood this and respected it, maybe because they wanted it from each other and never got it.

Loyalty among the Alcatraz inmates was better than in other prisons I had known. This was probably because of the special selection of men from the two major federal prisons who were sent there in the 1950s. Years later, I saw guys come to Springfield from the Rock who made some of us wonder how they got in there in the first place. I think this had a lot to do with the closing of the Rock and not the deterioration of the steel beams under the cellhouse, as some say.

It was common talk among the guys leaving there that the holes from behind the cells for the 1962 escape were cut from the utility corridors while new hot water pipes were being laid in the B corridor. The final digging for the escape may have been accomplished with spoons.

But loyalty was the mark of a solid con. He was one you could depend on in a tight situation. You would get references such as, "You can bank on Joe. He will be there when you need him." I have seen some put their lives on the line, like Schultz did several times. Charlie Harberbison had a fight with a black guy named Fuller who was bad with a knife, and when they got out of the hole, Fuller came to him on the yard and said they had to talk.

Because Charlie was a good friend of Schultz, Schultz said, "That nigger is trying to bully the kid." He walked over and asked, "What's the problem, Charlie?" Fuller said, "Hey man, I'm talking to the guy!" Schultz said, "I don't care if you're talking to President Eisenhower, nigger. I'll kick you through the side of that wall."

So, Fuller went and got a knife from another black and came to the bottom of the steps where Schultz was watching hand-ball. Fuller had a coat across his hand to hide the knife and said, "You think you're bad, don't you?" Schultz said, "No, I'm not bad. But when it comes to you or any other nigger, I'm the baddest sonofabitch you ever met! Now make your play, and I'll kick your guts out." Fuller never made his play.

Another example of loyalty dealt with Whitey Franklin, who worked in the hospital. A friend of his was in the hospital ward when Bigsey Gilford was serving the food off a portable steam table on wheels. Bigsey and Whitey didn't get along. In fact, he was the only person on the island who didn't like Whitey. So, he started cutting Brennen, Whitey's friend, short on his food. When Whitey found out, he told me that he waited until Bigsey went into the linen room and then darted in and closed the door.

He asked Bigsey why he was cutting Brennen short on food, and Bigsey, who was a big guy, started popping off. Whitey said, "Well, I didn't come to argue with you. I came to kill you," and he pulled out his knife. Bigsey started apologizing and said, "Hell, I didn't know he was a friend of yours. From now on I'll give him all he can eat." Whitey let him off the hook, because he was trying to get a transfer, which he finally got with the help of Warden Madigan. It was then that Whitey told me if he ever got a parole, "You can bet all your money I won't be back." I believed him. Both Schultz and I had a lot of respect for Whitey.

Years later, after I obtained my file from the FBI under the Freedom of Information Act and was perusing it, I came across a letter Whitey wrote to the prison psychologist about me. I guess he thought he was helping, because I don't believe he would have written it to harm me. Because he saw me as a fuckup, he was probably afraid I might sooner or later get violent. The letter was dated June 17, 1961 and reads as follows:

Dear Mr. York,

Sir, I believe this inmate Hopkins whom you assigned to cell with me is in serious need of further psychiatric treatment.

I had thought when he asked me if he could move in the cell with me, that he was only having trouble adjusting to this institution and that perhaps I might be able to help him with this adjustment. But it has become very clear that his problem is more than just a matter of adjustment. He is still mentally ill and needs psychiatric help.

When he first moved in here, he was disturbed but seemed rational. But as time went by, he became more morose and withdrawn and at times talked wildly and irrationally. During these times he seemed to be trying to associate himself with the "Superman" philosophy of Hitler and the Nazis.

It is easy to see, sir, that this man is in a mental turmoil and harbors deep seated resentments against people in general and is decidedly antisocial. He will go for days without speaking and just stares off in space. When he does talk it is generally about the Nazis and World War II, and his talk is disjointed and irrational.

Sir, I would not attempt to say what is wrong with him and I describe the symptoms for what worth they might be for someone who might be able to help him. If there is some way you can do it, I wish you would assign him to another cell. His irrational behavior, at times, indicates the possibility that he can become violent.

Sincerely,
Rufus Franklin

In July 1957, I got into a vicious fight with a guy by the name of Whitey Hill. He was a short, muscular man who had once fought with Joe Carnes. Some guys said Whitey was stir crazy. I don't know if he was or wasn't. All I know is that when he jumped Joe on the yard one day, I tried to help Carnes out. But two of Hill's buddies got in front of me, and before

I could go through them, the hacks had us surrounded. So, all three of us wound up in the hole.

A few weeks later, after we had been released from D-block and were on Broadway one evening, Whitey passed a note down to me, saying how pretty I looked and how he liked sex with other men. So, instead of giving him the finger or cursing him out, I waited until the next morning when it was time to go to the mess hall for breakfast. As he came down the steps, I left my cell and walked straight towards him with my fists flying.

My first punch hit him in the face, cutting his right eye open. He began bleeding so heavily that it covered his whole shirt, leading a guard to think I had a knife. Before the guard could reach me, however, I kicked Whitey about ten times in the head and in the stomach. Pork Chops was watching the whole contest and said, "Gee, man, Charlie, you're better with your feet than you are with your hands." Blue said, "I ain't fucking with you no more, because you come on like Sugar Ray Robinson." Simcox said later, "I know I ain't never fucking with you after seeing Whitey's eye."

Whitey was a bully at times, and Simcox came close to killing him over the fight we had. Simcox tried to provoke Whitey into a fight by asking his opinion of me so he could "legitimately" kill him. But Whitey was terrified of Simcox and kept saying, "Hoppy's a good guy. I have no dislike for Hoppy. He's a solid con."

Well, a guard had jumped in to break it up, and all of a sudden it became a three-way fight. The guard got roughed up a bit, and that afternoon Whitey and I were hauled into the Alcatraz court, which was run by the prison administration. The deputy warden held court in one of the A-block cells, where he had a desk set up. Officer Baker happened to be one of the guards sitting on the court that day, and because he liked me, he told me to tell Skinhead that Whitey and I had a fight over a ball game argument and he would favor keeping me out of the dark hole. Whitey and I were sentenced to three days in open front cells and then let go.

Simcox was a cold-blooded killer, but he had a warm spot in his heart for his friends. He would stand by them like he did for Carnes and me when I went to the hole and lost all my good time for giving him a knife.

He told some of the guys while I was locked up that I was the best friend he had, and if anybody ever hurt me, he would kill them. I'll describe this tragedy in detail further on.

When I was released from federal prison, I kept an unlisted number for almost twenty years, because even though I knew a lot of good guys, I also associated with a lot of dirt bags, too. Some of the guys were dealt a bad hand by Lady Fate and would never get rid of their hatred, depression, and tendency towards violence. Simcox was certainly a psychopathic killer, but at the same time he had real feelings for the right people. He had a big kid way about him that attracted some inmates. I remember that Jack Burnam, the San Francisco attorney, took a liking to him. If I said it once, I've said it a thousand times: fate put the wrong circuit breaker in Simcox's head.

One of the more controversial cons I made friends with in 1957 was Blackie Audett, an old-time gangster who wrote a book entitled *Rap Sheet* about his experiences on the Rock. He was about 5'8" and looked more like a lawyer than a hoodlum. I heard that 20 to 30 guards had him autograph his book in the officer's mess hall when it was published. [*]

Blackie was controversial, because some of the inmates, including Joe Carnes, felt he was a rat. There were rumors he had informed on certain cons. Joe hated his guts and said that much of what was written, either by Blackie or his ghost writer, was pure bullshit. I finally did get a copy of it, and I agree, there is a lot of bullshit in it. But he did this to sensationalize the book for better sales. Hell, he didn't care. But Blackie and I got along well enough. He used to talk about the time he spent in the dungeon on Alcatraz. The fact that there was a dungeon there was said over and over again by the eighteen or twenty old timers who had been called as witnesses for Henry Young in April 1941.

Blackie told me he had been in that dungeon and that it held about eight inmates. He said that all you got to eat was bread and water and a meal every fifth day, that the dungeon was always wet, and that it had rats. It was supposed to be below A-block, and an old army disciplinary barracks staircase led down to it. Blackie said that when you came out of the dungeon, the hacks put you in a cell in A-block that had a solid metal front with quarter-inch cracks you could barely see through. According to Blackie, they quit using the dungeon in 1939 and remodeled the solid metal doors. Jimmy Groves, who as I mentioned arrived on the Rock in 1934, never talked about the dungeon, although I bet he spent some time in it, since he was always in trouble.

I saw a lot of guys beat up by the guards at Raiford, Atlanta, Lewisburg, and Leavenworth. In most cases, the inmates were violent and aggressive toward the guards. As I mentioned, the guards on the Rock didn't abuse you physically. They did it mentally by treating you like you had a disease they might catch but I now know it was the official bureau policy they followed. I knew two or three guards who quit during their probation period because they couldn't tolerate the strain or the off-duty island lifestyle. One guard who I remember well was a young man named Hopkins. Because we were similar in age, he talked to me often. He had just started his training when I arrived, and he was just too nice to be a good prison guard. He couldn't fight and he didn't have the inner toughness.

Simcox was very loyal to his friends, and if someone messed with his friends, he was messing with Simcox. He enjoyed sticking a knife in someone he didn't like. It gave him some kind of release, made him feel better. Later, when he was released from D-block for stabbing Dog, Skinhead knew Simcox was going to kill Gauvin, so he and Captain Rychner figured, because Simcox and I were friends, I could talk him out of it.

They put Simcox in the cell next to mine, hoping that Simcox might listen to me. Even some of Gauvin's friends asked me to talk to Simcox about letting up, but all my talk didn't do any good. Simcox listened to no one except some weird person inside himself.

I had known Simcox since my first day on the Rock. He worked in the clothes room next to the showers in the basement. When I walked up to the cage of the clothing room to get my new clothes on that first day of my arrival, he smiled and said, "Hey, aren't you the cat they call 'Three Gun

Maniac?' I said, "No. That was my partner." Simcox said he was in the brig at Fort Leavenworth when I was on the loose and was rooting for me to get away. He said he kept up with my case after that. We became friends and stayed friends until the end.

When I was leaving Alcatraz for Springfield, he sent a message to me in the hospital by one of the medical technician's assistants who ran the hospital. The message was short and simple and I'll never forget it: "I hope I see you again someday under better conditions. You are always going to be my friend." Simcox is one of the few guys I knew in prison who I would want to see again today.

One afternoon I was idle in my cell when another guy hung himself. The guards put him on a stretcher, and they happened to walk with the stretcher past my cell on the flats. I looked down at his face, and he had a vacant stare. I told Larry Trumble, who was upstairs, that he was dead. Larry was the fellow's friend, and the guy had not mentioned one word that he was going to check out. Bigsey Gilford was working in the hospital then, and he told me later that he spent thirty minutes trying to revive him.

Bigsey said that the head MTA, a man named Charlie, was mad and kept saying over and over again that he would never again go against his better judgment. He had wanted to move the man to the hospital before he hung himself, but Skinhead told him not to. The MTA persisted, saying the guy was complaining about stomach pains and may have had cancer. But Skinhead said the con was faking.

The deputy warden was an evil bastard who hated everybody and was finally transferred to a country club–type prison in Milan, Michigan, because too many inmate deaths occurred under his control. I wrote my Florida Congressman, Spessard Holland, about this suicide. I felt sure Skinhead had caused it and explained how he framed me on several charges. Skinhead assumed (correctly) that I gave Simcox the knife he killed Gauvin with, but couldn't prove it. So, he took all my gain time away from me. Holland wrote back that he was asking someone else to look into my accusations. Less than a week later, Skinhead called me into his office and said, "If your congressman wants to be responsible for your incorrigible actions, then let him come and run this institution." The next morning, I was released from idle status. But within a year, another inmate committed suicide and another was killed, all due to Skinhead.

Everybody called Warden Madigan "Promising Paul." I saw him as basically a good man trying to control a prison population made up of the culls from all the other major federal prisons. These culls included gangsters, vicious killers, escape artists, treacherous Benedict Arnolds, and psychotics. Not one was a Boy Scout, not even Morton Sobell.

I remember Warden Madigan walking down Michigan Boulevard one day with a couple of celebrity visitors, and as they passed my cell, I started telling him about the mail room officer cutting up my goddamn *True* magazine. When he got rid of his visitors, he came to my cell alone and asked, "What was wrong with you Hopkins?" I explained about my magazine and he said, "Well, an article may have concerned one of the other inmates." He was real nice about it. I later got another copy of *True* from Tom Robinson that passed the censor without being scissored. The story that was clipped was about Dillinger and it involved Karpis. I hated cops back then, and I remember Karpis telling me that the cops had a job to do just like everybody else and warned me not to be a "jail-house gangster." If he hadn't liked me, he would have said nothing, since that kind of talk made you look bad and might get you a stab wound.

Jimmy Groves taught me about keeping a knife and how easy it was to kill somebody. As I mentioned, he and I had a run-in when I first got there, and he said, "I know you're a tough kid and like to prize fight, but don't fuck with me. If I have anything to say about you, I will say it to you."

Simcox told me later that Groves had already killed three guys, and I said, "Well, he can be killed, too." I found out some of the guys just liked to start trouble. But Jimmy and I became good friends. When I had my run-in with Blue, he asked me about it. Then he said, "I'll cut that motherfucker's guts out for you." As I said, Jimmy was black but thought like a white. He told me he was part Indian, and he looked it.

I mentioned that some of the guys kept a low profile on Alcatraz to the point that you forgot they were even there. Miranda was one. He was a Puerto Rican who shot up the US House of Representatives in 1954. The only thing I ever saw him do was walk the yard with Father Scannel, the Catholic chaplain. When I was on Michigan Boulevard, he celled above me on the second tier, and once in a while I would hear him call, "Jaleet!" This was Gillette, whom he got along with real well. Miranda looked about twenty years old and showed no signs that he was a violent revolutionary.

I found the guys in prison, and especially on the Rock, to be more honest and up front with you than the so-called Christian bureaucrats I have had to deal with on the streets. The biggest and only difference I can see between us is that we got caught and they didn't. If they tried to deal with the guys like we had on the Rock the same way they do with people on the streets, they wouldn't live more than two days.

On New Year's Day 1956, I watched Bullock kill Bebop over a pack of cigarettes that Bebop owed him. It wasn't over the amount; it was the principle of the thing. Bebop was twenty-four years old and a little overbearing. He pushed his luck until it ran out. What happened was that he owed Jimmy Bullock a pack of cigarettes from a poker bet and wouldn't pay. When Bullock demanded the pack, Bebop hit Bullock and knocked him down. Bullock got up with a knife in his hand and stabbed Bebop several times in the stomach. The blade also went through Bebop's hand a couple of times.

Bullock fell down, and when Bebop leaned over him to grab the knife, Bullock cut open the top of Bebop's shaved head. That's when the guard grabbed Bebop from behind. Bebop screamed, "Turn me loose. He's killing me!" The guard didn't see the knife and was bum-rapped for causing Bebop's death but Bebop was doomed even before the guard got involved. I was about ten feet away and watched it all.

Bebop walked about twenty feet towards the steps of the yard, made a sound like his lungs collapsed, and went down. All of this over a pack of cigarettes. But, the bottom line in Alcatraz was, if you said you would do something at 10:00 tomorrow, then it better be 10:00 and not 11:00, since your reputation depended on it—maybe even your life, depending on the circumstances. Bebop learned the hard way.

I watched Karpis and Pappy Kyle, who was Joe Cretzer's rap partner and Karpis' best friend, playing poker one day. A guy called Bill came up, and we got to talking about how he helped kill Mad Dog Coll for Dutch Schultz. I pointed out that Coll had killed some children one time, to get to another mobster. Bill said if he had the chance, he would kill the children of guards to get even. When I said that was bullshit to mess with their kids, he said, "It wouldn't bother you to step on a cockroach, would it?"

I figured he was a braggart and told Karpis that. But Karpis said Bill had been with Dutch Schultz, and in the late sixties I saw in the paper that he died in a courtroom in New York while talking to the judge. The Associated Press said he had been a killer for Dutch Schultz. Previously he had been a policeman but was fired because of his gangster connections. I quit talking to him, because to me, he was a no-good bastard. You don't kill kids for any reason.

When Skinhead had me before the board for a second time to take away all my good time, I told the court I knew guys were telling Skinhead things I was doing that I wasn't, because they didn't like me. Skinhead said, "No, that's just the problem. Everybody likes you, and that indicates to me that you're doing all the wrong things." He must have heard about me running Bill down, because he said, "You're finding out what kind of dogs some of these gangsters are, aren't you?"

One night while I was in the hospital, I heard the Birdman expressing an opinion to an MTA, and the MTA said, "Well, Bob, for a guy like you with no scruples, it shouldn't bother you." I talked to the Birdman a lot, and he never said some of the things I have heard others claim he said. I know he couldn't stand stupid people and would write his own opinion of them in notations on the "Letters to the Editor" page of the *Time* and *Life* magazines that we traded back and forth.

I liked the Birdman because he was sensible, tough as you need to be, and never broke, even after forty years in solitary. Bob Stroud died the same man he was when he came to prison. He wasn't a thief, but he killed his first man for beating up a saloon girl who supported him. The guard he killed was a sadist and deserves no sympathy. I remember his wife telling the news media that Bob caused her to raise her children in poverty, and I said then that her husband caused his children to suffer by his own cruel ways. Stroud was a likable guy and bothered nobody. It surprised me the way he could talk so much after spending so much time alone. He would always carry the conversation. I didn't have to do anything but listen.

Few people have ever heard the Birdman's version of how he killed the guard, which caused him to wind up in prison in the first place. He talked to me about it often, and I'm sure he was telling the truth—there would be no point in lying to me. Not only did the following account come straight from his mouth at Alcatraz, but also one day, when we sitting on the grass at Springfield.

The Birdman told me that his mother had come a long way to visit him when he first entered federal prison, and the day before visiting day, Stroud was put on report and therefore wouldn't be eligible for his mother's visit until after Stroud appeared before the staff court. Well, the next day, the guard who had placed him on report was on duty in the mess hall. Stroud raised his hand for permission to stand up so he could ask him to delay the report until after he visited with his mother. The Birdman said he asked the guard in a really nice way to help him out. But the guard shouted, "You son of a bitch! I thought you needed to use the toilet!" and raised his night stick to hit him.

The Birdman instantly pulled a knife that he carried for protection. Now, since Stroud was lefthanded, he grabbed the guard's right wrist, which held the night stick, with his own right hand and with his knife in his left hand came up as the guard fell over him. With the impact of his swing, Stroud's knife went right through the guard's heart. He told me, "The position we were in, with me being lefthanded, proved that it was self-defense and the killing was an accident. And the cons who testified that I deliberately killed him were lying, because they couldn't see what they claimed they saw from their angle."

Stroud loved his mother dearly; in fact, she was probably the only person he ever loved. He killed that asshole, which was the original reason for his imprisonment, out of loyalty for the girl the asshole assaulted. He didn't defend her out of love. Still, if anyone had known the Birdman as I knew him, they would have liked him, since he was so intelligent and would do anything for you if he liked you.

I have watched a lot of guys—Whitey Franklin especially—just sit and stare at one spot for a length of time, then start talking about anything. I pointed this out to Karpis one time, and he laughed. By the time I left there I had gotten the same way and still am. The Rock had a way of changing your personality and putting its stamp on you. Today, I can spot guys that have done hard time in a place like that. If the federal judges hadn't turned state and federal prisons into country clubs, they wouldn't be overflowing. Inmates today have it better than homeless people. I would like to see the chronic returners spend a month on Alcatraz in the fifties. Believe me, they would find God quick.

We had a Protestant chaplain on the Rock named McCormick who was one of the few who wasn't a hypocrite. He was a fine human being, not a bleeding-heart jerk. He was fired in 1958 and said they had asked him to sign a form that he had never carried messages in or out of the prison for inmates. He refused. McCormick would ask me every Sunday before he went into D-block if I had any messages for my friends. But I don't think he did or would carry any messages in or out of Alcatraz.

I had a couple of bad words with the pastor who was his replacement, since he insinuated that some of the charges against McCormick were true. This new man was a phony and should have been wearing a guard's uniform. I only talked to him once and didn't like this so-called man of God. Several guys, including Simcox and me, went to Reverend McCormick's services out of respect for him. He treated Simcox like a son and had tears in his eyes when he learned Simcox killed Gauvin.

I have read a couple of books by other Alcatraz inmates that say Simcox killed Gauvin over a homosexual relationship. Even Karpis said it in his book. But this is only what they heard, and rumors run rampant in jails. Rumors about sex, money, or murder are a good pastime. But I know exactly what happened, and I'm going to set the truth down once and for all. I participated in it by unintentionally providing the killing weapon. To this moment I'm ashamed. It is probably the worst thing I have ever done, and I can't describe the extent I'm sorry for what I did. ·

Gauvin was about 5'10" and weighed 150 pounds. He had black wavy hair, brown eyes, and was nice looking. He was well-liked by everybody and was in D-block serving as clean-up orderly for knifing a guy called "San Quentin Smitty." Simcox got mad at Gauvin in D-block for being too friendly with Bullock, who was black. Simcox kept shouting that Gauvin was a "fucking nigger-lover" and must be half black to associate with the vermin. So, one morning as he passed Simcox's cell, Gauvin spit in his face through the bars. From that second, Gauvin was doomed.

When I was trying to get Simcox to let it slide, he would say, "I tried man, but I can't. I thought I could, but the other day I saw him sweeping the floor when the D-door was open, and I started to boil. I know you like him, and if you want to quit talking to me, I'll understand but I must and I will kill that fucking son of a bitch."

Meanwhile, I kept talking to Simcox until I sounded like a broken record. I never worked so hard on anything. Even Gauvin's friends urged me to intervene. They kept saying, "He'll listen to you. He's your friend." But Simcox wouldn't listen and almost got mad at me because I kept after him. I told him to beat the hell out of Gauvin, to pound him into the concrete within a fraction of his life, but not to murder him. I tried to reason that killing him wouldn't prove anything.

I said, "Just spit in his face and break his arms and legs. But let him live. Hell, you started it!" Simcox would answer, "Hoppy, you just don't understand. Cutting his heart out will make me feel better! What the hell is wrong with you? He spit in my face over a lowlife nigger. I think about it day and night. I go to sleep thinking about it, I wake up thinking about it"

Then one day Skinhead called Gauvin into his office and started talking to him about a request he had made to get out of isolation. Skinhead later told me that Gauvin told him the trouble with Simcox was over and the deputy warden took him at his word. When Gauvin came back into D-block, he told me he had a rich aunt who had died and he was going to get a lot of money.

The next morning, June 6, 1957, he said Skinhead was letting him out of D-block, and he came by my cell to say goodbye. I told him not to go out into the yard, because he wouldn't live long. I said that I liked him and Simcox both, and that Simcox had already told me he hoped they would transfer Gauvin out of Alcatraz so he could avoid killing him. But Gauvin smiled and said, "Well, we will see what happens. I appreciate your concern, Hoppy." He was gone about an hour and a half when the D-block guard, named Robinson, shouted, "They're bringing in Simcox! He just stabbed Gauvin to death! He stabbed him in the shower room and split his heart wide open!"

My heart sank. In all my life I hadn't felt as low as I did that moment. In fact, the whole institution felt bad about it, even the guards, because they liked Gauvin, too. When Simcox was brought in, Larry Trumble asked, "What happened, Simcox?" And Simcox replied, "You know what the fuck happened, man. The guy threatened to kill me, and I beat him to it." Simcox later told me that when he saw Gauvin coming down the steps to the shower room, he went back and got his knife out of hiding and hid it under his belt.

FBI agents later testified that Simcox told them he hid the knife in his shoe. Simcox would not tell his interviewers how he got the knife downstairs, since it would have messed things up for the next guy who might want to try the same thing but there was no way the knife would have fit in his shoe, since it was more than 12 inches long and 1 ½ inches wide. In addition, it was ¼-inch thick. So, it was impossible to put such a thing into a shoe, let alone walk with it in there.

While Gauvin was taking a shower on the end next to the wicker wire, Simcox lit a cigarette, walked over to him, handed him the cigarette, and started talking. Three basement guards were present in the shower room, since they expected trouble. One walked up and said, "All right, Simcox, move on." Simcox said, "It's okay," and kept talking to Gauvin as Gauvin dried off and put on his shorts. Then suddenly Simcox pulled his knife and began stabbing Gauvin through the heart. It happened in a flash. When Simcox saw that Gauvin was finished, he walked away. But Gauvin got up and an inmate named Lewis put his hands on Gauvin's shoulders and asked, "Are you okay, kid?" and Gauvin whispered, "'Hell no, I'm not okay," and then fell to the floor.

Simcox told me that as he walked up the steps, he looked back and saw that Gauvin was bent over on his knees, looking up at him with hate in his eyes. Meanwhile, one of the basement guards was throwing rolls of toilet paper at Simcox, shouting, "Stop it! Stop it!" As Simcox was escorted into D-block by several guards, he stepped out far enough to look upstairs to where Larry Trumble and I were looking down. He had blood all over his right hand and wrist, and I suddenly felt sick. Goddamn it, I had furnished the fucking knife. But I also warned Gauvin not to go out into the yard that day. I urged him not to go back into the main population, since he might be transferred out of Alcatraz.

McKinney served as a witness for the defense and told the jury later that he overheard Gauvin tell Simcox in D-block that he was going to kill him. The jury found Simcox not guilty. Later, McKinney said that Gauvin's sister gave him such a sad look when he was testifying that he got a guilty feeling. Of course, McKinney was lying through his teeth. The judge then criticized the jury and told the jurors he would see to it they never again sat on another jury because their verdict of innocence was uncalled for and wrong. I learned later that Gauvin's people lived on Long Island and had money. Gauvin had a lot of courage and strength and was a better man than the guys who started rumors about him.

That summer I was transferred from a brief job in the library to the laundry and was assigned to the mangler, catching sheets as they came out and folding them up. It took two of us to do the job, and my partner was a guy from Hawaii called Pineapple Joe. He looked half-black and half-white, but he was considered white. He was a jam-up guy, my age, and built like a linebacker for the Green Bay Packers. Even most of the tough guys didn't want to tangle with him.

When we were caught up with our work, we would goof off until another load of sheets came through. Then we would walk back and forth and play tricks on each other, like kids do. I once loaded the end of a cigarette with match heads, then lit it and passed it to him. He took about three draws before it exploded, and instead of letting the cigarette drop from his mouth, he kept it there blown up and had us all laughing at him.

He often found notes to us from girls in the military clothes we laundered. One girl poured a whole bottle of perfume on a towel for us, and Pineapple Joe and I cut it in half. I cut my half in a bunch of pieces and shared them with my buddies. Even Karpis got a piece. I found a whistle once, and because it must have been made of brass and coated with stainless steel, I was able to walk right through the snitch box with it. At that time the snitch box wouldn't ring brass. But they later changed it so that it could.

But I had a lot of fun with the whistle I had found in the marine jacket. At night I would blow it as loud as I could, and a guard would come running around the corner looking for the source but I could see him in my mirror and kept one step ahead of him. It was a cheap laugh, but sometimes the cheaper the laugh, the better it is. I finally stopped when some of the guys started complaining I was messing with their sleep.

Red Winhoven was one of my best friends. He was a career bank robber and had the intelligence and the talent to be a success at anything he chose to do. He chose to rob banks. Red told me that once he was making an escape through some hilly woods one night after a bank job, and his partner dropped the brief case full of money, which slid on the rocks. He shot it full of holes, thinking he was being ambushed.

Most of the guys on the Rock had a knife, because you never knew when you would need it. Some of the knives were hidden in the library. Joe Carnes, who worked there, saw to it that these books were never checked out. Some knives were hidden in the bottom of toilets that had been cracked and resealed with soap. Some were hidden at the top of the bars by the slide box.

The hacks searched the library for Bullock's knife, but Jimmy Groves told me that he took it from Bullock and threw it over the wall in the direction of the water tower, where it probably lies today. This happened on a holiday, and the library was closed, so it's a mystery why the hacks thought it got into the library.

I had Red Winhoven make me a ten-inch knife out of brass in the industries. Even though it was a quarter-inch thick, I was able to walk right on through the snitch box with it, because it was brass. I gave it to Simcox to hide. Charlie Stegal was telling me on the yard that he went to court and lied for Simcox the time he stabbed Dog, but he said, "Well, at least I don't have to help Simcox now." And I said, "Yeah, I still feel bad about it, too." Jack Waites, who was standing nearby, said, "Hell, Charlie. You're the one who gave him the knife. No one else would give him a knife, because no one wanted Gauvin killed." I felt worse than ever.

Sugar Ray Robinson, the greatest fighter that ever lived, came through the laundry on a tour in July of that year and shook hands with Joe Schultz. Warden Madigan asked, "How many rounds do you think you could go with him, Joe?" Joe answered, "Give me six weeks' training and then see how many rounds he can go with me." Sugar Ray started laughing. He stopped and talked to all the inmates and told the sports reporters that he would dedicate his next fight to the boys on Alcatraz.

He was real popular with the guys out there, both black and white. Bill Russell, the basketball player, came through, too, and stood outside the mess hall as we returned to our cells. He looked about nineteen and kept staring at me. I guess he was wondering what I did to get there, since I looked about nineteen myself. I see him on TV today, and he looks like an old man. It just doesn't seem that long ago that he was there in the cell house.

During that summer, we were issued a rule book that served no purpose other than to stir up trouble. For example, we had no privileges, yet the book ordered us to do such stupid things as placing our shaving cup in a certain place on the shelf. It was really idiotic and had to be the brain child of Skinhead Latimer, since the warden wasn't that lame-brained.

Skinhead would go out of his way to stir up trouble so that it would feed his sadism. The first night a lot of guys started yelling and cursing and banging their bunks against the floor. Several tore their cells up. I set my rule book on fire and threw it out in the middle of the corridor. That started others doing it, and a whole lot more of the rule books came out on fire. The guards stayed on the ends of the cell house out of sight until we went to bed.

The second night of the strike, a young Indian named Red Wing, who celled above me, passed a small bomb down to me, tied to a string. This bomb was made out of match heads packed into a razor handle. I lit it and then threw it in front of the barber shop, but it never went off. Somehow, they traced it to Red Wing, and he spent a year in D-block for it. The hacks told him the FBI found his finger prints on it. But if they did, they would have found mine, too. I think somebody ratted.

The third day of the strike, Captain Rychner came through the laundry asking different guys what the problem was, and nobody wanted to talk about it. So, when he asked me, I said, "It's because you took Gunsmoke off the radio." Rychner, who took Captain Bergen's place as captain of the guards, said he liked Gunsmoke himself and saw no reason why we couldn't listen to it. He promised we could start listening to Gunsmoke that night. That afternoon they put notes on our cell beds to put our rule books on the library table when we came to breakfast the next morning. But nobody did, so they picked them up themselves. Rychner was a pretty decent fellow, and I liked him.

I had learned to make bombs by packing razor handles with match heads, like the one Red Wing made. In Atlanta I would put them under mop buckets under bunks and build small fires under them until they exploded like hand grenades. We heard through the grapevine that the warden asked the plumbing superintendent if there was any way we could plug up water pipes to make that kind of sound. I was never caught, but I brought my knowledge and experience of bomb making to the Rock, and once or twice a month for a while I would explode one, just to shake up the hacks. I think Skinhead suspected me but never said anything.

A "tush hog" at Alcatraz was a rough, tough, son of a bitch you couldn't whip. You had to kill him to stop him. Habacron was one of the worst tush hogs I ever met. He worked in the laundry with me and had already had his throat cut in Terra Haute by a buddy of mine. When he arrived on Alcatraz, he started to have trouble with some of Joe Schultz's friends. Schultz wanted to kill him "legally," so he picked a fight with him in the laundry and almost killed him before the guards pulled him off. But while Joe was being escorted up the steps into D-block, Habacron still had enough strength to jump Schultz's buddy Mike, who was pretty rough himself.

At that point, Allen West jumped on top of a table with some kind of a stick and started running his mouth. Joe Bentz walked up to the table, grabbed the stick out of his hand, and said, "Get down from there, you asshole. You ain't no leader." Pineapple Joe was standing next to me, and I told him how West used to pull stunts like that at Atlanta to make himself out like a hero. Joe said, "Yeah, West will run away and live to fight another day."

Well, the upshot was that Mike, Joe's friend, couldn't handle Habacron and took a solid beating. When Schultz was released from D-block a week later, he went to Habacron in the laundry and said, "You're going to hit me and Mike in the head with an iron pipe, huh?" Habacron asked, "Have you ever done anything to me?" Schultz answered, "Don't ask me if I've ever done anything to you. You're going to hit me in the head with an iron pipe!" Habacron said, "You're a lying motherfucker!" and threw a punch at Schultz.

Joe smiled, went into a crouch like Rocky Marciano, and countered with a left hook to Habacron's stomach that doubled him over. Then Schultz hit him with a right that knocked him into a tumbler with the door open. One guy shouted, "Turn the tumbler on!" But Schultz wouldn't do it. He let Habacron get out. Habacron came out swinging, but Joe blocked most of his punches and then knocked him down again. Habacron was bleeding so badly that Schultz offered to shake his hand and help him up. But Habacron tried to kick him. So, Schultz let him get up by himself then knocked him down again. The lieutenant had watched it all so that Habacron could get whipped, but he finally stepped in and broke it up. Later, Habacron, the ultimate tush hog on Alcatraz, jumped Mike for the second time.

As I mentioned when I emerged from D-block for the last time, I accused Lieutenant Ardway of trying to poison me. What happened was that one night I tore up my cell in hot anger. I don't even remember why but Lieutenant Mahan decided to put me in the hospital for observation rather than back in D-block. I tried to explain to Ardway and Mahan that I was having a recurring dream where I was in a boxing match and the referee would always wind up hitting me from behind with a black jack.

In the dream, I would also find myself talking to a horse that warned me I better watch out for Ardway, since he was tampering with my cell's water bottle, the type boxers use to rinse out their mouths with in between rounds. Because the dream was so real, I confronted Ardway about it. My accusation shook him up so much that he ordered several guards to observe me in the hospital's "big cell", a cell with a tiled floor, roof, and ceiling, but no fixtures.

Dr. Wolfson, who was in charge of the hospital, was a decent type of person who followed his medical oath and not the dictates of the custodial staff, and especially the deputy warden, like all the other prison doctors I had met. He wore $200 suits and looked like Clark Gable. He really tried to understand my increasing emotional outbursts. I explained that the outbursts were related to my dreams and that I wanted to return to the main population.

After observing me in the hospital for a few more days, he allowed me to return to the main cell house. But before I went down, I met with Wolfson and Dr. Whitsell, a psychiatrist, who advised me that I should be in an institution where prison psychiatrists could help me. Although I was leery about confiding in Dr. Whitsell, I wound up spending a good deal of time talking with him and a third San Francisco psychiatrist. Not only did they convince me to go to Springfield, where I probably should have been all along, but also put me on tranquilizers four times each day.

By the time I left Alcatraz, I had calmed down a lot and started thinking differently, so that I realized that Dr. Wolfson and Dr. Whitsell did me a big favor. If they hadn't helped me, I might still be in a prison somewhere. While I was in the hospital for observation, a lot of my friends were asking the elderly MTA on sick call how I was doing, and he was the only one who would tell them.

A few of my buddies came to visit me in the hospital, and Mr. York, an elderly guard who had started to work at Alcatraz when the place opened, would let them come back to the ward where I was under observation and talk to me for about ten minutes. I will never forget how nice Mr. York was and especially how he treated me. Because he was in his 70s, he was permanently assigned to hospital work.

While I was in the bug cage, I sometimes wouldn't eat or talk to any of the hacks. Mr. York would always leave a tray of food in the window, allowing me to make the decision later on if I wanted it. He did his job but tried to be as fair as he could. Whitey Franklin told me that Mr. York died right after I left Alcatraz. So did Dr. Wolfson. Both had heart attacks within a week of each other, and I felt a loss for both of them. Mr. York was more like a grandfather than a guard, and no inmate on Alcatraz disliked him. The deaths of Wolfson and York show once again that good men always go first.

One of my Indian friends named Kimo came to see me and apologized for beating up a young guy named Larry who was a buddy of mine. I said, "That's between you and him," because Kimo was my friend before Larry was.

Larry was a pathological liar, but he was likable and came to see me. Larry said he would help me break out of Alcatraz once he got out. I responded by saying, "I don't want to hear all that bullshit, man. This is why a lot of guys don't like you—you say crazy things." "Well," Larry said, "Fuck 'em. I'll break you out of jail whether you like it or not!" and then walked off. I told some of the other guys about it and they fell over laughing, saying he should be the one going to the nut house, not me. Another guy called "San Quentin Smitty" was sent to Springfield for not wearing any clothes because, he said, "Clothes always make my bones ache."

Talking about nut cases, I believe it was Joe Rivers who kept writing James V. Bennett, the director of US prisons, cursing him for vaccinating him in the ass with a twenty-penny nail. Rivers was later kept in 2-1 East, a wing for the real bad cases at Springfield. Howard Duncan, who had been on the Rock for about fifteen years, refused to go through the snitch box one day because he started screaming that it was wired to electrocute him. He was shipped off to Springfield.

A big black guy named DeLoach thought he was getting cancer by eating beef. I tried to explain that beef can't give you cancer, but pork can. I said, "Don't you know that pork always gives you trichinosis?" His eyes got wild and he asked, "Is that why every time I eat a piece of beef or pork, it knocks me on the floor?" He, too, made Springfield.

We had an elderly dentist on the Rock who would tire easily and come into the hospital to take a short nap. One day, Mr. York smelled alcohol on his breath, and while he was napping, he looked inside his briefcase and found a bottle of whiskey. The dentist was fired. That dentist fixed several of my teeth, and he always took his time and tried to do them right, unlike most prison medical workers, who couldn't care less if you died. Losing that dentist was a loss for the inmates. The first time he put a medicated filling in my tooth, I complained to Karpis about him calling me back and forth to the dentist's chair. Karpis said, "The dentist is treating your tooth so you won't lose it." I didn't realize that.

I was glad to learn I would soon be leaving the island but, in a way, I felt like I was leaving home. I had mixed feelings about it, because I had a lot of friends I didn't like leaving behind. But Skinhead was one son of a bitch I was glad to get away from.

CHAPTER EIGHT

SCREWING WITH THE MAFIA

"If God's designs are impenetrable, it is possible that he punishes what you call 'good' and rewards what you call 'evil'."
—Cocteau, Bacchus, Act II, Scene 4

I was surprised to see who was being escorted from their cells down in the basement for processing out of Alcatraz to Springfield. No one knew except the person involved that he was leaving, so it came as a surprise to see Joe Schultz, Alvin Karpis, Cricket, Johnny Iozza, Morton Sobell, and a few other buddies. It was a large group, and I was glad of the company for the long journey to Missouri.

We left Alcatraz about five in the morning, and I remember distinctly how the boat rocked in the water. But I can't say if it was storming. Karpis, who was on that same boat, said it was. I was so full of tranquilizers that I didn't notice much and so was Schultz. He was like a mad bull and didn't calm down at all. He kept cursing out everybody on the boat and later on the train.

We were bused from Fort Mason in San Francisco across the Bay Bridge to the Oakland train terminal, where we boarded a train with the special coach for inmates. Schultz was in the first seat, I was in the second, and Karpis sat in the third. Joe heard me telling Karpis not to feel bad about the things he was saying to him. So, the next time Joe turned around and started to curse, he looked at Karpis (who we called "Ray") and said, "I'm not talking to you, Ray."

Karpis responded, "I know, Joe."

Then Karpis told me how it took him 22 years to get away from Alcatraz and he was glad to see "you kids get away from it, too." Then he handed me a message for Harry Campbell, one of the members of his gang, who was the prison's shoemaker at Springfield. Harry made parole in

1959, and all his bitterness had by that time disappeared. I know he was a success after he got out.

All the guys on the train ignored Schultz and talked about how they intended to walk alone and never look back on their Alcatraz days. One guy said, "I used to knock them down and walk around them but now I'm just going to walk around them." Schultz commented, "Well, I'm gonna keep hitting them on the jaw and they are going to keep going down." On that train ride to Springfield, the lieutenant, who may have been Simpson, was telling us how he ran his family on a democratic basis.

For example, his family would actually vote on what television program they would watch. Sobell, the Atomic Spy, had to pass Schultz in order to get to the train's toilet. As he passed, he walked like a bird around a cat, but Joe never bothered him. He was more interested in the big guys and the bullies. As I've said, Schultz was really a good-hearted person who respected authority. But like so many others including myself, he had a certain kink in his brain that sent him in the wrong direction. On that trip to Springfield, once he cooled down, he told me that when he got out, he was going to stay out. Then he told a guard who stopped to listen how I had been locked up for the past eleven years and knew that I wouldn't be back.

The Springfield Medical Center for federal prisoners was for medical and mental patients and was built partly underground, with tunnel passageways. One section was the heavy security wing, and guys from the Rock were put in that area, called 10-North. We were kept there until the doctors said we were ready for the open wards, where no doors or gates were ever locked. In 10 Building, only the 10-A guys were allowed to go into the dining room. 10-G, D, C, F, E, and B ate in their own wards and were locked up at all times except when watching television in the day room at designated times. Like I said, 10-North held most of the ex-Alcatraz inmates, while 10-E was for homosexuals and those men who looked just like women.

I was assigned to the dining room area, cleaning off tables and refilling the coffee and tea pots, and one morning some of the black guys working in the back of the kitchen asked me to go to a table and ask a guy if he was the famous rock and roll singer Chuck Berry. I looked at the table and recognized him at once. So, I went to his table and said, "You're Chuck Berry, right?" And he said, "Uh-huh." He was so popular at the time that be had six or seven rock and roll hits. He was the black Elvis Presley. Chuck was assigned to the PC camp, which was part of Eight Building, a medical ward. The PC guys were there to do the work for the mental patients. Chuck was doing a three-year sentence for taking a fourteen-year-old girl across the state line for "immoral purposes." He got a five-year sentence first, but appealed and ended up with the three years that he had to do. Chuck was about 6'3" and carried himself with dignity, kept his hair slicked back, and talked very little.

One day after cleaning up the noon meal trays in the dining hall, he and I were waiting for the yard door to open so we could go to the recreation yard. Chuck got to teasing a sissy named Jackie who looked like a girl and actually believed he was. Jackie ran the music room and played records on the yard and over the radio. He tape-recorded the first concert Chuck put on for us and played it on the yard a lot.

On that day, Jackie got mad at Chuck because Chuck spurned his love, and he started mouthing that Chuck couldn't sing and that his album One Dozen Berries was a dud. To me, Jackie sounded like a woman scorned. Chuck just laughed and went on about his business. The incident was no big deal but it showed how nice Chuck was. Another guy might have knifed Jackie.

On another occasion, I was walking behind Chuck on the yard and watched him light a cigarette, then wait until he got to a garbage can before disposing of the match. I told my walking buddy, an Indian from Alaska, that Chuck showed presence of mind and a little class. My friend laughed and said, "Yeah, he ain't no bum. He always walks alone and acts like he respects himself and the planet." I figured he was doing hard time, but later I came to understand that Chuck was like most of the rest of us: we can't find peace of mind, and money can't buy us happiness. In fact, the only time I saw Chuck act happy was when he was playing guitar on the yard or performing for us. He seemed to be the happiest when he was doing comedy sketches for us, like when he wrote a letter from home to himself which he then read. That showed one more aspect of his overall talent.

Chuck teamed with a white inmate guitar player and introduced him to us as his twin brother. He could be funny when he wanted to but, when you lived around him, it just didn't seem to fit him. He was like Jekyll and Hyde. I talked to him briefly a couple of times when we left the dining room at the same time and headed in the same direction but he acted like a man detached and unhappy. I rarely saw him talk to anyone.

One day while working in the dining room, Chuck was standing at his steamtable ready to serve, just staring at the food, and a black guy asked, "You think you gonna make it, Chuck?" And Chuck said, "Whatta you mean? Hell, yes I'm going to make it." The guy tried to explain what he meant, and Berry said, "It's none of your business if I make it or not. Don't bother me!" He didn't talk to me much after that, although he seemed to like me.

One day he was sitting with me and Garcia, a Puerto Rican buddy of mine, just listening as we bullshitted, when a big black guy from the PC camp came up and said, "It takes a sorry motherfucker to put soap in milk." What had happened was that Garcia and I would always place a pitcher of milk in the ice chip box for our friends to drink at lunch. But the pitcher of milk kept disappearing. So, Garcia and I poured liquid soup in it.

Garcia, who smoked cigars constantly and had a wicked fight scar across his face, spoke English fluently, but Garcia didn't get along well with blacks unless they spoke Spanish. American blacks he hated with a passion. He was from Puerto Rico but lived in New York and was doing time for drug-dealing. The two of us and a Mexican named Morales worked in the dining room and stuck together.

Garcia looked up at the big black guy, stood up, and said. "l put the soap in it, not Hoppy. Now what are you going to do about it, you ugly shit-looking cocksucker?" The black guy said, "Well, I just want to say that I think it's chicken shit." Garcia said, "Look, we put the milk there for our friends. You steal it. If I had rat poison, believe me, I would have put rat poison in the milk and not liquid soap. Now what you gonna do about it?"

And the big guy said, "Well, I don't like you no way, Chico, because you don't like your own kind." And Chico said, "No I don't, because they ratted me out and that's why I'm here. And I'll tell you something else. You got big muscles, but I got something that will tear your muscles all to hell." At that point, Chuck Berry got up and moved away from us. The black guy then started saying he didn't want any trouble.

One day while Chuck was walking the yard by himself, acting like he was in deep thought, he stopped to watch a couple of white guys play the guitar. They asked him to play with them, and he said he would if they could get a better guitar. He said he couldn't get the true sound out of the ones they were using, so they found him one. Chuck started picking and singing the blues right then and there. The staff had him do a number of concerts for us, and he did them on the baseball diamond using amplifiers and a couple of white guitar players to back him up. They were all very good shows. He always did his famous duck walk on the clay diamond, followed by hilarious comedy sketches. He was truly a different person when he performed for us.

I watched an interview with Keith Richards of the Rolling Stones recently, and his opinion of Chuck Berry today is the same Chuck Berry I knew in jail, so it must have been his personality and not that he felt superior to the inmates. But with us it was always the same: I would pour out a ton of words and he would answer with a trickle. We were both going to night school to get our high school diplomas, and one night, as we waited for a movie to start, he came over and sat down by me and asked, "What's the movie going to be?" and offered me a cigarette. That was the last time I ever talked to him.

I went to night school for most of the time I was in Springfield and brought my education level up from the sixth grade to the tenth. I had a math teacher who was a whiz with a piece of chalk. But when I would ask him exactly why an algebra problem worked the way it did, he couldn't explain and would end up saying that some things just work the way they do and you have to learn to accept them. I responded that I will never accept anything I don't understand. When I said things like that, he would get irritated. He taught high school during the day and came to us at night.

The guy had a master's degree in math and art and showed us a modern painting entitled, *Nude Descending the Stairs*. I started laughing. When he finished his lecture, he asked, "What were you laughing about, Hopkins?" And I said, "It looked like a pile of lumber to me." He retorted, "That's because you don't understand abstract art." I said, "Do you know what Hitler said about abstract art?" And he said, "No, tell the class." I said, "Well, Hitler said that works of art that need a swollen set of instructions to prove their right to exist will no longer be allowed to reach the neurotics and morons who are receptive to such stupid nonsense. Artists who paint such garbage will be given eye tests, and if their eyes pass, they will be charged with fraud on the public and then sent off to the Russian Front." He said, "That sounds more like it came from somebody with a mental problem." I agreed, because by that time Herr Hitler didn't impress me anymore. But I must admit, our teacher taught me a lot about math and other general studies.

I got along well in Springfield and wasn't disciplined for anything other than fighting. Springfield was like being at home compared to the Rock. My whole attitude changed for the better, and I'm glad today that I was transferred. If it wasn't for Dr. Wolfson I would either be in jail or dead. And I liked the concept of Springfield, that is, what Springfield was supposed to do. When you had no hope in other federal institutions, when you lost all hope of ever being treated as a human being and of being punished in a humane way, Springfield would start the juices of life flowing again. I found myself feeling feelings again.

In June 1959, the inmates in blocks 10-G and E took control of the medical facility and seized several guards as hostages. The ring leader was a guy from Alcatraz named Earl Taylor. I was in 10-A, but the rioters never got to our block, and I was glad, since I wanted no part of it. I could hear the tank as it knocked a hole through the brick wall late that evening. The guards poured through the hole and beat the inmates with clubs, and one guy died of head injuries.

As I mentioned, the 10-North section was for violent or way-out patients, and the day they seized the guards in 10-G, we woke up in 10-A without the radio on and were kept locked in our rooms all day without food. We didn't know what was going on until 4:00 in the afternoon, when I heard the tank battering the side of 10-G. Then we found out that Earl Taylor and George Littlefield, my good friend from Atlanta, had seized control of 10-G, 10-F, and 10-E and beat the hell out of one guard they didn't like. My unit was separated from them by two gates across a corridor, and they didn't have a key. I wouldn't have joined them anyway, because by that time I had already begun to change and was nearing release.

Everyone involved in the takeover got beat on, and Dr. Anderson, a psychiatrist, started criticizing the rough ways of the guards after he treated some of the inmates for head injuries. He was immediately ordered by the superintendent, who was a doctor himself, to cool it and let the riot die down. The patients were not allowed to talk about it either, since one guy died from the beating. Nothing was ever done about it and no guard was reprimanded or dismissed.

At Springfield, you couldn't always tell if an inmate was a real mental case. Most of the guys appeared to be normal in most ways. For example, one guy who was a permanent fixture there wore a homemade army colonel's uniform because he said he had just assumed control of a nearby military base. Every minute of every day he issued orders for the military takeover of the country. But talking to him at mealtime, you'd think he was sensible.

One real military officer was there for shooting two other military men who had been teasing him about his wife. He would sit at a table alone, if one was available, or sometimes with me, since I ate alone a lot, too. In the main dining room, you could leave at any time you wanted and go back to your room alone, but he would always ask me if he could be excused before he would get up and leave the table.

One guy named Red Emory came there from the Rock in 1939 and was still in 10-North, although he was really out of it. He thought witch hornets were "persecuting" him, and he would try to sling them off with his fingers. If they got in his mouth, he would chew them up. We had a lot of laughs at Red's expense, even though we knew he shouldn't be laughed at. He tied strings on weather balloon parachutes and I was supposed to be his inspector. Every time I gave him one back, he would tell me to make the goddamn witch hornets leave him alone. Then he would start mumbling to them in a way you couldn't understand. His mumbling disturbed the other guys in 10-G when they were watching TV.

Red Emory was doing time for bank robbery and murder. One of the foremen in the Springfield industries told me Red had been a bad character when he was young and he had spent his first few years on the island in dead-lock status for assaulting guards. You could tell he had been a powerful man at one time.

Whitey Franklin told me in Atlanta that Red was in good shape when he left the Rock, so the Springfield environment may have made him crazy. I felt sorry for him. One day in 10-G I was in front of him in the chow line and he said I had cut in front of him the day before. He wasn't too coherent about what he was saying, and I knew it was in his mind, so I said, "Okay, Red, I won't do it again, I promise." A guy who would have fled from Red if he had been around when Red was a younger man said to me, "I ought to knock the hell out of him." I said it would be cowardly to take advantage of a guy in bad physical and mental health, the way Red was. Even though he was insane, Red was still more of a man than most of the Springfield jerks were.

An Indian from the Sioux reservation named Bad Horse had been there a long time, too. He probably killed someone back home. The yard had a circle of asphalt to walk on, and Bad Horse would walk around and around that circle, saying nothing to anyone. If somebody walking the opposite way was in his way, he would stomp his foot until you moved over and let him by. He was in 22-East, which was for totally insane guys like him.

Another Indian called Toney was on my ward and he never talked either, but could follow what you said to him.

Just before it would rain, he would always go to the sink, wash his hands, and get water all over him. Another Indian, an Apache named Chinchi who probably fought alongside Geronimo was so old that there was no record of his age. He was in the medical ward where I was assigned to clean the corridor, but I would always clean his room, too. I didn't have to, because it was his place to do it, but he was at least a hundred years old and I felt sorry for him. He had pride and self-respect and was still fierce and defiant, just like Geronimo. Some guys would try to humor him, but he didn't want any sympathy. Every day he would spend 30 minutes shaving himself and, in spite of his age, he walked without help or a cane.

An elderly black man known as Captain John was on 22-East and had been in the prison system since the turn of the century. When I talked to him, he showed no signs of being crazy. I asked him one day how old he was, and he said, "I was born in 1872. That ought to give you an idea of how old I am." He helped build Leavenworth Prison and always referred to it as the "new place." He told me the same story the Birdman did about Jack Johnson, the heavyweight champion of the world, eating a cat that an inmate sold him for a coon when he was in Leavenworth doing five years for taking a woman across the state lines. He said Jack pushed cement around in a wheel barrow while helping build Leavenworth.

In October 1959, I threatened a guy on 10-A, saying I would kick his head off, and the guy told a guard who in turn told the doctor who ordered me in 2-East. He had me scheduled for electro-shock therapy, but I told Doctor Anderson, who was in charge of the treatment, that I didn't need it. He explained to me that there was nothing wrong with it and that it was beneficial to a lot of people. I said I didn't want to be one of them, pointing to another patient being pushed by my room on a gurney, mumbling like crazy after getting a shock. Dr. Anderson finally sent me back to 10-A without going through it.

A couple of months later I was told by a board of doctors, after my second fight in a week, that I would get shock treatment if I continued fighting. I knocked one guy into Chuck Berry at the steam table for cursing me. He was in the PC camp and assigned to the kitchen. He told the lieutenants that I jumped him for nothing. The lieutenant said that because they had to restrain me, it made it look bad on me. A Mexican buddy of mine who worked the dining room told me that Garcia was now cursing that guy out every time he brought bread to the dining room. He would say, "Why don't you do something so I can kill you?" and the guy would ignore him. He was black, too. Garcia was a medical patient, so they couldn't do much to him.

One black named Jessie, housed on 10-A, looked just like Mr. Clean on the detergent bottle with his shaved head. But he was a Black Muslim and his mind was kept in a constant turmoil by the rhetoric put out by Elijah Muhammad. Other than that, he was a likable guy. He heard me telling some blacks in the TV room that the Civil War was fought over economics, that the North couldn't compete with the South on the European market because of free labor.

He started telling them how right I was and that I was the first white who was smart and honest enough to say it. From then on, he liked me. He said that some blacks deserved the treatment they got for being so stupid and watching TV all the time instead of going to night school like he and I were doing. He didn't like gays, and if one was moved to our unit, he would give them a hard time in order to make them move out.

Jessie was light-skinned and built like Hercules. He would have done better if he had left the Black Muslim literature alone, since he tried to follow their ideas about the white man being a devil. Yet, at the same time, he was smart enough to know it wasn't true. Jessie drew $230 a month from the army for his mental condition. He hated democracy and preached communism all the time and liked to make people mad by saying, "Hurry, Khruschev!" and "October 25th!"

Jessie would tell the guards that the money they were making and trying to save would be worthless after the communist revolution, since the new power structure would devalue the currency. He made a statue of a Muslim half star with a sword and the words, "Freedom, Justice, and

Equality," and it was displayed in the craft shop window. One guy on our ward asked, "What does that sword represent, Jessie?" He answered, "That's the sword that's going to cut your motherfucking head off after the revolution!"

We had a couple of homos on our ward. One night in the TV room I ran my mouth at one of them and he said, "My old man won't like it when I tell him what you said to me." His "old man" was a big weight lifter. Jessie, as I said, didn't like homos and didn't want any on our ward. Although he hated white people, he liked me, and one day he said, "I think you're okay for a white guy." Jessie was doing thirty years for bank robbery and assault.

I found that at Springfield and other institutions, the reputation of being on Alcatraz opened doors for you among the inmate population and you were treated with more respect. I had a lot of inmates, and a couple of guards, ask me about the bullshit stories put out mainly through movies about the way Capone was treated on the Rock by the inmates. I always told them what the old-timers told me: "He was a mean son of a bitch.

Karpis said he was about my height, which is 5'8", but weighed two hundred pounds and was built like a tank and scared of nothing." Both Blackie Audene and Jimmy Groves told me that when Jimmy Lucas tried to stab Capone in the basement as they all played instruments, Capone got a nick on his arm, then picked up a guitar and beat Lucas to the floor. Lucas tried to kill Capone in order to get publicity. A guard showed Whitey Franklin a statement Lucas made against him in the killing of a guard in their escape attempt, and Whitey said Lucas was sick.

In 1959, Reverend McCormick at Alcatraz went on a speaking tour and let it be known how the Birdman was being treated. Because of that, the US Bureau of Prisons transferred him to the medical center at Springfield and put him in the general population for the first time since President Woodrow Wilson commuted his death sentence. Bob hadn't been there long when a movie was made about his life, and Burt Lancaster, the movie actor, came to Springfield and asked to see him but was refused.

So, Lancaster tried to leave him some money and was told he couldn't do that, either. The superintendent told the news media he couldn't understand how some people could make a hero out of a hardened killer like Stroud.

The Birdman was good at making leather goods and, about three weeks before being released, I asked him to make me a case for my sun glasses. He offered me his, because he said he wasn't making things in the craft shop anymore, but I wouldn't take it. I was released September 20, 1963 and he died November 21, 1963, almost exactly eight weeks later.

I saw in the news that he was dead from cancer. I couldn't believe it. He looked so healthy just two months before. I have heard a lot of negative things said about him, especially by guards and prison officials, but I found him to be a proud and defiant man, and most of the guys who talked about him didn't know him that well.

I went to work in the Springfield industries in September 1958 and stayed in that job until my transfer in 1961. I had accumulated about eight months extra time off my sentence, plus the assignment was real good therapy for me. Along with the medication I was taking, I started to change a lot of my ways of thinking. I wasn't fighting anymore and felt a whole lot less angry.

But my buddy Joe Schultz was still angry and fighting. When he first arrived at Springfield with me, he got into fights, a whole lot of fights, and when I left, he was still fighting. Joe fought with anyone and especially enjoyed fighting black inmates. The reputation he brought with him from Alcatraz didn't help matters, either. Even though most of the inmates walked around him, the real sickos managed to find him, and a fight would ensue.

Interestingly, the more he fought. the less insane he grew. His bouts with depression lessened, and by 1961 he was almost back to his old ugly and mean self. No one was ever killed fighting Joe Schultz, although you could string a Christmas tree with the teeth he knocked out. When I was transferred to Atlanta, I gave him an autographed picture I had of Ralph Dupas, a top-ten boxer I knew from the gym in Miami. I still think of

Schultz often and hope everything turned out all right, because he really was a guy who deserved it.

In the spring of 1960, I asked to be transferred to Atlanta, and Doctor Herman told the board he didn't advise it. But the administration transferred me anyway. I laid over in isolation at Leavenworth for two weeks, and several guys from the Rock were there. They sent me cigarettes and whatever I needed. If you're the right kind of guy, that's the way it goes with your friends.

Jimmy Groves had just been transferred there after 26 years on the Rock, and he told me he wasn't happy and would rather go back to the Rock. About seven months later, he killed himself by somehow sticking a knife through his own heart during the night in a cell he had all alone. I felt bad about it because he, too, was a decent guy. I'll never forget Jimmy.

When I appeared before the classification board in Atlanta, I asked about getting a single cell, and the deputy warden, who was there when I left for Alcatraz, made fun of me by saying I should have brought my single cell on Alcatraz with me. That comment really got me off to a bad start. Most of the guys that were there when I left were gone, but word got around that I had come back from the Rock, and I was accepted like an old buddy.

I got a job in the Atlanta industries, since I had already had a similar one at Springfield, but I couldn't stand the laundry lint or the noises of the machines. I was assigned to yard clean-up, and my attitude started getting bad again. I cursed out the clothing room guard but the deputy warden in charge of corrections didn't punish me. He only locked me with full meals for a week then talked to me about it. I told him I wanted to work in the plumbing shop, so he sent me to take a test for it, and the superintendent in charge of trade schools told me I failed the test but that he would put me in the plumbing shop anyway.

Mr. York, the deputy warden, had told him he wanted me in the plumbing shop, and he was the boss. I enjoyed going all over the institution, doing repair work. A guy named Johnson who was a plumber on the streets worked with me, and he would let me do the job while he told me what to do. We would visit guys in cells and drink coffee and go under the basement of the dining room to watch guys with similar jobs cook steaks. There is a space underneath the kitchen in Atlanta that is deep enough to stand, and a lot of stolen steaks were cooked under there.

Before I first left Atlanta for the Rock in 1954, I was in a cell with George Darby and three other guys. George was hard on anybody he found out was talking to the authorities. He forced several to move out of our cell. When I returned after leaving the Rock, he had everybody in his cell sign a request to the deputy warden, asking that I be placed in their cell after orientation.

George had one guy in his cell who he liked but who I couldn't bring myself to trust. I have always been good at spotting squealers, and about four months later, a new guy showed Darby a news clipping on this guy that said he had testified against his rap partner. Darby took it to the guy and said, "Read this." The guy said, "Wait a minute. Let me explain," and began saying he had to testify because his wife was pregnant. Darby said, "You motherfucker! I don't care if your mother was pregnant. You don't put people in jail. And, I'll tell you something else. Don't let the door close on you tonight. You be out of our cell."

I was in the plumbing shop at the time, and we had a big guy working in there who I thought was a rat. He was telling some of the plumbers what he would do if anybody set his stuff outside the cell door like Darby had done. Several guys and I said, "Where we came from, they don't set people's stuff outside their cell. They throw them off the tier!" He never made any more comments. Most of the guys in plumbing stayed out of trouble.

Later, Vito Genovese's chief lieutenant, DiPalermo, who ran the tool room and issued tools to the plumbers, told me he liked the way I handled myself. He said, "You got style, man, and that's lacking in most of these jerks." The guard who ran the plumbing shop was a master plumber but also a guard, and he used to watch me when I would be running down rats or making antiestablishment statements but never said a word to me. I knew he was probably making bad reports on me, but at the time I didn't care that much.

In 1953 and 1954, I had run with an Atlanta prison clique, prison slang for gang, and we looked out for each other the way blacks in prison look out for each other today. In fact, we beat the shit out of a black named Jimmy Davenport who had boxed as a heavyweight on the streets. In 1961, a huge black guy just like Davenport, who worked in the kitchen basement, was bullying a small guy, so the little guy and his friend, who worked in the kitchen, caught the black guy leaning over a barrel of pickles and hit him on the head with an iron pipe.

While he was unconscious, they stabbed him to death. The killing went unsolved for a couple of weeks. But I knew who had done it, because I told them how not to give him the opportunity to hurt them. I told them not to give him the same break he wouldn't give them. When they were finally charged with his death, I told them to take the stand and tell the jury how big guys like him tried to sexually molest young guys, and that they were just defending themselves.

This is exactly what they did, and the jury found them guilty of involuntary manslaughter. They got off with a three-year sentence. One guy named Cox who knew what I had advised them to say started calling me "professor." This may have been what the deputy warden had in mind when he told me I knew how to go about starting trouble, and he would send my ass back to the Rock soon enough. Although he never mentioned it to me, talk gets around in prison, and that's why the fewer people who know about your business, the better. The right kind of guys don't want to know your business unless they are involved.

In Atlanta, the laundry was joined to the clothing room by a tunnel, and the clothes were transported back and forth through it. In the summer of 1954, a guy named Gross stabbed a bully in the tunnel, threw his body in a clothing basket, pushed it off to the side, and covered it with clothes. He bumped into another guy while moving the body and said, "Sorry, man, excuse me," and was sincere in his apology for accidentally bumping the guy.

Red Royal, a buddy of mine in Atlanta in 1954, was classified by the prison psychologist as psychotic. Red was transferred to Leavenworth instead of Springfield, and within a month he killed Larry Trumble's rap partner. The officials couldn't try him for it because of the diagnosis and classification made on him in Atlanta. He was still in Springfield with the 1954 murder charge when I was released, ten years later. Red had a P-number, which meant he was not able to stand trial.

To talk to him, you would never think he was a mental case. The two of us hung around together a lot in Atlanta, and when Red was transferred, he seemed normal enough to me but I was told by an inmate office worker that he had been recommended for psychiatric care. I think he told the psychiatrist in Atlanta that he felt like killing somebody. The same office worker gave a friend of mine a psychological report about me that stated that I appeared to have developed higher than average intellectual functions. It also stated that I was the type of personality who wanted to change the world, and that I was under the impression I would be disposed of in the same manner as John Dillinger.

I didn't know very much about the German World War II spy Erich Gempel at Atlanta. I think he landed in Canada from a submarine with three or four other saboteurs, and he came to Atlanta in 1954 from Alcatraz. I talked to him a lot, and he told me that he was under direct military orders from Hitler to spy on America and, if he had had a choice, he wouldn't have come. He spoke fluent English and looked a lot like former Supreme Court Justice Warren Burger. He was about 6'2", weighed about 200 pounds, and looked younger than his age. He had silver-gray hair and showed a lot of class in the way he handled himself. Erich liked to read and went to the library a lot. He told me that I was a typical looking German.

He, I, and another guy ended up in the hole together in 1955 when I was waiting for transfer to the Rock. But the other guy wasn't too strong and couldn't stand to be locked up. I explained he could get a fever by eating soap, so he ended up eating a whole bar of soap while making all kinds of faces doing it. The guy wasn't very smart, either. But it gave

Gempel and me a good laugh. After he had eaten about half the bar, he asked Gempel if it would really work. Gempel said, "Yeah, but it may take more for you than for someone else." The guy ate the whole bar of soap and, of course, never got a fever. All he got was the urge to throw up.

Gempel was thrown in with us for refusing to give up a lower bunk to an inmate whom the prison doctor had specified should receive the lower bunk. He was called in and reprimanded. When he returned to the hole, he said he told the associate warden he insisted on returning to Alcatraz. "I been here two years and I can't make it here!" he shouted at us.

A guard opened our solid front door and told him to cool down and not say anything further, because he had overheard the associate warden say they were drawing up papers to return him to West Germany. In January 1955, Gempel's time was cut to what was served, and he was finally deported.

In all prisons, about 60 percent of the trouble is sex-related, and the rest is started over gambling or by stir-crazy psychos over stupid little things. The first week I was back in Atlanta, I challenged a guy in an eight-man cell for staring at me, and he said he wasn't. He probably wasn't. But I was a bit looney then and very, very paranoid. A couple of days later, an Italian buddy of mine, who was a little psycho himself, challenged the same guy about staring at him, and the guy said, "Goddamn, I'm getting out of this cell today. You fucking guys are crazy. I'm the only sane one in here." And Tony, my friend, said, "You better get the fuck out of here and don't even be staring at me or Hoppy again. And believe me, you're the crazy one in here. Not me and Hoppy."

Meanwhile, word got back to us in Atlanta that George Littlefield was still in segregation at Springfield because he led the hostage takeover in 1959. He was young and good looking, and since he was in segregation, as were many of the Springfield sissies, the sissies were after him. I had to laugh at that.

When George and I were in Springfield in the early 1950s, the sissies would ask him to fix me up with them. But George would tell them that I was a sex maniac convicted of cutting off men's dicks. He said he told the sissies he would ask me anyway, because I was missing something good. He beat one guy up in the tunnel for cursing me out for not going over.

Johnny Iozza was doing all right at Atlanta and was scheduled to be released soon. He boxed in competition at Atlanta and knocked out all but two of his opponents. Word reached him that Frankie Carbo, one of the mobsters who controlled boxing in New York, wanted him to contact him once he was released. Johnny told me, "I sent word back that I respected his interest in me, but I was retiring from boxing to become a cop."

JOHNNY IOZZA

Before Johnny's reputation got around Atlanta, one muscle-bound Yankee guy with an attitude problem went to the front of the line in the mess hall, and Johnny said, "Hey buddy, the line forms at the rear." The guy looked at Johnny and said, "Go get fucked." So, Johnny waited until he got through the line and had room to fight, and went up to the guy. They started swinging, and John knocked him out cold with the first punch he landed on the guy's jaw.

A week later John fought two black guys on the Atlanta yard, and the guys who saw it said John hit one of them so hard it spun him around and his watch flew off his arm. Schultz said to me one time, "Big John is a tank and you're the pilot." In other words, Johnny would listen to my suggestions. I was bad about listening to other people back then myself, and it caused me a lot of trouble. Today I don't listen to anyone. I think counselors are for people who are either weak-minded, can't think for themselves, or like to wallow around in self-pity.

Lots of people have a self-pity problem. I have tried to teach my daughter Lisa, since she was two years old, to do things for herself and never feel sorry for herself. When she was eight years old, I let her change a flat tire for me on the side of the road, and today she doesn't depend on a man to do it for her.

Wherever I was in the federal penitentiary system, whether in Lewisburg, Atlanta, Leavenworth, or Alcatraz, I mingled in one way or another with mobsters from crime families. We all knew who was who, and it made absolutely no difference if he was a member of the Bonanno family, Lucchese, Gambino, Genovese, Patriarca, Magaddino, or Marcello. I heard there were probably 6,000 or 7,000 members of twenty or thirty families throughout the country, and at least a quarter of them were in various federal prisons for one thing or another.

At Atlanta in the early 1960s, I would say there were at least 75 Mafia-connected figures. I didn't pay much attention to any of them, because they kept to themselves and left the other inmates alone. They served their time quietly and generally carried themselves with confidence and dignity. If you respected them, they respected you. They certainly weren't into the childish bullshit of fighting, stealing, being angry, or fucking with the guards and administration. They had two major intents: one was to conduct business as usual from their penitentiary cells, and the other was to get the hell out as soon as possible.

The Mafia guys I got to know pretty well and who seemed to like and trust me were Johnny DioGuardia, Frank Costello, Vito Genovese, and Joe DiPalermo. For each of them I did minor things like smuggling or delivering messages. If something needed to be stolen or information gotten about someone, I'd handle it. They paid me in various ways, and I got to be accepted in their circles. They talked freely in my presence until it got serious, and then they would switch from speaking English to the Sicilian or Calabrese dialect of Italian.

Several of the Mafia friends I made had Italian friends who wouldn't say a word to me, even if I were with their buddies. Johnny Iozza told me, "Those are the wops who give made guys a bad name. They only associate with their own kind. I've told them, 'When you see my friend walking with me, you say hello to him, too!'" But they wouldn't do it. Johnny said he didn't like those kinds of Italians. One guy Iozza especially didn't like looked exactly like Sammy "The Bull" Gravano, the mobster who ratted on his boss, John Gotti. This guy's hair was slick and parted on the side, the same way Gravano parted his hair. They could have been twins, as far as I was concerned. But this guy stayed out of trouble, although I felt that if anyone ever gave him any shit, he would throw him off the tier.

One Mafia figure, a guy who had changed his name to K.O. Kornenberg, was beaten up by a guard and the mobster actually sued the guard in federal court but in court, all the other guards swore under oath that the mobster was beaten up by other inmates and not by the guard. The judge in the case said he believed a lot of perjury had been committed, but that there was nothing he could do about it since there was no proof.

Well, Kornenberg had his associates on the outside trace the guard's address. They then took pictures of the guard's wife and kids, playing in the front yard, around the neighborhood, and at school. Kornenberg then showed the guard the photos. The guard was in shock for days and from then on, Kornenberg regularly asked the guard, "How's the wife and kids?" Kornenberg and the other Italians never had any problems from that guard or any of his friends ever again.

I liked Johnny DioGuardia a lot. "Johnny Dio," as we called him, was a soldier in the Thomas Lucchese crime family. He had a brother, Tommy, whom he used to visit, and they talked about their "investments." They were the nephews of James "Jimmy Doyle" Plumeri, a captain in the Carmine Tramunti family. I read that he was murdered in 1971 because of some mob war going on in New York. But Johnny was known around Atlanta for making headlines in 1955 when he had a newspaper man blinded for writing bad columns about him. All the guys I knew applauded him, because they had all experienced how some reporters exaggerated small incidents or minor facts way out of proportion to get sensational stories. In the early 1960s I didn't care much for newspaper men, either, but I can't say I wanted any of them blinded.

To look at Johnny Dio and watch his actions, you wouldn't think he committed the mob murders and other crimes he was accused of. He always donated money to inmate welfare funds and was a big contributor to the United Way. I noticed he was always touched by tear-jerking movies. But he wasn't all that popular with the inmates who thought for themselves, because he had a huge ego and let a crew of Italian guys do things for him.

One day a buddy of mine named Bodeen was waiting in the canteen line when one of Johnny's bodyguards said, "Hey, how about letting Johnny in front of you?" Bodeen asked, "Johnny who?" The guy said," Johnny Dio, man!" Bodeen said, "Fuck Johnny Dio! And fuck all you goddamn greasy guineas at the same time." I thought Johnny's man was going to kill Bodeen on the spot. But DioGuardia walked over and, without saying anything, nudged his man to the end of the line. Nothing was ever said, because Johnny wasn't going to spend one extra second in jail over some ten-cent hick's racist comment about Italians.

Frank Costello was in Atlanta twice. The first time was in 1953. At that time, I was assigned to the linen room, passing out clothes, and one day an inmate told a buddy of mine called Robbie, who later also went to the Rock, "Gimme Frank's clothes, man!" Robbie said, "Fuck Frank! Tell him to get his own clothes!" It wasn't because Robbi didn't like Costello, because we all did, but because the guy asking for his clothes was a kiss-ass yes man. So, a few minutes later, Costello came over from the shower room and asked, "How about it, kid? Can I get my clothes?" He seemed to respect Robbie for it.

Frank Costello's real name was Francesco Saveria, and he was a big New York Mafia boss who ran things for Lucky Luciano when Lucky was deported to Italy in 1946. Costello looked like a cold-blooded person, but he was good to the guys in his cell who had no money. Once a month in Atlanta, you could spend $15 at the canteen, and Frank always spent most of it on them and only got smokes and shaving gear for himself. Cigarettes were 20 cents a pack and candy bars were 5 cents each. Nothing was taxed, which meant that $15 went a long way.

Frank Costello was known as "The Prime Minister," both by his criminal associates in the outside world and at Atlanta, where he was liked and respected by the inmates. Both Costello and Dio had only Italians in their eight-man cell. Costello got caught cooking a steak by putting it in a coffee bottle and letting hot water run on it until it was done. But instead of Costello taking the rap for it, all his other cellmates denied it, insisting the bottle came with the steak in it. So, the deputy broke the group up and put each in a different cell.

Just before Costello's release in 1954, he was transferred to Milan, Michigan, and then to a federal detention center in New York. I saw in the paper that he was caught there with a fancy sturgeon dinner in his cell, and prison officials were investigating who brought it in. Right after his release, a hit man named Vincent "The Chin" Gigante shot him in the head, but the bullet glanced off his skull, and Frank said he had no idea why somebody would want to shoot him. Every time I hear about Costello, I think about how cold and penetrating his eyes were. He could look right through you, even when he was laughing and joking with you.

The most respected gangster at Atlanta was Vito Genovese. Vito was a New Jersey crime boss and would later die in Springfield in 1969. The

Italians called him "Don Vitone," and he was close to Frank Costello and Lucky Luciano, at least in the early days. He was feared at Atlanta by both inmates and guards and had a bodyguard who went everywhere he did. Vito was quite well-spoken and carried himself with class. But he always had a determined look about him, as did Costello.

One of his chief lieutenants was there with him. His name was Joe DiPalermo, but he was better known as Joe Beck. Joe was in for narcotics violations and worked in the plumbing shop with me. I got to know him pretty well. Whenever he was expecting Genovese to stop by the plumbing shop after Vito saw his lawyer, he would ask me to wait on the steps outside or deliver a message for him. Later on, when I was placed in the Atlanta psycho ward, he talked to the inmate orderlies and told them I was good people and if there was anything I needed to let him or Vito know.

Joe Valachi, who.was a Genovese soldier turned informer, was also at Atlanta. He later told the McClellan Senate hearings that DiPalermo had been ordered by Vito to kill him. Valachi accidently killed a guy he thought was DiPalermo. Joe just killed the wrong guy. The inmate who set up the unintended victim was later murdered by a Genovese soldier so he couldn't talk to the prison officials. After Valachi beat the wrong guy to death with a pipe, he said, "Well, sometimes mistakes happen in this business of ours." I always believed that Valachi talked to the senators because he was scared of the electric chair.

It was around 7:30 a.m., June 22, 1962, that Joe Valachi, who had been convicted as a heroin trafficker, grabbed a two-foot piece of iron pipe lying on the ground near some construction work in the yard and, before anyone knew what was happening, rushed up to a fellow inmate from behind and in just a few seconds beat his head into a bloody pulp. Valachi was 58 years old and strongly built, like Joe Schultz. He was 5'6" and weighed more than 190 pounds. He had gray hair, and his eyes always had a cold expression to them. He would look at me when I'd pass him and say "Hello," and I knew he would be wondering, "What the hell does that son of a bitch mean by that?"

Joe made the headlines in the mid-1960s because he was the first man to tell the whole story of the Cosa Nostra. I heard that his incarceration at Atlanta caused a heck of a debate among the bigshots in the Bureau of Prisons and also in Atlanta. The Atlanta people didn't want him that close to Vito Genovese and his crime partners, but Valachi was strong. He never broke his Mafia blood allegiance, although word was out in the prison that he was a marked man by the very people he wouldn't rat on.

All of us respected him and couldn't see what the problem was between him and Vito. During that spring I saw him in the mess hall and around the yard all the time. Sometimes I spotted him and Vito walking together in deep conversation. But in May and June he appeared to grow more and more nervous. He was always looking back over his shoulders, as if he were expecting someone to come up from behind him. I knew that DiPalermo was involved, because I could see the hate in his eyes as he watched Valachi. And since DiPalermo was Vito's chief lieutenant, I guessed that Genovese ordered him to kill Valachi. I heard from some of the guys that DiPalermo offered Valachi a steak sandwich he stole from Joe in order to provoke him into fighting so they could kill him.

So, on that morning in the yard, half-crazy from worrying that he would be killed, Valachi went berserk on a man he thought was DiPalermo, but DiPalermo was on his way to the laundry with me. I knew the unfortunate guy whose head Valachi bashed in. He was John Saupp, a forger and mail robber. He was not a mob guy and he didn't know Vito, DiPalermo, or Valachi. He was just an ordinary guy who stole nickels and dimes and was minding his own business.

Everybody liked him, including me. The only reason Valachi killed him was because be bore a remarkable resemblance to DiPalermo. I heard from one of the clerks in the warden's office that Valachi was really upset when he learned he killed the wrong guy. He kept saying, over and over, "I went crazy. I went crazy."

I was with DiPalermo when he got the news. At first, he was stunned, then he grinned from ear to ear, as if to say, "Well, at least I don't have to put myself on the spot by killing him." Then I saw Vito and Johnny Dio and a couple of other guys come into the laundry and huddle in the back room. They were laughing a lot, but I don't know if it was because of the mistaken killing. DiPalermo never talked to me about the matter and just went about his work, as if nothing had happened. I always felt a lot of sorrow for John Saupp and a little pity for Valachi. He became an informer only after that incident, when the mob guys wanted to kill him. Otherwise he was a stand-up guy, and if he indeed was talking to the FBI, he wasn't giving them any worthwhile information.

DiPalermo was a small guy but one day I saw him put boxing gloves on with a black guy in the yard to settle a dispute, and when the guard saw they were trying to hurt each other, he broke it up. I don't know why Vito brought DiPalermo into killing Valachi other than for the reason of trusting him. But I did learn from the inmate grapevine, which was always pretty reliable, that it wasn't DiPalermo Joe meant to kill. Life Magazine did a story on Genovese when he was first busted and put his personal wealth at $15 million. This always impressed us. There were several guys in Atlanta whom Vito could have paid to kill Valachi, and Joe wouldn't have had a chance.

When I was in the Atlanta psycho ward, which was located in the basement of the hospital, two of the inmate orderlies helped the medical technician assistant subdue an inmate one night. When word got out to the population about it, someone cut the legs off of the pants of the prison official and his assistants and put notes in them saying that this was just a sample of what was going to be done to them. One of the orderlies asked me to send word out to all the guys that they were okay. I said I couldn't get involved, so they asked a Mexican orderly whom I was friendly with to ask me to send word to DiPalermo and some of the guys from the Rock that they were okay. The Mexican told them the same thing. I don't know whatever happened to them, because shortly after that I was sent back to Springfield.

When the new Atlanta deputy warden took over, he called me to his office and started talking to me about Hitler and some letters I wrote the Secretary of the Army about Southern chain gangs being worse than the camps Hitler set up. I started running down the capitalist system and how it only benefited the people intelligent enough to know how to manipulate it. I said that 80 percent of the people in this country were left out. The deputy warden said, "Well, I've been reading some of your letters to the Secretary of the Army"—which he wasn't supposed to do— "and they sound more like the first chapter of a book you're writing about us. I don't appreciate that. And you have been complaining about how bad the food is and that a canine would pass it up. Plus, you're the type who knows how to go about starting trouble. You may be classified as a psycho, but you're no dumb bunny. You're a pretty smart fellow. Now you say you would rather be on the Rock. Well, I'll send you back to the Rock."

I responded by saying, "So, because I don't agree with a system that lets smart people take advantage of the less intelligent, you think I belong back at the Rock." He said, "Probably, but I'm not punishing you for all your letter writing. I'm going to put you upstairs and tell the guards to leave your door open during the day so you can help feed all the others, (I was an orderly at the time) especially your Mafia dago friends." The guards never bothered me at all, and about a week later I was moved to the hospital.

After an outside psychiatrist came to talk to me one night, the head medical technician assistant told me I was being transferred to Springfield. And a couple of days later, I left for Springfield. I think the Bureau of Prisons ordered the deputy warden to send me back to Springfield for further supervision rather than the Rock, where he wanted me to go for discipline. The psychiatrist talked to me at length about Hitler and how Germany was divided. They questioned my opinions about how the Allies had corrupted the German people and destroyed the German Army officer corps.

I think the two things the deputy didn't like me doing was mixing with the mob and defending communism in the cell house, because it made some of the jealous inmates mad, especially the less educated and the guys with low IQs. Rudolph Abel, the famous Russian spy who was on my tier, could hear me argue with the guys in my cell about communism. When he passed my cell, he would look at me and nod in approval, although we never spoke.

About ninety days after that, he was traded for an American spy. Abel was a colonel in the Russian Army. As he was leaving Atlanta, a guard stopped him and made him stand in a position that had him facing a gun tower. He was then told to hold a painting up for inspection, and all the time a television camera was in the tower shooting a secret video of him. Robert Kennedy was attorney general at the time, so he had to okay it, since it was forbidden in the prison system prior to Kennedy. Abel was a good portrait painter and worked in the industries. He kept to himself and bothered nobody. About a week before I left for Springfield, he was all over the news again when he appeared at a bridge in Berlin for the spy swap.

I got along better in Springfield than in any other institution I have ever been in. I probably should have stayed there, like Dr. Herman said. The doctors restored my lost gain-time after a couple of years, and before I left for home, the deputy warden in charge of security called me into his office and talked to me about the big changes in my attitude and behavior. He said he would like for me to write down the things I thought helped me, so that my statements could help others. I saw guys who acted like tigers put on Thorazine, and in a week they were kittens. I don't know how they ultimately turned out, but it sure calmed them down.

When I was released to go home in 1963, I had almost $800 saved. I wanted to locate in Miami but was told I had to return to Jacksonville. The officials and I had a big argument about that. I had done my time and felt like it wasn't any of the Bureau's business what I did after release. One guard at Springfield said, "With your attitude, you won't be out long." I responded that I wasn't a boot licker or simple-minded and didn't need somebody telling me what to do after I had done my time.

When I reported to the parole officer in Jacksonville, the man who was in charge of my case told me that I wouldn't be bothered. "Just find a job and keep me informed of your address, income, and place of employment," he advised. He then he told me I shouldn't say anything to people I might see staring at me, since they might think they knew me. I guess he was going by my prison record and the times I jumped and beat up people for staring at me.

He was a stern and tough old man, but he always tried to be fair with me. He said he would help me as long as I didn't get arrested, and if I did, not to call him. A few years later when I had a job that required me to go out of town, he said, "You go right ahead, and if anything comes up about it, I'll cover for you." You couldn't go out of town without written permission from your parole officer in those days, which meant you were limited in terms of the jobs you could get.

The first job I got after my release was at a truck stop near St. Augustine, Florida. The place had just been raided in the past year by the FBI for transporting hookers across the state line. My parole officer told me he was concerned about me working there but didn't ask me to quit. I quit anyway, because I saw that Dorothy, the woman who owned it, fired a guy who had been with her for a long time for going to visit one of the females in her trailer.

The guy just wanted some companionship, but Dorothy felt that because of it he was being disloyal. But I felt she was disloyal to him, and I don't deal with people who are disloyal. She liked me and later often called my brother's house, trying to locate me. I finally talked to her on the phone one day and she wanted to know why I quit. She said, "Just like you heard things about me, I heard things about you but I never paid any attention to them. Diane was a troublemaker, and I had to get rid of her." I said, "Diane had nothing to do with me leaving. You did."

My parole officer called a union chief he knew in Jacksonville and asked him to put me to work, which he did. He let me pay my union entrance fee on a weekly basis. His assistant wouldn't send me out to work until he checked with Leon, the chief. He told me it was unusual for the chief to hire ex-cons. But Leon told me he always tried to work with Mr. Bullock, the parole officer, since you never know when you will need a favor.

I became disgusted with the hypocrites who expected ex-cons to stay out of trouble but didn't believe in hiring them. Soon I started planning a bank robbery with a buddy of mine. But fortunately, a friend put me in touch with a man named Jack Mayo who owned several carpet and tile stores in Jacksonville, and he put me to work. Soon, he started treating me like a brother. He never asked me about my background even though he knew all about me.

I was always the first one to work and the other fellas and I would have to wait for him to arrive and let us in. So, one day he gave me a key to the front door and told me to open up and let the guys start loading trucks and cutting carpets while I supervised until he arrived. Sometimes in the evenings after work, he would send me to the liquor store to get some scotch for him and some beer for me. We would talk about everything except my background.

One day he told me that he trusted me and that we thought alike. He was good about letting guys without a car drive a truck home. He told me that when he first came back from Korea, he took a job with a vending machine company and the owner let him drive a truck home, and he never forgot the courtesy. His father-in-law got him started in the business, and it really took off, since he had a good business head. I used to listen to him talk business at night with representatives from the carpet mills, and he knew how to deal.

If one was new, Jack would let him know that if he ever crossed him, that he better not come back. He donated a lot of money to Israel and had pictures of him and Moshe Dayan, the hero of the 1967 war. After Jack died, I talked to his wife, and she started running him down. I told her he had been like a brother to me, and she shut up. Then she asked me to come back to work for her and her daughter, since they got the business when he died. But I couldn't do the work anymore because of my bad back.

After my release I had some pretty girlfriends, although most said they couldn't understand me. I tried to explain to each of them that before going to prison, I was popular with the women. But once I got to the Rock, I had a personality change. Well, that didn't seem to matter. They said I was a strange person and backed off. One or two even told me they were afraid of me, adding that I had to learn to give as well as take. But during these brief flings, 1 couldn't seem to get close to anyone. For some reason I kept a wall between us.

In those years that followed after my release, I thought a lot about the true feelings I had for the first girl I ever loved. That was when I was twenty. Marquita, whose name is still tattooed on my right arm, was a pretty, blue-eyed blonde who was only fifteen. As I mentioned earlier in my autobiography, I saw her in a restaurant, and after she left, I asked the waitress, whom I knew, to introduce me.

After the waitress introduced me to her, we started dating a lot. Her mother seemed to like me and gave her permission for us to see each other. Later, the way the FBI got on my trail was through letters from her found in a suitcase that I had to abandon during the chase, which eventually led to my capture. Under FBI pressure, Marquita's mother gave them my photograph.

In 1965, when Marquita flew to Jacksonville from Simi Valley, California, to attend her grandmother's funeral, we got together. She told me she still loved me and only married in order to get away from home. Marquita said that when my photograph was on the front pages of all the Florida newspapers, her mother brought a few of them home. She then started abusing Marquita for having run around with me, as if her daughter could have known how I was going to turn out.

When Marquita returned to California, she told her husband she was going to leave him. She didn't mention me or that she was going to return to Jacksonville. Well, after Marquita returned to Jacksonville, he somehow learned about me, and one night while we were at her aunt's, he called and started crying.

He said he was going to find me and kill me, no matter how long it took. I got on the line and tried to explain that I had loved Marquita a long time before he met her and to please leave us alone. I had not meant to break up their marriage, I said, and if he had treated her better all along, she would undoubtedly have remained with him. A few weeks later, he wrote her a letter and told her I had done him a lot of good. That letter seemed to wake her up, and when she left me to go back to him, she cried softly and said that no matter what directions our lives would take from that moment on, she would always love me.

I told her to do what she felt was right. To this day, I have not heard a word from her. I wish both her and her husband well, since I honestly feel it wouldn't have worked out anyway. No man has the right to come between a couple already married.

About eight months after my release, I met a girl named Kim at a service station-bar. She was a strip-tease dancer, and I saw her off and on for two years. Through her baby sitter, I met other girls. Kim was twenty-three, and most of the other girls were about that age. They all worked in nearby bars. One girl named Loretta, who was twenty-two, worked at the R & R Lounge in Jacksonville as a go-go dancer, and I ended up marrying her, which was a big mistake but I did buy the house she picked out that I still live in today. I'm proud to say that house has been paid off for the past ten years.

I met another girl named Barbara who was the sister of a guy I worked with. This fellow and I used to go to bars, and one day I took him home. Barbara had just arrived from Texas and was celebrating her twenty-first birthday. I dated her for two months and then married her. It lasted five years.

One weekend she came home after spending a couple of days with her parents in Green Cove Springs, Florida. She woke me up on the sofa and showed me one of my shirts with lip stick on it. She said how much she loved me but was leaving because she couldn't put up with disloyalty. I knew the lipstick wasn't on my shirt because of any messing around I did.

Hell, I didn't even notice it. Later, when I talked to her daddy, he told me she had left my daughter Lisa with them and went to a bar where she met a guy named Mike, and she was spending a lot of time at his apartment. When I found out this part, I said, "Good riddance!" She had put that lipstick on the shirt as an excuse.

I was hurt, since Lisa, who was too young to understand, was caught in the middle. I took my daughter home every weekend, and one Saturday night about six months after Barbara married Mike, Barbara arrived on my doorstep about 2:00 in the morning with all her clothes. She said Mike beat her up, and she had left him. I told her I wasn't getting involved in it and that she couldn't stay with me. So, she went back to Mike. Mike and I became friends later, and when she left him for another man, I told him he should have known she would. If she did me that way, she would do him that way, too.

I have been single since and have no desire to get married. That's for lonely people, and I'm not lonely. Loretta is going to church now and has tried to get me to go to church with her several times, but I don't want to get involved with her again. The only one of my past girlfriends I still care about is Diane Perryman, because she is loyal, has class, and is as pretty as they come. She works as a secretary now and even supported her ex-husband for a while when he was out of work. How much more classy can anyone be?

I first met Diane on New Year's Eve in 1967. I had been out all the previous ·night with my friend, Buddy Miller. Meanwhile, my best friend at the time, Richard Kane, left a note on my door that he was in town with a girlfriend, indicating the hotel and address. So, on New Year's Eve, I drove over to the hotel and knocked on his door. When Richard opened the door, I saw Diane laying on the bed in a minidress, reading a book. When she looked over at me and into my eyes, it burned a hole in my heart that, to this day, has never gone away. I have never told her how I felt, for she was my best friend's girl, and he asked me to leave her alone.

A few years later, after Richard served some time for some trouble he got in, I signed him out of pre-release. That afternoon, when we stopped at an intersection on the way to the beach, Diane happened to drive by. Richard said, "Damn, there goes Diane. I hope she isn't headed to the same beach we're going to. I don't want to run into her." I knew then that he really loved her and was glad I hadn't come between them.

I've always thought that it takes a weak character to double-cross your friends, whether it's love or war or whatever. That afternoon at the beach, Richard asked if I would take Diane off his hands. I laughed and said it was a little too late for that, even though I knew I was lying to the both of us.

To this day, Diane has been one of my best friends. She is a good old Georgia girl, and all she needed was a good man. She's now married to Lacy, a very nice guy. Diane could have had her pick of the men in Jacksonville, and she chose wisely. Lacy and I are good friends, and I told him that I was proud of his wife getting away from Richard.

He said that Diane speaks highly of me and that he wasn't jealous about our friendship. I would always be welcome in their home and could call anytime. Lacy is a real man, a guy with confidence in himself. I respect him. Today, Lacy and Diane own their business. They contract for room additions and house siding. Diane runs the office while Lacy does the work.

Most of the other women I took out in those years wanted to sit in bars or go to bars where their friends were or worked. Anything else bored them. I'm actually surprised that with all the women I ran around with I didn't pick up a disease but I was pretty careful. At one point in 1970, I had two girls who were friends. Both of them actually cried over me while I was going out with other girls who were their friends. They couldn't understand that I like them equally.

I tried to explain that if you're lonely, you'll sometimes go out with anybody, just to shake off the loneliness. I never told any of these women I loved them, because the last thing I wanted to do was build up any hope in any of them. I just wanted friends. But my thoughts always returned to Diane.

On the Rock, Simcox had gotten me started on astrology, which I felt had a lot of things going for it. Diane is Sagittarius and I'm Pisces. All I know is that I always got along good with Leos and Sagittarius. This even goes for the inmates and guards I knew.

I did construction work out of the union hall for a couple of years and, as I mentioned, then got a job in carpet installation through the son of a friend of mine. I laid wall-to-wall carpeting until 1980, when I pulled a disc in my back and had to have surgery. The first job I got after the surgery was as a safety and security officer for St. Luke's Hospital. But because you have to be licensed to do security work, the state turned me down for a license until the chief parole officer for the middle district of Florida and Jack Mayo, the owner of the carpet stores who had employed me for thirteen years, wrote letters on my behalf.

The hospital was in a high-crime area. I was the best security man they had, since I knew how to deal with the people we had to keep from coming into the hospital. Most of the guards were scared and overlooked a lot. I escorted a lot of the transients out of the hospital, because they came in to steal from the patients' rooms and to look for drugs at the nursing stations.

I caught two young blacks going through the drug cabinet at one station, just out of sight of the nurse, and I escorted them to the door and told them not to come back. They were glad to get out. I could have held them for the police.

The director of security told the chief administrator that he needed more men like me. I turned down a sergeant's stripes for three years, because it would have changed my weekends off and also because it can create petty jealousies among the more simpleminded guards, and we had plenty of those around.

Once, the captain, who was being promoted to the new post of supervisor of security, asked if I would take his job, and I said yes but it somehow went to someone else. I'm sure jealousy and politics had something to do with it. When they were in the process of building a new hospital, the director of security, Ernie Felguth, asked me if I would do him a personal favor and take the sergeant's stripes so I could run security at the old hospital while he and the supervisor spent most of their time at the new hospital, getting security established.

I said I would, and sure enough, the petty jealousies started. Even the supervisor, Johnny, who was afraid Ernie would give me his job, sabotaged everything I did. If he saw Ernie and me walking around talking, he would come running, like a jealous kid. I finally quit and went to work running an Exxon station at night. I liked it so much that I have been doing that job for seven years now. I meet all kinds of people from different walks of life. I now know the mayor of Jacksonville as well as a high-powered lawyer who ran for governor.

Not so bad for a former incorrigible who survived Alcatraz.

AFTERWORD

By Don DeNevi

When I sat down to assist Charlie Hopkins in writing his story, I did so for two reasons. First, I wanted to reciprocate for all the marvelous help he gave me in developing my book Riddle of the Rock: The Only Successful Escape from Alcatraz. Second, he was a close friend of the late Clarence "Joe" Carnes, a former Alcatraz inmate I collaborated with in the late 1970s on several books and the film treatment for the NBC Movie of the Week, *Alcatraz: The Whole Shocking Story*. If Clarence, who associated with only a handful of prisoners, chose to befriend Charlie, then that was all I needed to know. Working closely with him was like being with Clarence again.

This manuscript was originally drafted in 1991 and is presented here just as it came from Charlie. The only editing that has been performed has been to correct minor spelling and grammatical errors or to provide slight clarification of some statements.

With a gift for remembering details, Charlie told me tales of his incarcerations in various federal prisons as well as the ways of the hopelessly incarcerated: behaviors at times laughable, but more often dark, cruel, and pitiful. Only Clarence could match Charlie's intimate knowledge of the styles, moods, and ideas of the prison underworld culture, especially at Alcatraz during that penitentiary's most violent years, 1955–59.

The manuscript was developed from my direct interviews with Charlie, his written responses to my questions, and several hundred pages of court transcripts and other official sources and documents. Not once during his recollections did he indulge in any self-pity. There were no verbal theatrics, no whining that he got bum raps or never had decent breaks. He shed no crocodile tears nor sniveled repentance. Hoping in a small way to help potential criminals who may be headed to long-term imprisonment, Charlie spoke directly, honestly, courageously, warmly, and with insight.

This mild-mannered man who was once the nemesis of his keepers asked recently, "How do I explain to my friends, the public, and especially my twenty-four-year-old daughter [when the manuscript was originally completed], Lisa, that I was once declared intractable and irreclaimable? In fact, I didn't even tell Lisa until just a few months ago on the ferry to Alcatraz for the tour of the prison that I had even served time there, much of it in isolation. What will I tell her children? Is there something to be proud of in my life? Do I wish I could get in that car of Hill's all over again and drive off to commit that insane crime spree? The only thing I don't regret is meeting and making friends with a lot of other supposed incorrigibles who were not incorrigible but who were looked down on as incorrigible. Joe Schultz, Johnny Iozza, Alvin Karpis, and others taught me dogged persistence and ferocious tenacity, things that help me in life today. Joe Carnes taught me to never, never, never, never break or quit. I hope some of the kids today bent on crime read my story and straighten out before it's too late, before they or someone else is harmed. The old saying that crime doesn't pay is more true than their wildest dreams can imagine."

Although Charlie submitted himself to degradation and brutality in the prison systems, he never gave up, because in the final analysis, he belonged to himself. Today he is making an honorable and honest place for himself and his daughter in the Jacksonville community. It was my luck to meet him and help him tell his story. He will always be my friend.

THANK YOU FOR READING!

If you enjoyed this book, we would appreciate your customer review on your book seller's website or on Goodreads.

Also, we would like for you to know that you can find more great books like this one at www.CreativeTexts.com

www.ingramcontent.com/pod-product-compliance
Lightning Source LLC
Chambersburg PA
CBHW032131020426
42334CB00016B/1117